T0202989

Communications in Computer and Information Science   1177

Commenced Publication in 2007
Founding and Former Series Editors:
Phoebe Chen, Alfredo Cuzzocrea, Xiaoyong Du, Orhun Kara, Ting Liu,
Krishna M. Sivalingam, Dominik Ślęzak, Takashi Washio, Xiaokang Yang,
and Junsong Yuan

Editorial Board Members

More information about this series at http://www.springer.com/series/7899

Michelangelo Ceci · Stefano Ferilli ·
Antonella Poggi (Eds.)

Digital Libraries: The Era of Big Data and Data Science

16th Italian Research Conference
on Digital Libraries, IRCDL 2020
Bari, Italy, January 30–31, 2020
Proceedings

 Springer

Editors
Michelangelo Ceci ⓘ
University of Bari
Bari, Italy

Stefano Ferilli ⓘ
University of Bari
Bari, Italy

Antonella Poggi
Sapienza University of Rome
Rome, Italy

ISSN 1865-0929   ISSN 1865-0937 (electronic)
Communications in Computer and Information Science
ISBN 978-3-030-39904-7   ISBN 978-3-030-39905-4   (eBook)
https://doi.org/10.1007/978-3-030-39905-4

This Springer imprint is published by the registered company Springer Nature Switzerland AG
The registered company address is: Gewerbestrasse 11, 6330 Cham, Switzerland

Preface

The Italian Research Conference on Digital Libraries (IRCDL) is an annual forum for the Italian research community to discuss the research topics pertaining to digital libraries and related technical, practical, and social issues both on the computer science and the humanities side. Since 2005, it has served as a key meeting for the Italian digital library community. During these years, IRCDL has touched upon many of the facets of digital library, adapting its topics of interest to the evolution of the research in this domain and of the whole process of scholarly communication.

The theme of the 2020 edition of the conference was "Big Data and Data Science." This theme was motivated by the characteristics of data resources of many modern digital libraries, requiring existing library services to use methods that are able to face the main issues of big data: volume, variety, and velocity. This also paves the way to new forms of data analysis from big digital libraries that go far beyond the classical techniques of data analysis from digital libraries adopted in the last decade.

This volume contains 18 selected contributions accepted for presentation at the 16th Italian Research Conference on Digital Libraries (IRCDL 2020), which was held at the Department of Computer Science of the University of Bari Aldo Moro (Bari, Italy) during January 30–31, 2020. These contributions touched a rich range of topics: information retrieval, big data and data science in digital libraries, digital libraries for cultural heritage, and open science. The papers were selected after a rigorous evaluation of a Program Committee composed of 19 members, including representatives of the most active Italian research groups on digital libraries.

We are proud to present a rich scientific program, including high-profile keynotes and many technical presentations.

To conclude, we would like to express our gratitude to all our colleagues for submitting papers to IRCDL 2020 and for helping to finalize this volume in due time. We would like to thank those institutions and individuals who made the conference and this volume possible. In particular, we would like to thank the Program Committee members, the Steering Committee members, the Advisory Board members, and the Organizing Committee. We would also like to thank Artificial Brain S.r.l. for the helpful conference secretariat and the Department of Computer Science of the University of Bari Aldo Moro for supporting and hosting the event.

January 2020

Michelangelo Ceci
Stefano Ferilli
Antonella Poggi

Organization

Program Committee Chairs

Michelangelo Ceci	University of Bari Aldo Moro, Italy
Stefano Ferilli	University of Bari Aldo Moro, Italy
Antonella Poggi	Sapienza University of Rome, Italy

Advisory Board

Tiziana Catarci	Sapienza University of Rome, Italy
Floriana Esposito	University of Bari Aldo Moro, Italy
Costantino Thanos	ISTI-CNR, Italy

Steering Committee

Maristella Agosti	University of Padua, Italy
Alberto Del Bimbo	University of Florence, Italy
Stefano Ferilli	University of Bari Aldo Moro, Italy
Costantino Grana	University of Modena and Reggio Emilia, Italy
Antonella Poggi	Sapienza University of Rome, Italy
Carlo Tasso	University of Udine, Italy

Program Committee

Lorenzo Baraldi	University of Modena and Reggio Emilia, Italy
Nicola Barbuti	University of Bari Aldo Moro, Italy
Valentina Bartalesi	ISTI-CNR, Italy
George Bruseker	FORTH, Greece
Leonardo Candela	ISTI-CNR, Italy
Fabio Ciotti	Tor Vergata University of Rome, Italy
Marilena Daquino	University of Bologna, Italy
Giorgio Maria Di Nunzio	University of Padua, Italy
Achille Felicetti	PIN S.c.R.L., Italy
Nicola Ferro	University of Padua, Italy
Elena Giglia	University of Turin, Italy
Fabio Leuzzi	Polizia di Stato, Italy
Claudio Lucchese	Ca' Foscari University of Venice, Italy
Paolo Manghi	ISTI-CNR, Italy
Nicola Orio	University of Padua, Italy
Eloy Rodrigues	University of Minho, Portugal
Marco Schaerf	Sapienza University of Rome, Italy
Giuseppe Serra	University of Udine, Italy

Luigi Siciliano   University of Bolzen-Bolzano, Italy
Gianmaria Silvello   University of Padua, Italy
Anna Maria Tammaro   Bibelot, Italy
Fabio Vitali   University of Bologna, Italy

Invited Talks

Context-Aware Distributed Mobile Search

Fabio Crestani

Faculty of Informatics, Università della Svizzera Italiana

Abstract. Distributed Information Retrieval (DIR) has been around for a while, yet in this talk I will present an approach to using uncooperative DIR in a mobile environment. We called this Unified Mobile Search (UMS). I will present how this concept extends that of DIR by considering fully the context in which the search is carried out and present our first approach to target application selection for mobile devices. I will then expand on this idea toward a conversational assistant for context-aware distributed mobile search, providing a view on what we should expect coming to our mobile phones very soon.

Short Bio. Fabio Crestani is a full professor at the Faculty of Informatics of the Universita' della Svizzera Italiana (USI) in Lugano, Switzerland, since 2007. Previously he was a professor at the University of Strathclyde in Glasgow, UK. He holds a degree in Statistics from the University of Padua (Italy) and a MSc and PhD in Computing Science from the University of Glasgow (UK). Prof. Crestani is an internationally recognized researcher in Information Retrieval, Text Mining, and Digital Libraries. In these areas he has published over two hundred refereed papers on both theoretical and experimental investigations. He has also served in the Organizing and Program Committees of several conferences and the editorial boards of several journals.

Aiuto – ho troppi dati! Digital Library Users and Their Challenges With Big Data

Elke Greifeneder

Institut für Bibliotheks- und Informationswissenschaft,
Humboldt-Universität zu Berlin

Abstract. Digital libraries have many users: the repository holder, the repositories' day to day managers, the users who provide big data for storage and use in the digital library, the researchers as end-user who benefit from large data sets, the industry firm who seeks large, free amounts of data for commercial reuse, and many others. Yet, they all have something in common: the initial enthusiasm for the simple availability of a magic thing called "big data" often changes to an attitude of despair, frustration, and defense within months of working with big data. This presentation uses a personal approach and explains the various needs and practices of those user groups, and depicts their pain points when it comes to operating with big data.

Short Bio. Prof. Elke Greifeneder is a full professor at the Berlin School of Library and Information Science at Humboldt-Universitaet zu Berlin (Germany). She is currently leading the research group on information behavior and focuses on methodological questions, in particular on empirical research completed in digital environments. She was tenured in Berlin in 2019 and was previously an assistant professor at the University of Copenhagen (Denmark). She has been very active in the field as reviewer and Program Committee member, as well as program chair of the iConference, ASIST chair for International Relations, IFLA section member on library services to people with special needs, and has been the co-editor of Library Hi Tech for 10 years.

Contents

Cultural Heritage

Open Science

Information Retrieval

Reproducibility of the Neural Vector Space Model via Docker

Nicola Ferro$^{(\boxtimes)}$ (iD), Stefano Marchesin$^{(\boxtimes)}$ (iD), Alberto Purpura$^{(\boxtimes)}$ (iD),
and Gianmaria Silvello$^{(\boxtimes)}$ (iD)

Department of Information Engineering, University of Padua, Padua, Italy
{nicola.ferro,stefano.marchesin,
alberto.purpura,gianmaria.silvello}@unipd.it

Abstract. In this work we describe how Docker images can be used to enhance the reproducibility of Neural IR models. We report our results reproducing the Vector Space Neural Model (NVSM) and we release a CPU-based and a GPU-based Docker image. Finally, we present some insights about reproducing Neural IR models.

1 Introduction

Reproducibility of models and systems is central for the verification of scientific results ans it is one of the cornerstones of the system of sciences. In the field of Information Retrieval, reproducibility has been the object of thorough analyses and efforts; only in the last two years we have seen the rise of many reproducibility-oriented events like the CENTRE evaluations at CLEF [2], NTCIR [7] and TREC [8], the SIGIR task force to implement ACM's policy on artifact review and badging and the *Open-Source IR Replicability Challenge at SIGIR 2019 (OSIRRC 2019)*.

In this paper, we advocate OSIRRC 2019s vision that is to build Docker-based[1] infrastructures to replicate results on standard IR *ad hoc* test collections. Docker is a tool that allows for the creation and deployment of applications via images containing all the required dependencies. Relying on a Docker-based infrastructure to replicate the results of existing systems, helps researchers to avoid all the issues related to system requirements and dependencies. Indeed, *Information Retrieval (IR)* platforms such as Anserini, Terrier, or text matching libraries such as MatchZoo rely on a set of software tools, developed in `Java` or `Python` and based on numerous libraries for scientific computing, which have all to be available on the host machine in order for the applications to run smoothly.

We explore the use of Docker images for the reproducibility of *Neural IR (NeuIR)* models, which is a challenging domain that has seen only a few reproducibility efforts so far [1,5]. NeuIR models are particularly hard to reproduce

---

[1] https://www.docker.com/.

The full paper has been originally presented at the OSIRRC@SIGIR workshop [3].

© Springer Nature Switzerland AG 2020
M. Ceci et al. (Eds.): IRCDL 2020, CCIS 1177, pp. 3–8, 2020.
https://doi.org/10.1007/978-3-030-39905-4_1

because they are highly sensitive to parameters, hyper-parameters, and pre-processing choices. Also, these models are usually compatible only with specific versions of the libraries that they rely on (e.g., `Tensorflow`) because these frameworks are constantly updated. The use of Docker images is a possible solution to avoid these deployment issues on different machines as it already includes all the libraries required by the contained application.

For this reason, (i) we propose a Docker architecture that can be used as a framework to train, test, and evaluate NeuIR models; and, (ii) we show how this architecture can be employed to build a Docker image that replicates the *Neural Vector Space Model (NVSM)* [9], a state-of-the-art unsupervised neural model for *ad hoc* retrieval.

2   Background

Repeatability, replicability, and reproducibility are fundamental aspects of computational sciences, both in supporting desirable scientific methodology as well as sustaining empirical progress. These concepts have been discussed and analyzed in depth in [4], that focuses on the core issues and approaches to reproducibility in several fields of computer science. Relevant to these concepts is the *Platform, Research goal, Implementation, Method, Actor and Data (PRIMAD)* model, which tackles reproducibility from different angles. The PRIMAD paradigm has been adopted by the IR community, where it has been adapted to the context of IR evaluation – both system-oriented and user-oriented. In this context, our contribution lies between replicability and reproducibility. Indeed, we rely on the NVSM implementation available at [6] and described in [5] to replicate the results of a reproduced version of NVSM.

NVSM is a state-of-the-art unsupervised model for *ad hoc* retrieval. The model achieves competitive results against traditional lexical models and outperforms state-of-the-art unsupervised semantic retrieval models, like the Word2Vec-based models. NVSM jointly learns distinct word and document representations by optimizing an unsupervised loss function which minimizes the distance between sequences of n-grams and the documents containing them. Such optimization objective imposes that n-grams extracted from a document should be predictive of that document. After training, the learned word and document representations are used to perform retrieval. Queries are seen as n-grams and matched against documents in the feature space. Documents are then ranked in decreasing order of the cosine similarity computed between query and document representations.

3   Docker Image Architecture

We developed two Docker images reproducing NVSM, one CPU-based and another GPU-based.

The CPU-based version of NVSM is written in Python and relies on `Tensorflow v.1.13.1`. For this reason, we developed a Docker image based on the official Python 3.5 runtime container, on top of which we install the Python packages required by the algorithm – such as `Tensorflow`, `Python NLTK`, and `Whoosh` – we also install a C compiler, i.e. `gcc`, in order to use the official `trec_eval` package[2] to evaluate the retrieval model during training. Since this docker image still relies for some functions (i.e. random number generation) on the host machine, despite being very similar, the results are not exactly the same across different computers – while they are consistent on the same machine.

The GPU-based version of NVSM is based on `Tensorflow`, which is a machine learning library that allows us to employ the GPU on the host machine in order to perform operations more efficiently. There are many advantages of employing GPUs for scientific computations, but their usage makes a sizable difference especially when training deep learning models. The training of such models requires in fact to perform a large number of matrix operations that can be easily parallelized and do not require powerful hardware.

In our experiments, we observed that `nvsm_gpu` does not produce fully consistent results on the same machine. In fact, `TensorFlow` uses the `Eigen` library, which in turn uses CUDA atomic functions to implement reduction operations, such as `tf.reduce_sum` etc. Those operations are non-deterministic and each operation can introduce small variations. Despite this problem, we still believe that the advantages brought by the usage of a GPU in terms of reduction of computational time – combined with the fact that we detected only very small variations in the *Mean Average Precision at Rank 1000 (MAP), Normalized Discounted Cumulative Gain at Rank 100 (nDCG@100), Precision at Rank 10 (P@10)*, and *Recall* – make this implementation of the algorithm a valid alternative to the CPU-based one.

4   Evaluation

To test our docker image we consider the Robust04 collection, which is composed of TIPSTER corpus Disk 4&5 minus CR. The collection counts 528,155 documents, with a vocabulary of 760,467 different words. The topics considered for the evaluation are topics 301–450, 601–700 from Robust04. Only the field *title* of topics is used for retrieval. The set of topics is split into validation (V) and test (T) sets. Relevance judgments are restricted accordingly. The execution times and memory occupation statistics were computed on an 2018 Alienware Area-51 with an Intel Core i9-7980XE CPU @ 2.60 GHz with 36 cores, 64 GB of RAM and two GeForce GTX 1080Ti GPUs.

To train the NVSM model, we set the following parameters and hyperparameters: word representation size $k_w = 300$, number of negative examples $z = 10$, learning rate $\alpha = 0.001$, regularization lambda $\lambda = 0.01$, batch size $m = 51200$, dimensionality of the document representations $k_d = 256$ and n-gram size $n = 16$. We train the model for 15 iterations over the document collection and we select the model iteration that performs best in terms of MAP.

---

[2] https://github.com/usnistgov/trec_eval.

When comparing the `nvsm_cpu` image and the `nvsm_gpu` image, we observe is that the CPU Docker image takes less space on disk than the GPU one. This is because the former does not need all of the drivers and libraries required by the GPU version of `Tensorflow`. In fact, these libraries make the `nvsm_gpu` image three times larger than the other one.

In Table 1, we report the retrieval results obtained with the two shared Docker images. From these results, we observe that there are small differences, always within ±0.01, between the runs obtained with `nvsm_gpu` on the same machine and with the ones obtained with `nvsm_cpu` on different machines.

Table 1. Retrieval results on the Robust04 (T) collection computed with the two shared Docker images of NVSM.

	MAP	nDCG@100	P@10	Recall
CPU (run 0)	0.138	0.271	0.285	0.6082
GPU (run 0)	0.137	0.265	0.277	0.6102
GPU (run 1)	0.138	0.270	0.277	0.6066
GPU (run 2)	0.137	0.268	0.270	0.6109

The MAP, nDCG@100, P@10, and Recall values obtained with the images are all very similar, and close to the measures reported in the original NVSM paper [9]. Indeed, the absolute difference between the reported MAP, nDCG@100, and P@10 values in [9] and our results is always less than 0.02. As a side note, the MAP values obtained by NVSM are low when compared to the other approaches on Robust04 that can be found in the OSIRRC 2019 library – even 10% lower than some methods that do not apply re-ranking.

In order to further evaluate the performance differences between the runs, we begin computing the RMSE considering the MAP, nDCG@100, and P@10 measures. The RMSE gives us an idea of the performance difference between two runs – averaged across the considered topics. We first compute the average values of MAP, nDCG@100, and P@10 over the three `nvsm_gpu` runs on each topic. Then, we compare these averaged performance measures, for each topic, against the corresponding ones associated to the CPU-based NVSM run we obtained on our machine. These results are reported in Table 2. From the results of this evaluation we can observe that the average performance difference across the considered 196 topics is very low when considering the MAP and nDCG@100 measures, while it grows when we consider the top part of the rankings (P@10). In conclusion, the RMSE value is generally low, hence we can confidently say that the models behave in a very similar way in terms of MAP, nDCG@100, and P@10 on all the considered topics.

In Table 3, we report the Kendall's τ measures associated to each pair of runs that we computed. This measure shows us how much the considered rankings are similar to each other. In our case, the runs appear to be quite different from

Table 2. RMSE between the NVSM CPU Docker image and the average of the 3 runs computed with the NVSM GPU Docker image.

	NVSM GPU (average)
RMSE (MAP)	0.034
RMSE (nDCG@100)	0.054
RMSE (P@10)	0.140

each other, since the Kendall's τ values are all close to 0. In other words, when considering the top 100 results in each run, the same documents are rarely in the same positions in the selected rankings. This result, combined with the fact that the runs achieve all similar MAP, nDCG@100, P@10, and Recall values, leads to the conclusion that the relevant documents are ranked high in the rankings, but are not in the same positions. In other words, NVSM performs a permutation of the documents in the runs, maintaining however the relative order between relevant and non-relevant documents.

Table 3. Kendall's τ correlation coefficient values between the NVSM GPU and NVSM CPU runs.

	GPU (run 0)	GPU (run 1)	GPU (run 2)	CPU
GPU (run 0)	1.0	0.025	0.025	0.018
GPU (run 1)	0.025	1.0	0.089	0.014
GPU (run 2)	0.025	0.089	1.0	0.009
CPU	0.018	0.014	0.009	1.0

5   Final Remarks

In this work, we performed a replicability study of the *Neural Vector Space Model (NVSM)* retrieval model using Docker. First, we presented the architecture and the main functions of a Docker image designed for the replicability of *Neural IR (NeuIR)* models. Secondly, we described the image components and the engineering challenges to obtain deterministic results with Docker using popular machine learning libraries such as `Tensorflow`. We also share two Docker images of the NVSM model: the first, which relies only on the CPU of the host machine to perform its operations, the second, which is able to also exploit the GPU of the host machine, when available.

We observed some differences between the runs computed by the `nvsm_cpu` Docker images on different machines and between the runs computed by the `nvsm_cpu` and `nvsm_gpu` Docker images on the same machine. The differences between `nvsm_cpu` images on different machines are related to the non-determinism of the results, as Docker relies on the host machine for some basic operations which influence the model optimization process through the generation of different pseudo-random number sequences. On the other hand, the differences between `nvsm_gpu` images on the same machine are due to the implementation of some functions in the CUDA and `Tensorflow` libraries. We observed that these operations influence in a sizeable way the ordering of the same documents across different runs, but not the overall distribution of relevant and non-relevant documents in the ranking. Similar differences, that are even more accentuated, can be found between `nvsm_cpu` and `nvsm_gpu` images on the same machine. Therefore, even though these differences may seem marginal in offline evaluation settings, where the focus is on average performance, they are extremely relevant for user-oriented online settings – as they can have a sizeable impact on the user experience and should thus be taken into consideration when deciding whether to use NeuIR models in real-world scenarios.

References

1. Dür, A., Rauber, A., Filzmoser, P.: Reproducing a neural question answering architecture applied to the SQuAD benchmark dataset: challenges and lessons learned. In: Pasi, G., Piwowarski, B., Azzopardi, L., Hanbury, A. (eds.) ECIR 2018. LNCS, vol. 10772, pp. 102–113. Springer, Cham (2018). https://doi.org/10.1007/978-3-319-76941-7_8

2. Ferro, N., Fuhr, N., Maistro, M., Sakai, T., Soboroff, I.: Overview of CENTRE@CLEF 2019: sequel in the systematic reproducibility realm. In: Experimental IR Meets Multilinguality, Multimodality, and Interaction. Proceedings of the Tenth International Conference of the CLEF Association (CLEF 2019) (2019)

3. Ferro, N., Marchesin, S., Purpura, A., Silvello, G.: A docker-based replicability study of a neural information retrieval model. In: Proceedings of the Open-Source IR Replicability Challenge co-located with 42nd International ACM SIGIR Conference on Research and Development in Information Retrieval, OSIRRC@SIGIR 2019, vol. 2409, pp. 37–43. CEUR-WS.org (2019). http://ceur-ws.org/Vol-2409/docker05.pdf

4. Freire, J., Fuhr, N., Rauber, A.: Reproducibility of data-oriented experiments in e-science (Dagstuhl Seminar 16041). In: Dagstuhl Reports, vol. 6, no. 1, pp. 108–159 (2016). https://doi.org/10.4230/DagRep.6.1.108, http://drops.dagstuhl.de/opus/volltexte/2016/5817

5. Marchesin, S., Purpura, A., Silvello, G.: Focal elements of neural information retrieval models. an outlook through a reproducibility Study. Inf. Process. Manag. **34** (2019). print

6. Marchesin, S., Purpura, A., Silvello, G.: A neural vector space model implementation repository (2019). https://github.com/giansilv/NeuralIR/

7. Sakai, T., Ferro, N., Soboroff, I., Zeng, Z., Xiao, P., Maistro, M.: Overview of the NTCIR-14 CENTRE task. In: Proceedings of the 14th NTCIR Conference on Evaluation of Information Access Technologies, Tokyo, Japan (2019)

8. Soboroff, I., Ferro, N., Sakai, T.: Overview of the TREC 2018 CENTRE track. In: The Twenty-Seventh Text REtrieval Conference Proceedings (TREC 2018) (2018)

9. Van Gysel, C., de Rijke, M., Kanoulas, E.: Neural vector spaces for unsupervised information retrieval. ACM Trans. Inf. Syst. **36**(4), 38:1–38:25 (2018)

Towards a Decision Support Framework for Forensic Analysis of Dynamic Signatures

Daniela Mazzolini[1], Patrizia Pavan[1], Giuseppe Pirlo[2], and Gennaro Vessio[2(✉)]

[1] Dipartimento Peritale, Associazione Grafologica Italiana (A.G.I.), Ancona, Italy
[2] Dipartimento di Informatica, Università degli Studi di Bari, Bari, Italy
`gennaro.vessio@uniba.it`

Abstract. This paper presents a preliminary easy to explain and effective framework for supporting dynamic signature analysis in forensic settings. The proposed approach is based on measuring similarities among signatures by applying Dynamic Time Warping on easy to derive dynamic measures. The long term goal of our research is to provide forensic handwriting examiners with a decision support tool to perform reproducible and less questionable inference.

Keywords: Dynamic signatures · Forensic analysis · Signature verification · Decision support systems

1 Introduction

Traditionally, forensic handwriting examiners (FHEs) are asked to verify the authenticity of a signature by relying on its *static* version, i.e. on an image of the signature acquired after the writing process has already occurred. However, with the increasing use of new technology, such as digitizing tablets, PDAs and smart phones, FHEs are more and more often confronted with *dynamic* signatures, i.e. the ones that can be acquired while the writing process still occurs [2]. Examples of application include information access and document analysis in digital archives. A dynamic signature is characterized not only by the geometrical position of the pen, but also by temporal, inclination and pressure information. In addition, most of modern tablets capture pen movement not only when the pen is on the pad surface, but also when the pen is in proximity of the surface, i.e. "in-air". While these new measures provide FHEs with a basis for quantitative and semi-automatic examinations, they also pose new challenges mainly due to a shift of paradigm from a qualitative analysis to a statistical and mathematical one they may be not familiar with.

Historically, the field of signature verification is of interest also to the biometric community. Excellent verification performance have been obtained in a number of studies employing pattern recognition and machine learning strategies to provide an automatic answer about the authenticity of a questioned signature

M. Ceci et al. (Eds.): IRCDL 2020, CCIS 1177, pp. 9–14, 2020.
https://doi.org/10.1007/978-3-030-39905-4_2

[1]. State-of-the-art methods have also been used in the forensic scenario [6,7]. However, the majority of these systems are characterized by complex solutions and high dimensional data making them perfect "black-boxes" to FHEs. Unfortunately, the use of these systems make difficult to FHEs to explain the rationale behind their final evaluation, which is strictly required in a working setting.

Therefore, there is the need for an easy to explain yet reliable framework for supporting dynamic signature verification in forensic scenarios. The present paper aims at moving a step towards this direction: a preliminary framework is proposed and the results of a simple case study are reported. Recent research started to address this problem, raising limitations and opportunities [4]. Unfortunately, especially in Italy, there is the lack of cross-fertilization between the forensic and biometric community. The present research is the result of an interdisciplinary collaboration and it is thus aimed at promoting fruitful exchanges.

2   Proposed Method

The proposed method is intended to provide guidelines for the FHE to follow for evaluating the authenticity of a questioned signature, given the time series raw data sampled by the acquisition device. It is worth to remark that it is inspired by the quantitative analysis recently proposed by Linden et al. [4]. The main difference concerns the introduction of a majority voting decision scheme to assist the FHE when multiple evidences arise. Moreover, as we will show in the Next Section, the proposed method has been tested on completely legible signatures instead of less complex initials.

The first main requirement is to have a meaningful set of genuine signatures (around 20), against which to compare the questioned signature, otherwise no convincing conclusion can be obtained.

The main attributes acquired by a digitizing tablet are the x and y coordinates of the pen position and their time stamps. Moreover, pen tablets capture pen pressure and pen inclination. The last measure is the so-called button status, which evaluates 0 for pen-downs and 1 for pen-ups. Kinematic features of the handwriting process can be calculated starting from the computation of the pen displacement during movement: $d_i = \sqrt{(x_i - x_{i-1})^2 + (y_i - y_{i-1})^2}$, where $i = 2, \ldots, N$, N is the number of sampled points and $d_1 = 0$. In other words, displacement corresponds to the straight line distance between consecutive sampled points. Given the typically high sampling frequency of the tablet, it provides a good approximation of the pen trajectory. From displacement, the tangential velocity and acceleration of the pen can be straightforwardly calculated as the first and second derivative of displacement, respectively: $v_i = \frac{d_i}{dt}, a_i = \frac{v_i}{dt}$, where $dt = t_i - t_{i-1}$, $i = 2, \ldots, N$, and $t_1 = v_1 = a_1 = 0$. Our focus is on these kinematic features, together with pressure, as they are directly provided by most of commercial software, such as *Firma Certa Forensic* (https://www.namirial.com/it/), typically used by FHEs. Therefore, they do not require additional derivations.

The guiding principle of this kind of analysis is that a high quality forgery can either appear precise but not fluent, or it could have been written fluently while looking imprecise. However, difficulties arise because of the inherent within writer variability, which makes signatures different even if produced by the same writer. While the trajectory pattern of the pen as well as the velocity, acceleration and pressure profiles can be easily plotted as scatter plots, these representations provide only a qualitative way to perform the signature analysis. Much more convincing conclusions can be obtained by performing a quantitative evaluation.

The comparison between a questioned signature and the given set of genuine specimens can be carried out by measuring how the signature to be investigated is positioned against the statistical distribution of the within writer variability of the genuine set. Of course, the classic Euclidean distance cannot be used to compute the similarities among signatures, given the non-perfect alignment of the corresponding time series. To overcome this issue, we use the well-known Dynamic Time Warping (DTW) algorithm. DTW has been extensively described in the literature: its goal is to measure the similarities between temporal sequences varying in speed. In the present study, we used the *FastDTW* Python implementation [5].

The proposed method involves computing all distances, with respect to a specific feature, among the N genuine signatures in the reference set. This results in $\frac{N(N-1)}{2}$ distances which capture the within writer variability and can be plotted as a box plot. Then, the mean distance from the questioned signature and each specimen of the reference set can be calculated and plotted against the previously obtained box plot. If the questioned signature places itself within the main variation, i.e. between the first and third quartile, then it can be considered as a genuine specimen. Otherwise, if it falls outside the main variation, i.e. below or above the first or third quartile, it can be considered to some extent as a suspicious signature. It is worth noting that different degrees of reliability of the conclusion can be obtained depending on how far the questioned signature is from the main variation. This approach is helpful for the FHE to analyze how well the questioned signature is separated from the distribution of genuine signatures. The same analysis can be performed for each of the time-dependent features: velocity, acceleration, pressure. The final conclusion can be provided as the most occurring outcome derived from the previous analysis. For instance, if the questioned velocity and acceleration fall outside the main variation, while pressure does not, the conclusion is that the signature can be a forgery. In other words, a majority vote is taken.

3   Case Study

In order to evaluate the effectiveness of the proposed framework, we performed a case study involving a genuine writer and a skilled forger. More specifically, we asked a FHE to provide 20 signatures of an invented person, equally split between two acquisition sessions in two different days for accounting for the within writer variability. Then, we asked the same writer to provide 5 genuine test specimens, performed in another day. Finally, we asked the daughter of the main signer, i.e. one which shares some physiological characteristics with her,

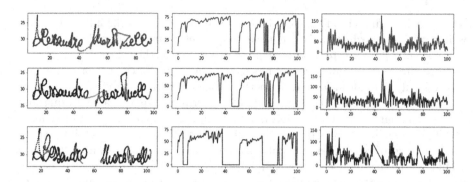

Fig. 1. Visual inspection of data. From top to bottom: a genuine signature; a genuine test specimen; a test forgery. From left to right: the signature rendering; the pressure profile; the velocity profile. Similarities between genuine samples and dissimilarities between them and the practiced forgery are quite recognizable.

to perform several forgery signatures and to choose the best 5 signatures, after practice, to be used as a test.

The samples were acquired through the Wacom STU-530 sign-pad, featuring 1024 pressure levels and 200 pps of report rate. It is one of the most common and professionals pads used at the POS or at customer contact points.

3.1 Qualitative Analysis

The geometrical position of the pen and the main dynamic attributes lend themselves to a qualitative analysis performed by considering their visual representation as scatter plots. Figure 1 shows the rendering of the signatures (including both on-surface and in-air trajectories) as well as the pressure and velocity profiles of a test genuine specimen and a test forgery. The solely visual inspection can provide meaningful insights into the signature apposition process. However, more reliable conclusions, especially in more ambiguous cases, cannot be drawn. In fact, the solely visual inspection of the characteristics of a dynamic signature, even if non-redundant with its static version, could provide less reliable evaluations than those performed in the traditional way based on the composition, direction, fluency, etc., of the signature.

3.2 Quantitative Analysis

This analysis involves the automatic comparison of time series using DTW. First of all, it is interesting to note the pronounced variation between signatures provided by the same individual in the two different days (Fig. 2). Then, we collapsed the overall reference set into a unique distribution against which to compare each test signature. Figure 3 shows the verification comparison, with respect to velocity, of a test genuine sample and a test forgery: differences are pretty evident.

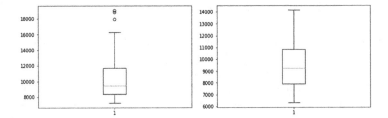

Fig. 2. Variability of the reference set among sessions with respect to velocity.

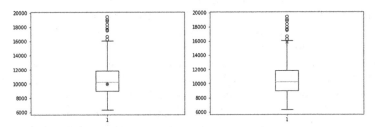

Fig. 3. Illustrative outcome of the verification comparison between a test genuine specimen (the blue dot on the left) and a test forgery (the red cross on the right). The first one clearly falls within the normal range; the other one appears to be an outlier. (Color figure online)

Table 1 reports the results obtained on the test set. They confirm the effectiveness of the proposed majority voting strategy as, although the individual features sometimes failed in providing the right answer, their combination improved the verification accuracy. Indeed, only the third signature in the forgery set was mistakenly categorized as genuine. Interestingly, acceleration revealed itself as the best predictor for verification, while pressure was the worst performing feature in accurately classifying the forgery class.

Table 1. Verification performance of the proposed method. On the left, the results concerning the test genuine (G) set; on the right, those concerning the forgery (F) one. The ✓ symbol indicates that, based on the corresponding feature, the method correctly classified the given signature as genuine or forgery, respectively. The final decision is taken has the majority vote of the individual features.

#	Velocity	Acceler.	Pressure	Decision
1	✓	✓	×	G
2	×	✓	✓	G
3	✓	✓	✓	G
4	✓	✓	✓	G
5	×	✓	✓	G

#	Velocity	Acceler.	Pressure	Decision
1	✓	✓	×	F
2	✓	✓	×	F
3	✓	×	×	G
4	✓	✓	✓	F
5	✓	✓	✓	F

4   Conclusion and Future Work

In this paper, we have proposed an easy to use yet effective framework for assisting the FHE during the analysis of dynamic signatures. Since the proposed approach is based on simple methods, provided by most of free statistical packages, and easy to derive features, it can be well tolerated by non computer science experts and can be easily explained to non professionals. Moreover, it provides FHEs with an objective evaluation tool which is independent of the specific examiner performing the analysis, resulting in reproducible and less questionable inference. The long term goal of our research is to develop guidelines accepted and used by the forensic community working with dynamic data. Our goal promotes synergies between the forensic and biometric community, as they can provide complementary and non mutually exclusive perspectives.

Several issues surely demand further research. First, the effectiveness of the proposed method should be tested against a large sample of specimens, involving a large variety of writers. Second, more refined thresholds, other than the first and third quartile, should be studied, based for example on outlier analysis. Third, the results here reported only concern with global characteristics of the signatures under consideration: future work should also take into account local approaches based, for example, on the segmentation between on-surface and in-air strokes. Fourth, more refined decision schemes could be investigated, weighting the available features by their different discriminating importance. Finally, device interoperability should also be taken into account, as it can strongly affect the verification results [3].

References

1. Diaz, M., Ferrer, M.A., Impedovo, D., Malik, M.I., Pirlo, G., Plamondon, R.: A perspective analysis of handwritten signature technology. ACM Comput. Surv. (CSUR) **51**(6), 117 (2019)
2. Harralson, H.H., Miller, L.S.: Huber and Headrick's Handwriting Identification: Facts and Fundamentals. CRC Press, Boca Raton (2017)
3. Impedovo, D., Pirlo, G., Sarcinella, L., Vessio, G.: An evolutionary approach to address interoperability issues in multi-device signature verification. In: Proceedings of the 2019 IEEE International Conference on Systems, Man, and Cybernetics (IEEE SMC 2019), pp. 3028–3033. IEEE (2019)
4. Linden, J., Marquis, R., Mazzella, W.: Forensic analysis of digital dynamic signatures: new methods for data treatment and feature evaluation. J. Forensic Sci. **62**(2), 382–391 (2017)
5. Salvador, S., Chan, P.: Toward accurate dynamic time warping in linear time and space. Intell. Data Anal. **11**(5), 561–580 (2007)
6. Tolosana, R., Vera-Rodriguez, R., Fierrez, J., Ortega-Garcia, J.: Feature-based dynamic signature verification under forensic scenarios. In: 3rd International Workshop on Biometrics and Forensics (IWBF 2015), pp. 1–6. IEEE (2015)
7. Vera-Rodríguez, R., Fiérrez, J., Ortega-García, J., Acien, A., Tolosana, R.: e-BioSign tool: towards scientific assessment of dynamic signatures under forensic conditions. In: 2015 IEEE 7th International Conference on Biometrics Theory, Applications and Systems (BTAS), pp. 1–6. IEEE (2015)

An Information Visualization Tool for the Interactive Component-Based Evaluation of Search Engines

Giacomo Rocco and Gianmaria Silvello(✉)

Department of Information Engineering, University of Padua, Padua, Italy
gianmaria.silvello@unipd.it

Abstract. In this paper, we present an InfoVis tool based on SanKey diagrams for the exploration of large combinatorial combinations of IR components – the *Grid of Points (GoP)*.

The goal of this tool is to ease the comprehension of the behavior of single IR components within fully functioning off-the-shelf IR systems without recurring to complex statistical tools. In order to assess the quality of the proposed SanKey-based InfoVis tool we conduceted an initial user study that led to interesting conclusions, yet to be validated in a future and more comprehensive study.

Keywords: Information Retrieval · Evaluation · Grid of Points · Information visualization · Sankey

1 Motivations

Information Retrieval (IR) systems are constituted of "pipelines" of components such as stop lists, stemmers and IR models, which are stacked together in order to process both documents and user queries and to match them returning a ranked result list of documents in decreasing order of estimated relevance. The performance of IR systems are evaluated in terms of *effectiveness* that can be determined only after that the system has been built; indeed, no effectiveness prediction about a specific component can be done before it has been tested within a fully functioning IR system.

Currently, the only viable means to determine the contribution to the system effectiveness of single components is to measure their impact on the overall performances by testing all the different combinations of such components. This leads to a very high number of cases to be considered, making the space of system combinations large and complex to explore.

Besides requiring a great deal of effort and resources to be produced, these combinatorial compositions constitute a challenge when it comes to explore, analyze, and make sense of the experimental results with the goal of understanding how different components contribute to the overall performances and interact together. Indeed, it is typically needed to resort to rather complex statistical

© Springer Nature Switzerland AG 2020
M. Ceci et al. (Eds.): IRCDL 2020, CCIS 1177, pp. 15–25, 2020.
https://doi.org/10.1007/978-3-030-39905-4_3

tools (e.g. multi-way *ANalysis Of VAriance (ANOVA)* models) requiring a careful experimental design and producing results which call for a considerable extent of expertise to be interpreted [6]. To this end, we developed an extensive set of $612 \times 6 = 3,672$ systems – i.e. the *Grid of Points (GoP)*[1] – arising from the combinatorial composition of several open-source publicly available components such as stop lists, stemmers, and IR models, and run against 6 different public test collections shared by the *Text REtrieval Conference (TREC)* international evaluation initiative. Thanks to this GoP, in [8] we presented the deep statistical analyses we run and the insights we gathered about the individual contributions of single IR components to the overall performances of fully working IR systems.

In this paper we present an InfoVis system based on SanKey diagrams – often used in physics to represent energy inputs, useful output, and wasted output – to allow the exploration of the GoP to quickly understand which combinations perform best under specific criteria, how components behave across a wide range of cases, and how they interact together. Our main goal is to give IR researchers and practitioners a fast and easy way to understand and analyze the GoP without recurring to demanding and complex statistical tools.

Hence, the InfoVis tool we present enables the analysis and comparison of a complex set of measures associated with a large combinatorial space of IR systems and the intuitive exploration and understanding of many component configurations. It is thought to be simple to use and to favor interaction, thus it provides functionalities as component filtering, measure selection and tooltips presenting statistical information easy to interpret. We present a user study to validate the presented tool.

The rest of the paper is organized as follows: Sect. 2 presents the related works, Sect. 3 describes the experimental setup and the Grid of Points we are considering for the visual tool, Sect. 4 describes the visual tool based on the Sankey visualization detailing the main components and its use, Sect. 5 reports the results of the user study which compared the present tool with another state-of-the-art visual tool though for the same task and Sect. 6 draws some final remarks.

2   Related Work

InfoVis techniques are typically exploited for the presentation and exploration of the *documents* managed by an IR system [16]. Typical examples are: identification of the objects and their attributes to be displayed [9]; different ways of presenting the data [13]; the definition of visual spaces and visual semantic frameworks [15]. The development of interactive means for IR is an active field which focuses on search user interfaces [10], displaying of results [4] and browsing capabilities [11].

Less attention has been dedicated to the application of InfoVis techniques to the analysis of experimental evaluation results. One example of a system

---

[1] http://gridofpoints.dei.unipd.it/.

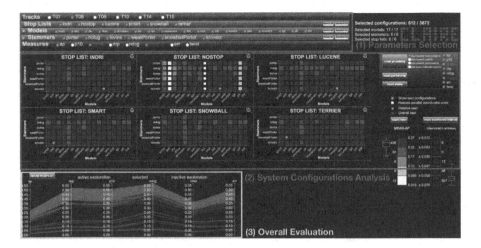

Fig. 1. The overall view of the CLAIRE visual analytics tool [1].

applying visualization to IR is *Visual Information Retrieval Tool for Upfront Evaluation (VIRTUE)*, a visual analytics tool supporting performance and failure analysis [2]. In the same vein, [3] presents an analytical framework trying to learn the behavior of a system just from its outputs for obtaining a rough estimation of the possible effects of a modification to the system. More recently, [12] presented an InfoVis tool to explore pooling strategies.

However, to the best of our knowledge only one solution – i.e. the CLAIRE tool [1], see Fig. 1 – exists for dealing with large sets of IR systems – the GoP [6,7] – generated by many IR components which allows the inspection of both configurations and measures. CLAIRE is based on a totally different visual paradigm since it uses tiles, parallel coordinates and boxplots to explore system configurations. *Combinatorial visuaL Analytics system for Information Retrieval Evaluation (CLAIRE)* is composed of three main areas: (i) the *Parameters Selection* area, dealing with the exploration coordinates; (ii) the *System Configurations Analysis* area, enabling the performance analysis of the system configurations; and, (iii) the *Overall Evaluation* area, where the system configurations performances are evaluated.

The visual tool we present in this paper follows the same overall organization, but it relies on a different visual paradigm allowing for an intuitive, yet less deep comprehension of the evaluation results over the considered Grid of Points. Indeed, CLAIRE has a strong focus on Visual Analytics, whereas the SanKey-based InfoVis tool we present here is specifically tailored to Information Visualization. The main difference is that visual analytics aims at exploiting visual clues to actually inform or modify analytical or algorithmic tools working over some data; on the other hand, information visualization aims at providing visual tools to better understand complex and possibly high-dimensional data.

Overall, CLAIRE is a more complex system than the SanKey-based Info-Vis tool presented here, even though they are comparable for the information visualization part since they both allow the user to select different evaluation collections and measures. Both the systems aim at intuitively visualize multi-dimensional data from different perspectives. Moreover, they both allow the user to select different IR system components and understand how they interact with one another also grasping the overall contribution of a single component over the whole search pipeline.

3   Experimental Setting

The GoP data adopted by our InfoVis tool is based on three main components of an IR system: stop list, stemmer, and IR model. We selected a set of alternative implementations of each component and, by using the Terrier v.4.0[2] open source system, we created a run for each system defined by combining the available components in all possible ways. The selected components are:

- *Stop list*: `nostop`, `indri`, `lucene`, `snowball`, `smart`,`terrier`;
- *Stemmer*: `nolug`, `weakPorter`, `porter`, `snowballPorter`, `krovetz`, `lovins`;
- *Model*: `bb2`, `bm25`, `dfiz`, `dfree`, `dirichletlm`, `dlh`, `dph`, `hiemstralm`, `ifb2`, `inb2`, `inl2`, `inexpb2`, `jskls`, `lemurtfidf`, `lgd`, `pl2`, `tfidf`.

Overall, these components define a $6 \times 6 \times 17 = 612$ runs. The stop lists differ from each other by the number of terms composing them; specifically, `indri` has 418 terms, `lucene` has 33 terms, `snowball` has 174 terms, `smart` has 571 terms and `terrier` 733 terms. Stemmers can be classified into aggressive (e.g. `lovins`) and weaker stemmers (e.g. `porter`).

The models we employ are classified into the three main approaches currently adopted by search engines: (1) the vector space model – e.g. `tfidf` and `lemurtfidf`; (2) the probabilistic model – e.g. `bm25` and the *Divergence From Randomness (DFR)* models; and, (3) the language models – e.g. `dirichletlm`, `hiemstralm` and `lgd`. We considered 6 standard and shared collections with 50 different topics each: *TREC Adhoc tracks* `T07` *and* `T08`; *TREC Web tracks* `T09` *and* `T10`; and, *TREC Terabyte tracks* `T14` *and* `T15`. We evaluate the GoPs by employing 8 evaluation measures: AP, P@10, Rprec, RBP, nDCG, nDCG@20, ERR, and Twist.

Summarizing, the GoP we visualize with the proposed InfoVis tool consists of 612 runs over 6 collections with 50 topics each and evaluated with 8 measures, which amounts to almost 1.5M data points.

---

[2] http://www.terrier.org/.

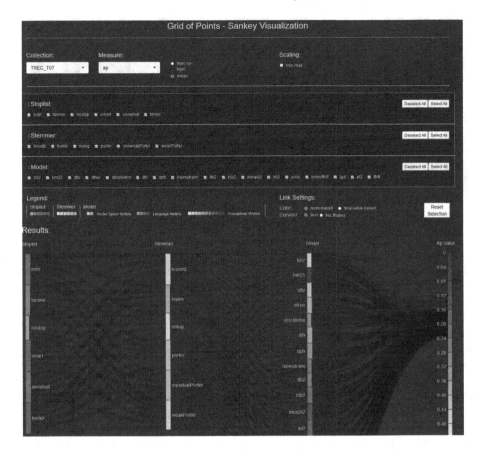

Fig. 2. The overall InfoVis system; on the top there is the parameter selection area and on the bottom the dynamic SanKey diagram.

4   The InfoVis Tool

The InfoVis tool we realized, see Fig. 2 is composed of two main areas:

Parameters selection area: (top of Fig. 2) it allows the user to load the runs relative to the desired experimental collection, to select the components s/he wants to consider and the evaluation measure to be used.

System analysis area: (bottom of Fig. 2) it allows the actual analysis and exploration of the various components and their evaluation on the basis of the parameters selected above.

4.1   Parameter Selection Area

In Fig. 3 we can see a detailed view of the parameter selection area.

The first two parameters that can be selected (in the green box) are the experimental collection and the evaluation measure of interest. On the left of

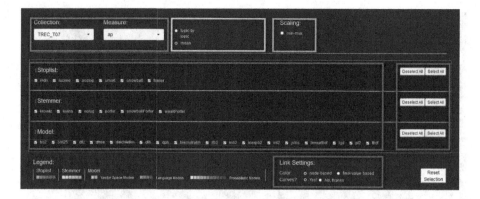

Fig. 3. A detailed view of the parameter selection area (Color figure online)

these two drop down menus we can choose to visualize the system performances topic-by-topic (if this option is selected a new drop-down menu appears allowing the user to select the topic of interest) or on average (e.g. MAP). The "scaling" option enables a normalized visualization of the SanKey diagram (only actual min-max values or the whole range such as $[0, 1]$ for AP). The blue box in Fig. 3 shows the control panel enabling the dynamic selection of component families to be visualized in the SanKey diagram.

The three component families (stoplists, stemmers and IR models) can be re-ordered by a simple drag-and-drop action, leading to a dynamic re-ordering of the axes of the Sankey diagram; this is particularly useful when during the data analysis phase we want to highlight the components interaction. The default axes order better shows the interaction between stoplists and stemmers and between stemmers and IR models, but by re-ordering the axes we can highlight, for instance, the stoplists-models interaction.

Below the blue box we can see the legend of the SanKey diagram where three chromatic variations are used to differentiate between the components of each family and sub-family of components: fuchsia for stoplists, green for stemmers, light blue for vector space models, purple for language models and dark blue for probabilistic models. The fuchsia box highlights the link settings where we can choose the shape of the SanKey curves and their color schema – i.e. based on component selection or based on evaluation measure value selection.

Every single interaction with the parameter selection area produces an effect on the SanKey diagram which is rendered dynamically and in real-time; this is intended to ease the interaction with the system and the data analyses to be performed.

4.2   System Analysis Area

On the bottom of Fig. 2 we can see the entire analysis space where all the available components are displayed by the SanKey diagram, whereas in Fig. 4 we can see a restricted analysis area where only some specific components have been selected and highlighted for an in-depth analysis of their performances and interactions.

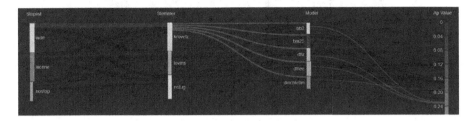

Fig. 4. A detailed view of the system analysis area where some components have been filtered out and some other are highlighted for an in-depth analysis of the interactions. (Color figure online)

The rightmost column presents the evaluation measure values divided into 25 rectangles of equal size, each one representing a 0.04 value interval. The color of each rectangle follows the red-yellow-green schema where reddish rectangles are assigned to lower values and the greenish ones to higher values. By the means of a drag-and-drop mouse action it is also possible to re-order the rectangles representing family components. Each single link insisting on these rectangles represents one of the 612 systems and their overall performance values.

A single system is represented by a path, i.e. a series of links connecting one component with the next one. The user can select a set of components (left click on one or more rectangles) to highlight the paths of interest as shown in Fig. 4 where we selected the `indri` stoplist and the `krovetz` stemmer.

The component columns present a number of rectangles equal to the components selected in the parameter selection area and the size of the rectangle gives a visual idea of the performances of the component it represents. This is done by calculating the marginal arithmetic mean of the performance values obtained by the systems using a specific component; the means are dynamically re-calculated every time a component is filtered out or added to the visualization. In Fig. 4, we can see that `krovetz` has a bigger rectangle than `lovins` and `nolug` (meaning no stemmer) showing the positive effect of the `krovetz` stemmer when interacting with the `indri` stoplist and the selected models.

The same idea is applied to the link size: the thicker the line the better the interaction between the components it connects. For instance, in Fig. 4 we can see that the stoplist-stemmer pair `indri-krovetz` has higher performances than the pair `lucene-krovetz`.

With a mouse-over action on a rectangle or a link, a tooltip reporting the top 5 systems using the selected component (rectangle) or the selected components pair (link) is visualized to the user. The InfoVis system also runs the Dunnett [5] statistical test to determine if the reported means are statistically different one

(a) Component tooltip   (b) Link tooltip

indri	
Average:	0.1978
Best Path:	
indri,krovetz,bb2	0.2290
Top Group (Dunnett's test):	
indri,krovetz,dfree	0.2227
indri,krovetz,bm25	0.2192
indri,krovetz,dfiz	0.2180
indri,lovins,bb2	0.2034
indri,lovins,bm25	0.1998
First five results	

Link:	
nostop → nolug	
Average:	0.1288
Best Path:	
nostop,nolug,dfree	0.1854
Top Group (Dunnett's test):	
nostop,nolug,dirichletlm	0.1526
nostop,nolug,dfiz	0.1357
nostop,nolug,bm25	0.1214

Fig. 5. (a) The tooltip visualized with a mouse-over action on the indri stoplist component and (b) the tooltip visualized with a mouse-over the nostop-nolug link.

from the other. In Fig. 5(a) we can see the tooltip visualized when the indri stoplist is selected: we show the average measure (AP in this case) of all the system using this stoplist, the best system adopting the stoplist and the top group of system adopting the indri stoplist that are not statistically different one from the other. In Fig. 5(b) we see the tooltip reporting the statistical information related to the nostop-nolug link.

5   User Evaluation

We did an initial user study with nine users (i.e., master degree students in Information Engineering) with a basic knowledge and previous experience with IR systems and experimental evaluation in the field; the study had a twofold goal, to compare the SanKey-based InfoVis tool with the CLAIRE system and to conduct an in-depth analysis of the newly proposed SanKey-based InfoVis tool. Of course, CLAIRE is a more complex system providing a wide range of functionalities, but we focused on the common features which regards the exploration of the combinatorial space of IR system pipelines.

The test was organized in three phases: (i) in-depth description of the two visual tools and hands-on phase to get to know them; (ii) *comparative study:* execution of three tasks with both CLAIRE and the SanKey-based InfoVis tool (in this phase we divided the users into two groups where one group used firstly CLAIRE and then the SanKey-based InfoVis tool and the second group did the opposite); (iii) *in-depth analysis:* execution of five tasks by using only the SanKey-based InfoVis tool. The tasks were centered around core activities enabled by the two visual tools such as the ability to determine the best IR system, the best combination of components, the comparison between two or more alternative components and so on. After the resolution of the first group of tasks the users were required to fill closed questionnaire. After the resolution of the second group of tasks the users were required to fill in an open questionnaire.

The questionnaire relative to the first set of tasks required to get a preference between the SanKey-based InfoVis tool and CLAIRE, was composed of two sets of questions; the first set with three questions: (Q1) How intuitive was the SanKey-based InfoVis tool (CLAIRE) tool? (Q2) In your opinion how much useful is the SanKey (CLAIRE) tool to understand the performances of IR systems? (Q3) How much effective was the SanKey (CLAIRE) tool to solve the given tasks? Each question of the questionnaire had to be answered by using an interval Likert scale ranging from 1 to 5 in which each numerical score was labeled with a description: {1: not at all, 2: a little, 3: enough, 4: a lot, 5: quite a lot}.

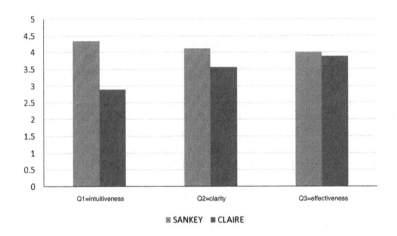

Fig. 6. Average answers for the first set of questions of the comparative study

In Fig. 6 we can see that both systems were evaluated as clear to use (Q2) and effective (Q3) in both cases with a slight preference for SanKey; but SanKey was considered more intuitive than CLAIRE (Q1).

The second set of questions for the comparative study was: (Q1) Which system does represent better the experimental data? (Q2) Which system does offer the most intuitive interface to interact with the data? (Q3) Which system is more complete to solve the assigned tasks? (Q4) Which system did you prefer to use? Each question of the questionnaires had to be answered by indicating a strong preference (a "2" in our interval scale) or a mild preference (a "1") for CLAIRE or SanKey where a "0" value indicated equality between the systems.

In Fig. 7 we can see that on average SanKey was preferred by the users with the only exception of Q3 where the systems were judged equivalent.

6   Final Remarks

The InfoVis tool we presented has the goal to ease the exploration and analysis of large experimental GoP enabling IR researchers and practitioners to better

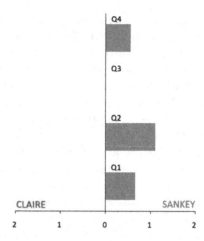

Fig. 7. Average answers for the second set of questions of the comparative study

understand the performances of single components, their interactions and their impact on off-the-shelf IR systems. The InfoVis tool we propose is highly interactive and remarkably simple as shown by the user study we conducted, yet offering advanced statistical information and analytics functionalities. Note that the user study has to be improved, thus the quality assessment of the SanKey-based InfoVis tool is initial and has to be further investigated to lead to more solid conclusions.

The presented tool is available on-line at the URL:

http://gridofpoints.dei.unipd.it/sankey/

and the source code is openly shared at the URL:

https://github.com/giansilv/sankey_eval

References

1. Angelini, M., Fazzini, V., Ferro, N., Santucci, G., Silvello, G.: CLAIRE: A combinatorial visual analytics system for information retrieval evaluation. Inf. Process. Manag. (2018). https://doi.org/10.1016/j.jvlc.2013.12.003. in print
2. Angelini, M., Ferro, N., Santucci, G., Silvello, G.: VIRTUE: a visual tool for information retrieval performance evaluation and failure analysis. J. Vis. Lang. Comput. (JVLC) **25**(4), 394–413 (2014)
3. Angelini, M., Ferro, N., Santucci, G., Silvello, G.: A visual analytics approach for what-if analysis of information retrieval systems. In: Perego et al. [14], pp. 1081–1084 (2016)
4. Crestani, F., Vegas, J., de la Fuente, P.: A graphical user interface for the retrieval of hierarchically structured documents. Inf. Process. Manag. **40**(2), 269–289 (2004)
5. Dunnett, C.W.: A multiple comparison procedure for comparing several treatments with a control. J. Am. Stat. Assoc. **50**(272), 1096–1121 (1955)

6. Ferro, N., Silvello, G.: A general linear mixed models approach to study system component effects. In: Perego et al. [14], pp. 25–34

7. Ferro, N., Silvello, G.: 3.5K runs, 5K topics, 3M assessments and 70M measures: what trends in 10 years of Adhoc-ish CLEF?.Inf. Process. Manag. 53(1), 175–202 (2017)

8. Ferro, N., Silvello, G.: Towards an anatomy of IR system component performances. J. Am. Soc. Inf. Sci. Technol. (JASIST) **69**(2), 187–200 (2017)

9. Fowler, R.H., Lawrence-Fowler, W.A., Wilson, B.A.: Integrating query, thesaurus, and documents through a common visual representation. In: Fox, E.A. (ed.) Proc. 14th Annual International ACM SIGIR Conference on Research and Development in Information Retrieval (SIGIR 1991). ACM Press, New York, USA (1991)

10. Hearst, M.A.: "Natural" search user interfaces. Commun. ACM (CACM) **54**(11), 60–67 (2011)

11. Koshman, S.: Testing user interaction with a prototype visualization-based information retrieval system. J. Am. Soc. Inf. Sci. Technol. (JASIST) **56**(8), 824–833 (2005). https://doi.org/10.1002/asi.20175

12. Lipani, A., Lupu, M., Hanbury, A.: Visual pool: a tool to visualize and interact with the pooling method. In: Kando, N., Sakai, T., Joho, H., Li, H., de Vries, A.P., White, R.W. (eds.) Proceedings of 40th Annual International ACM SIGIR Conference on Research and Development in Information Retrieval (SIGIR 2017). ACM Press, New York (2017)

13. Morse, E.L., Lewis, M., Olsen, K.A.: Testing visual information retrieval methodologies case study: comparative analysis of textual, icon, graphical, and spring displays. J. Am. Soc. Inf. Sci. Technol. (JASIST) **53**(1), 28–40 (2002)

14. Perego, R., Sebastiani, F., Aslam, J., Ruthven, I., Zobel, J. (eds.): Proceedings of 39th Annual International ACM SIGIR Conference on Research and Development in Information Retrieval (SIGIR 2016). ACM Press, New York (2016)

15. Zhang, J.: TOFIR: a tool of facilitating information retrieval - introduce a visual retrieval model. Inf. Process. Manag. **37**(4), 639–657 (2001)

16. Zhang, J.: Visualization for Information Retrieval. Springer, Heidelberg, Germany (2008)

3D Average Common Submatrix Measure

Federica Franco, Alessia Amelio$^{(\boxtimes)}$ (iD), and Sergio Greco

University of Calabria, DIMES, Via Pietro Bucci 44, Rende, CS, Italy
{a.amelio,s.greco}@dimes.unical.it

Abstract. This paper introduces a new measure for computing the similarity among 3D objects as the average volume of the largest sub-cubes matching in the objects. The match is approximate and only verified within a neighbourhood from the position of the sub-cubes. Preliminary tests performed on random and synthetic datasets prove the efficacy of the similarity measure in capturing the visual similarity among the 3D objects and a reduction in the execution time when the neighbourhood is considered.

Keywords: 3D objects · Pattern matching · Image similarity

1 Introduction

In multimedia retrieval, a similarity measure is used on a digital library of 2D images, 3D objects of medical imaging, and other data for finding the k-most similar items to a query item. The problem of automatically computing the similarity in the context of the digital libraries is still challenging, due to the gap between the human perceived appearance of the data and their features which are captured by the machine (semantic gap) [10].

In the last years, different approaches based on the concept of *common sub-matrix* have flourished for similarity computation in image retrieval tasks, whose advantages versus competing methods have been deeply investigated in the literature [1,2,4]. Specifically, [3] introduced the *Average Common Submatrix* (ACSM) measure for computing the similarity of images represented as matrices. ACSM computes the similarity between two images as the average area of the largest sub-matrices matching in the two images. A more efficient version of ACSM was proposed in [4] using a tree data structure for indexing the sub-matrices. To avoid the time and space requirements of constructing the tree index, [1] introduced an approximate version of ACSM, where the match between two sub-matrices is only verified for a portion of pixels at regular intervals, with any additional data structure. Finally, [2] framed ACSM within a new framework laying the theoretical foundations of the *common sub-matrix* concept and extending it. It noticeably reduced the temporal cost of computing the similarity without using additional data structures or omitting the match of a portion of pixels.

© Springer Nature Switzerland AG 2020
M. Ceci et al. (Eds.): IRCDL 2020, CCIS 1177, pp. 26–32, 2020.
https://doi.org/10.1007/978-3-030-39905-4_4

The *common sub-matrix*-based methods have been introduced for 2D objects so far, thus making not possible their usage in multidimensional contexts, including video retrieval [6] where the semantic gap still remains an open problem, medical image registration [11], and extensions in the context of multidimensional network analysis [7–9]. Especially in medical image registration, the correct selection of a similarity measure is a key aspect for reliably monitoring the time evolution of a patient's state for critical pathologies (e.g. stroke lesions) [5].

In this paper, we focus on extending the concept of *common sub-matrix* revisited in [2] for 3D objects, which is a brand new idea in the state-of-the-art. In particular, we provide the following contributions: (i) the ACSM measure is extended for objects in three dimensions, (ii) the match is verified in a neighbourhood of the objects, (iii) the match is approximate and computed in terms of the Hamming similarity extended in three dimensions. Accordingly, we aim to provide in progress results of our research.

2   The Proposed Method

In this section, we present 3D Average Common Submatrix (3D-ACSM), a new similarity measure for 3D objects extending the revisited version of ACSM introduced in [2]. Specifically, we use this new measure for computing the similarity between data in three dimensions, which can be represented as parallelepipeds.

2.1   3D Average Common Submatrix

Intuitively, let A, B and C be three parallelepipeds of volume $v = n \times p \times m$ defined on the same alphabet Σ. Then, A can be considered as more similar to B than to C if the average volume of sub-cubes of A matching approximately in B is larger than the same average volume in C [5].

More specifically, for each position (i, j, z) of A, 3D-ACSM finds the largest sub-cube in A starting at that position and with edge length greater than or equal to α approximately matching with a sub-cube in B within an ε-neighbourhood from (i, j, z). Restricting the area of search makes the similarity evaluation more efficient while it preserves the accuracy. The parameter α represents the minimum edge length of the sub-cubes to consider for the match. The parameter ε is related to the size of the neighbourhood with centre in (i, j, z) where a sub-cube can be found. Two sub-cubes approximately match to each other if the number of identical elements at the same positions exceeds or is equal to a given similarity threshold τ. From all aforementioned, 3D-ACSM between A and B is computed as follows:

$$S_\alpha(A, B) = \frac{1}{v} \sum_{i=\alpha}^{n} \sum_{j=\alpha}^{p} \sum_{z=\alpha}^{m} W(i, j, z), \quad s.t. \ W(i, j, z) \geq \alpha \tag{1}$$

where $W(i, j, z)$ is the volume of the largest sub-cube starting at position (i, j, z) in A of edge length greater than or equal to α approximately matching a sub-cube of B within an ε-neighbourhood from (i, j, z) in B.

Algorithm 1. 3D-ACSM algorithm

```
1: function compute3D-ACSM(A, B, α, τ, ε)
2:     Wα(A, B) = 0; Wα(A, A) = 0; d = 0; k = 0;
3:     for i = α ... n do
4:         for j = α ... p do
5:             for z = α ... m do
6:                 k = min{i, j, z};
7:                 Wα(A, A) = Wα(A, A) + k³;
8:                 found = false;
9:                 while (k ≥ α ∧ ¬found) do
10:                         if matchApproximate(A^k_{i,j,z}, B, ε) ≥ τ then
11:                             Wα(A, B) = Wα(A, B) + k³;
12:                             found = true;
13:                         end if
14:                         k = k - 1;
15:                 end while
16:             end for
17:         end for
18:     end for
19:     return SNα(A, B) = Wα(A, B)/Wα(A, A);
20: end function
```

A value $SN_\alpha(A, B)$ between 0 (minimum similarity) and 1 (maximum similarity) can be obtained as the ratio of $S_\alpha(A, B)$ with $S_\alpha(A, A)$, which is the similarity of A with itself.

2.2 Algorithm

The Algorithm 1 shows the steps for computing the 3D-ACSM similarity between two parallelepipeds A and B, given the minimum edge length of the sub-cube α, the similarity threshold τ and the ε size of the neighborhood. We denote with $A^k_{i,j,z}$ the sub-cube at position (i, j, z) in A whose edge length is k.

Firstly, for each position (i, j, z) (lines 3–5), the algorithm computes the ideal matching at that position. This value, denoted by $W_\alpha(A, A)$, is given by the volume of the maximal sub-cube matching itself, whose value is k^3 (line 7).

The global match of parallelepipeds A and B is denoted by $W_\alpha(A, B)$ and is computed by accumulating at each step the values of the matching between sub-cubes of A and B, respectively. In particular, at each step, the algorithm looks for the maximal sub-cube $A^k_{i,j,z}$ in A, with size k and start position (i, j, z), having a match with a sub-cube of B, with size k and start position in a neighbourhood of position (i, j, z) of size ε (lines 8–15). To determine the maximal size of the sub-cube k, it starts with a maximal size $k = min\{i, j, z\}$ and, at each step, if the matching value (computed by function $matchApproximate$) is not greater than or equal to a given threshold τ, decrements the size of the sub-cube k. If a feasible match is not found, the position (i, j, z) gives no contribution to $W_\alpha(A, B)$.

Finally, the ratio of $W_\alpha(A, B)$ with $W_\alpha(A, A)$ is returned (line 19).

The core of Algorithm 1 is given by the method $matchApproximate$, which finds the match of a sub-cube $A^k_{i,j,z}$ in B. The match is verified in a neighbourhood with centre at (i, j, z) in B and extent of ε hops along the three dimensions (where possible). Also, the match is approximate and resembles to the notion

Table 1. CPU time of Algorithm 1 on the first dataset with $m = \{15, 20\}$. For $\varepsilon = \{1, 3\}$, Δ_α is the average absolute time difference between $\alpha = 3$ and 1, and $\alpha = 5$ and 3. For $\alpha = \{1, 3, 5\}$, Δ_ε is the average absolute time difference between $\varepsilon = 3$ and 1

m	15						20					
ε	1			3			1			3		
$(n = p)/\alpha$	1	3	5	1	3	5	1	3	5	1	3	5
4	0.02	0.01	–	0.06	0.03	–	0.02	0.01	–	0.08	0.06	–
16	0.44	0.24	0.19	1.06	1.02	0.92	0.34	0.37	0.34	1.67	1.62	1.47
64	4.28	3.41	4.07	8.22	8.13	7.92	6.91	6.19	6.23	16.24	17.02	15.32
128	15.40	16.44	16.35	24.30	23.98	22.86	41.32	31.54	31.57	50.88	49.09	48.60
256	68.20	65.67	64.39	78.49	77.12	74.93	146.58	140.04	129.75	161.07	158.35	151.89
512	273.83	261.29	255.56	278.01	269.51	262.20	565.34	549.59	538.24	570.80	554.49	551.86
Δ_α	–	2.86	1.56	–	1.73	2.19	–	5.47	4.35	–	3.61	2.29
Δ_ε	4.66	5.46	5.65	–	–	–	6.70	8.82	12.60	–	–	–

of Hamming similarity [2] and its direct extension to 3D objects. Specifically, a match between two sub-cubes exists if their Hamming similarity (number of identical elements at the same positions) is greater than or equal to a threshold parameter τ, $0 \leq \tau \leq 1$.

3   Experiments

Preliminary experiments have been conducted for testing the performances of 3D-ACSM on two different datasets. The experiments have been performed in Matlab R2017a on a computer laptop with CPU Quad-Core 2.30 GHz, 8 GB RAM and Windows 7 (64 bit) operating system.

The first dataset includes a set of randomly generated numerical parallelepipeds of size $n = p$ varying from 4 to 512 and depth m varying from 5 to 20 with steps of 5. The size of the alphabet $|\Sigma|$ is set to 2. This dataset is used for testing the CPU time (in seconds) of Algorithm 1 at different values of the input parameters $\varepsilon = \{1, 3\}$, $\alpha = \{1, 3, 5\}$, and $\tau = 0.5$.

The second dataset includes a set of synthetic parallelepipeds each composed of three greyscale illusory and colour miscellaneous images of size 128×128 ($n = p = 128$ and $m = 3$). The used images are extracted from the online database of the Computer Vision Group, University of Granada[1]. They represent synthetic objects with frequent patterns and shapes useful for assessing the effectiveness of the similarity measure. The 3D-ACSM similarity is computed for each pair of parallelepipeds at different values of the input parameters $\varepsilon = \{1, 2, 3\}$, $\alpha = \{1, 4, 8\}$, and $\tau = \{0.5, 0.6, 0.7\}$. In the end, the obtained 3D-ACSM similarity is compared with the visual similarity, which is the similarity as perceived by the human eye.

---

[1] http://decsai.ugr.es/cvg/dbimagenes/.

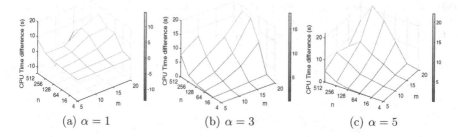

(a) $\alpha = 1$ (b) $\alpha = 3$ (c) $\alpha = 5$

Fig. 1. CPU time difference between $\varepsilon = 3$ and 1

Fig. 2. Sample parallelepipeds A, B and C from the second dataset. The size n, p is 128 with depth m equal to 3

Table 2. 3D-ACSM similarity computed among the sample parallelepipeds in Fig. 2

τ	ε/α	1		4		8	
		$SN_1(A,B)$	$SN_1(A,C)$	$SN_4(A,B)$	$SN_4(A,C)$	$SN_8(A,B)$	$SN_8(A,C)$
0.5	1	0.999	0.963	1.000	0.964	1.000	0.946
	2	1.000	0.994	1.000	0.994	1.000	0.988
	3	1.000	0.999	1.000	0.999	1.000	0.999
0.6	1	0.999	0.853	0.999	0.842	1.000	0.864
	2	0.999	0.931	0.999	0.924	1.000	0.930
	3	0.999	0.972	0.999	0.969	1.000	0.973
0.7	1	0.978	0.700	0.977	0.680	0.966	0.615
	2	0.991	0.819	0.990	0.807	0.985	0.739
	3	0.995	0.870	0.995	0.863	0.991	0.792

4   Results and Discussion

Table 1 reports the CPU time of Algorithm 1 on the first dataset of randomly generated numerical parallelepipeds with $m = \{15, 20\}$. It is worth noting that changing ε determines a higher time variation than changing α (the average absolute time difference Δ_ε is higher than Δ_α), which confirms the need of restricting the match within a neighbourhood.

Also, Fig. 1 shows the CPU time difference between $\varepsilon = 3$ and 1 for $\alpha = \{1, 3, 5\}$. It is worth noting as the time difference increases when the 3D objects become larger (higher size n, p and depth m) regardless of the α value. It confirms that restricting the neighbourhood can be time-saving especially for large 3D objects for which the CPU time has the tendency to normally increase (see Table 1).

Finally, Table 2 reports the 3D-ACSM similarity values for three sample parallelepipeds from the second dataset (see Fig. 2). From a visual inspection, it can be observed that A is more similar to B than to C, since the first and second slices of A and B are exactly the same. From Table 2, it is worth noting that 3D-ACSM similarity is compliant with the human perception of similarity, since $SN_\alpha(A, B)$ is higher than $SN_\alpha(A, C)$ for all parameters' combinations. It confirms that reducing the neighbourhood size still obtains reliable results with the advantage of reducing the execution time.

5   Conclusions

This paper introduced the 3D-ACSM measure as an extension of the ACSM similarity measure for 3D objects. Preliminary experiments were presented as a part of an ongoing work employing 3D-ACSM in the medical context of CT images. In such a context, an efficient 3D similarity measure is required in the registration process for monitoring the correct evolution of a patient's state [5]. Also, a comparison of 3D-ACSM similarity is being performed with other state-of-the-art measures. Finally, the Matlab code of the project is going to be available in open source for the scientific community.

Acknowledgments. This work was performed during the student internship of the first author at DIMES, University of Calabria.

References

1. Amelio, A.: Approximate matching in ACSM dissimilarity measure. Proc. Comput. Sci. **96**, 1479–1488 (2016). Knowledge-Based and Intelligent Information & Engineering Systems: Proceedings of the 20th International Conference KES-2016
2. Amelio, A.: A new axiomatic methodology for the image similarity. Appl. Soft Comput. **81**, 105474 (2019)
3. Amelio, A., Pizzuti, C.: Average common submatrix: a new image distance measure. In: Petrosino, A. (ed.) ICIAP 2013. LNCS, vol. 8156, pp. 170–180. Springer, Heidelberg (2013). https://doi.org/10.1007/978-3-642-41181-6_18
4. Amelio, A., Pizzuti, C.: A patch-based measure for image dissimilarity. Neurocomputing **171**, 362–378 (2016)
5. Amelio, L., Amelio, A.: CT image registration in acute stroke monitoring. In: 2018 41st International Convention on Information and Communication Technology, Electronics and Microelectronics (MIPRO), pp. 1527–1532, May 2018
6. Gurrin, C.: Content-based video retrieval. In: Liu, L., Özsu, M.T. (eds.) Encyclopedia of Database Systems, pp. 466–473. Springer, Boston (2009). https://doi.org/10.1007/978-0-387-39940-9

7. Hu, W., Xie, N., Li, L., Zeng, X., Maybank, S.: A survey on visual content-based video indexing and retrieval. IEEE Trans. Syst. Man Cybern. Part C (Appl. Rev.) **41**(6), 797–819 (2011)
8. Kankanhalli, M.S., Rui, Y.: Application potential of multimedia information retrieval. Proc. IEEE **96**(4), 712–720 (2008)
9. Li, Y., Gu, C., Dullien, T., Vinyals, O., Kohli, P.: Graph matching networks for learning the similarity of graph structured objects. CoRR abs/1904.12787 (2019). http://arxiv.org/abs/1904.12787
10. Patel, T., Gandhi, S.: A survey on context based similarity techniques for image retrieval. In: 2017 International Conference on Innovative Mechanisms for Industry Applications (ICIMIA), pp. 219–223, February 2017
11. Roche, A., Malandain, G., Ayache, N., Prima, S.: Towards a better comprehension of similarity measures used in medical image registration. In: Taylor, C., Colchester, A. (eds.) MICCAI 1999. LNCS, vol. 1679, pp. 555–566. Springer, Heidelberg (1999). https://doi.org/10.1007/10704282_60

Big Data and Data Science in DL

Lost in Translation: Can We Talk About Big Data Fairly?

Matilde Fontanin$^{(\boxtimes)}$ ⓘ and Paola Castellucci ⓘ

University La Sapienza, Rome, Italy
{matilde.fontanin,paola.castellucci}@uniroma1.it

Abstract. Big data and data science are global, there is no alternative in our connected, digital world. Yet, for a truly open and fair science, cultural biases and different opportunities across different countries must be taken into consideration.

English has become the international language for the scientific debate: a single language is most convenient, moreover it is undergoing a process of refinement and adaptation to the science register. On the other hand, laboratories are populated by researchers from all over the world, and much research takes place in non-English-speaking countries, where research tradition often develops moving from different perspectives, influenced by the cultural context.

A fair and open science would miss an opportunity if it did not take into consideration the multilingualism and multiculturalism of the researchers as individuals and members of specific communities, and could also waste precious time and energies, as language barriers prevent cooperation.

The paper will discuss the above-mentioned issues with examples and reflect on the changing role of librarians and information specialists within a global scientific community.

Keywords: Communication of data science in English · Multilingualism · Decolonising digital libraries

1 Overview

Big data and data science rely on a large international scientific community; scientists from different disciplinary fields, of multilingual and multicultural backgrounds share, openly and fairly, data including *"original scientific research results, raw data and metadata, source materials, digital representations of pictorial and graphical materials and scholarly multimedia material"* as in the Berlin Declaration [1].

In cyberspace, language is both a source of data and a tool to discuss them globally, it is necessary to put them in context, reason about them and to create metadata and, since researchers from different countries speak different languages, the need for a common language is as strong as the one for a shared technical jargon. Even on common disciplinary grounds, cultural differences remain, related to gender, provenance, social and educational backgrounds: to work together effectively, a linguistic and cultural mediation is needed.

© Springer Nature Switzerland AG 2020
M. Ceci et al. (Eds.): IRCDL 2020, CCIS 1177, pp. 35–46, 2020.
https://doi.org/10.1007/978-3-030-39905-4_5

Last year at IRCDL the authors [2] had reasoned on the barriers to a truly open access to science and the role of librarians. We will focus here on the predominance of English as a language for international communication among scholars, though if "*Our mission of disseminating knowledge is only half complete if the information is not made widely and readily available to society.*" [1], the concept of *cultural justice*, as defined by Ross [3], connected to *citizen science* and cultural context is in the background – though it would deserve a treatment of its own, which is beyond our scope. An ethical approach is needed if we share the view that "*Everyone has the right freely to participate in the cultural life of the community, to enjoy the arts and to share in scientific advancement and its benefits*" [4]. There is agreement that "*the Internet now offers the chance to constitute a global and interactive representation of human knowledge* [1]: in scientific communication, open to scholars and laymen, this implies different views, languages and jargons, as well as resorting to different codes, as images and even videogames [5]. Communicating to the general public research that may impact on their lives entails choosing carefully the tools; moreover, being aware of cultural and language barriers is beneficial to the multicultural community of scientists too. In this respect, librarians and other information workers feel involved since, according to IFLA Code of Ethics [6], their mission is to organize information and the services to access it for their users – be they scholars or laymen.

The paper will discuss with examples these issues, reflecting on the role librarians can play in a global scientific community and closing with some proposals.

2 Language Issues in the International Science Community

2.1 Discourse About Science: Language and Political Issues

The data collectively produced and analyzed are expressed in many formats, not necessarily text. Real objects and visual formats may be self-evident, nevertheless, to understand the deeper meaning of objects or the value they represent, a narration is necessary, as Hans Rosling demonstrates, creatively unleashing the power of statistical data [7] to popularize science. Data mapping the *geopolitics of science* show a definite, political hegemony of English. The ensuing marginalization and scarce visibility of other languages and cultures could be tackled effectively if we considered *openness* in the wider, political sense described by Chan [8], one of the signatories of the BOAI statement in Budapest [9].

Machine learning and Artificial Intelligence help analyze and understand the digital universe of data that people produce everyday simply by living online. The span of these fields of studies is increasingly multidisciplinary. A new, global science cannot ignore that AI affects the way people build their selves in a digital world. As Cheney Lipold suggests, "*Who we are in terms of data depends on how our data is spoken for. And in general, our data is spoken for with a language fashioned from these models. [...] systems of classification algorithmically authenticate us online*" [10]. Meaning that data themselves might cause biases and that they need to be reinterpreted before they can build the basis for scientific discoveries: reasoning about them implies linguistic communication. Language in science requires a specific register and the sharing of a common jargon, crucial to success in international research environments, as is awareness that the cultural background influences the meanings people read in words and actions.

The globalisation of science through the internet means not only that it is possible to communicate across continents: research data, technology - the digital revolution, the internet of things – impact on the representation of our own *selves* and the world. Floridi [11] underlines that *"we do not make science by mere accumulation of data"*, so *"the real epistemological problem with big data is small patterns. […] the pressure […] is to be able to spot where the new patterns with real added-value lie in their immense databases. […] This is a problem of brainpower rather than computational power"*. Since there is no dedicated academic path ready yet, *"philosophers might not only have something to learn, but also a couple of lessons to teach"* [11]. The *Harvard Business Review* describes the data scientist *"as a hybrid of data hacker, analyst, communicator, and trusted adviser"* [12]. To synthesize, different kinds of scientists are already *doing* data analysis and a multidisciplinary approach is advisable.

At international conferences like IRCDL researchers from different fields exchange views being displaced from their *safe havens*, obliged to explain anew issues that they are used at taking for granted, starting from nomenclature. False friends such as *library*, *collection*, *archive* evoke completely different images in the minds of a Library and Information Science (LIS) professional and of a computer scientist. The translation needed is not only to mediate between English and other languages, but also between the language of science and that of the humanities, to cross a chasm which has been perceived for a long time, at least since Snow defined it in his Reed Lecture [13] as a *"gulf of mutual incomprehension"*. At a conference recently organised at the University "La Sapienza" upon the lecture's 60th anniversary, the theme of language surfaced in the challenges of defining the object of study and communicating science. In this respect, the name of Otlet [14] and the creation of the Universal Decimal Classification were mentioned: born of the urge to supply science with a further tool for its progress, his taxonomy was meant to assign a code number to disciplines, thereby helping highlight the relations between sciences, so that new science could be developed by the observation of the same object from different points of view. His idea was to overcome misunderstandings by means of the numeric notation.

For all that, the issue remains of what language is to be used within the scientific community, made increasingly global by the internet communication tools and the changing habits with respect to the publication process. Publication formats such as books and journal articles developed into preprints and raw data; their sharing happens via social media or, alternatively, in journals, institutional repositories or large open-access databases such as PubMed, ArXiv or the like. In any case, the language most widely used is English. PubMed homepage states that the database comprises over 30 million citations, but a language search returns over 25 million English records, whereas Chinese, Italian and Spanish score less than 400.000 records each, Russian over 600.000, French over 700.000. To date, a Scopus search by language yields 65,417,222 results in English, 1,413,945 in French, 751,903 in Spanish, 1,026,903 in Russian and 1,769,605 in Chinese. Though PubMed is US-based and open access, Scopus is a proprietary database produced by a Dutch corporation with a long, European history. Yet English rules in both cases.

Open and fair data implies a cultural translation; using languages other than English, also in contexts like *citizen science*, will promote *cultural justice* across nations, ethnicities, social strata, gender, age (the elderly, for example), foster the dissemination of the results of socio-relevant research, and hamper the potential imperialism of the English language. An example is MeSH, the medical thesaurus of the US National Library of Medicine, which, next to the medical jargon, enriches its Spanish version with the common language terms for illnesses: plurality of languages and registers.

2.2 Why English? English as a World Language

Pullum, co-author of the Cambridge English Grammar, while stating that the reasons do not matter anymore, and that we should simply accept English as a *lingua franca* and the advantages of having a common language at all, underlines that English did not gain this position because it was the language best suited for the purpose and *"it's rather important that people should realize, if they're English speakers, that this is their great piece of underserved good luck"* [15]. Wiener complained that Latin had failed as an international language, though it had once had the possibility of becoming *"an adequate international language far superior to the artificial ones as Esperanto"* [16]. English is here to stay, it works, therefore we are keeping the tool.

An effective strategy is a multilingual approach, as in the European Union *"mother tongue-plus-two"* principle enunciated in Barcelona, aiming at enabling *"citizens to be fluent in two languages in addition to their mother tongue"* and at raising *"awareness of the linguistic diversity of European society and turn it into an asset for intercultural dialogue and competitiveness"* [17]. This second goal is particularly meaningful in a multicultural and interdisciplinary research environment, moreover the idea is relying on the preceding UN choice of using more official languages - besides English also French, Spanish, Russian, Chinese, Arabic. Other international organisations, as IFLA, follow the example.

2.3 English as the Language for Science

Being an international language does not necessarily make English a language for science. This further development is definitely rooted in the history of science around World War II, the European diaspora of scientists first from the Nazi regime and later from the Soviet bloc. It was the time of Big science, the time when Wiener criticized the habit of certain classicists to freeze language in time and forbid its development into an effective tool for communicating. He pointed out that *"the Greek language of the time of Aristotle was ready to compromise with the technical jargon of a brilliant scholar, while even the English of his learned and reverend successors is not willing to compromise with the similar needs of modern speech"* [16], so English had a long way to go. Gordin seems to agree with Pullum, that *"There's nothing about English that makes it intrinsically better for science than any other language."*. He foresees that it *"could split into three languages: English, Chinese and another language, such as Spanish, Portuguese or Arabic."* [18], yet, it is the common language now, and it *"is perfect for science: it's precise and straightforward"*, says Bosch Grau [19]. This is the result of a process: scientists adapted to using English and provoked a reverse process of adaptation of the language to science, so that nowadays "*English has acquired a vocabulary for concepts and processes*" [12].

Without the adaptive process there may be no English for international communication at all. Interestingly, it does not seem to be intrinsically more refined than other languages; for example in French, German or Russian, the term "science" encompasses "*scholarship in a broad sense, including the social sciences and often also the humanities*" [18] while its meaning in English is narrower. Yet, "*scientific activity is communicated in a language. I do not simply mean 'in words'; I mean in a particular, specific language, shared by a community of speakers*". Gordin distinguishes between *identity* – speaking of our inner feelings, in our native language, in different contexts - and *communication*, when we speak to be understood by a specific audience. "*If you are a native speaker of English, your language of identity equals your language of communication; your burden is reduced to the irreducible problem of saying what you mean.*" [18]. Non-native speakers face a harder task.

Nature published an article following an incident at a US University, when a professor reproached some Chinese students for speaking their own language on Campus. Seven scholars, selected for their personal or professional experience with language barriers, offered their views on English as a *lingua franca* for science [19] and referred of episodes which witness to the advantages and disadvantages of English for scientific communication. Most agree that as a tool it is well developed: Chinese is a rich language, but "*it still lacks much of the vocabulary that's needed to describe physical science*", says Cheng, Physicist at Cornell University, for whom it would be difficult to give a presentation on her research topics in her native language. Elsewhere [20] she declares that it was precisely her English competence which allowed her to "*science*" her way out of her country and of a limiting social background. She remarks that a low English competence is often confused with a lack of skills or of clarity of mind, and witnesses that Chinese researchers who are not fluent in English do not feel like trying her path. The same happens for Spanish speakers, and, as Clarissa Rios Rojas underlines, that it is not just a matter of reading and writing literature in English, but of understanding the process and culture of science: this is why she founded a mentoring program, Ekpa'palek, "*that helps students from Latin America to navigate academia*" [19]. The same seems to be on the mind of Montserrat Bosch Grau, from Spain, presently Director of *in vitro* studies at Sensorion in Montpellier, France, who claims that to master the language means to advance both in research and on the job market. She worked hard to raise her English competence to a good level while studying 12 months in France when English was not in the syllabus. Vera Sheridan, Language and intercultural relations researcher at Dublin City University, is of Hungarian origin and understands what it is like to learn a foreign language. She compiled a list of resources for foreign researchers from all over the world and points out that language skills need to be taught, they cannot be implicitly absorbed [19].

2.4   The Contribution of Multicultural Research Perspectives

Relying totally on English for scientific communication could cause *open* and *fair* science to miss some opportunities in understanding the world diversity. The concept of *open* was asserted through the BBB Declarations between 2002 and 2003, the concept of *fair* stands for *Findable, Accessible, Interoperable, Re-usable*, as synthesised in 2011 by FORCE11 [21]. If *open* and *fair* have become the pivotal principles of the Digital Libraries in our days, this is due to the redefinition of values brought about by the Post-Modernist thought and particularly due to the kind of critical perspective proposed by the Post-Colonial, Cultural and Gender Studies. A multicultural and interdisciplinary community, as the one represented at IRCDL, will seize on these values and integrate them in their *technical* choices.

Diversity. The perspective of the UN Millennium Goals regarding diversity is that problems must be faced globally, whereas non-English research is more difficult to spot and read out. When studying issues linked to local territories, the international community might miss out quite a few points. Irawan, hydrogeologist at the Bandung Institute of Technology, following the example of the first-ever open world repository, arXiv, founded *INA-Rxiv* [22] to increase visibility of papers in Indonesian – the language of one of the countries with the highest biodiversity in the world - that describe issues of geology, biodiversity, geography linked to that territory.

Tatsuya Amano [19], Zoologist at the University of Queensland, Brisbane, after realising that 36% of over 75,000 biodiversity conservation papers published in 2014 in PLoS Biology were in languages other than English, therefore less accessible, started a research for non-English literature in the field, struggling to have it translated into English. In other words, "*Just because something's not in English doesn't mean you should ignore it*" [23], says Bond, a senior conservation scientist at the Royal Society for the Protection of Birds in Sandy, UK.

Field research would benefit from a multilingual approach. Shena Dharwadkar, from the Centre for Wildlife Studies in Bengaluru, India, is a herpetologist and remarks that scientists from Western countries prefer to hire English-fluent guides to carry out field research in her area, yet, she underlines, "*locals understand the problem better*" [19], no matter whether they speak English or not. Moreover, as she points out, science should reach out to residents and be beneficial to everyone. Wildlife researcher Owen Bidder [23] explains that, being proficient in German, he can get precious information from German hunters during his field research.

Managing Interaction and Career. Much research is led globally, in large laboratories, involving international, multicultural and multilingual research groups, where every member has different tasks. To work well together, they must feel comfortable: Chen [19] observed that normally European researchers speak in their native language, whereas Chinese and South-Koreans just do not feel comfortable at doing the same. Conversely, Clarissa Rios Rojas seems to feel that being from abroad has some advantages, as she, being a native Spanish speaker, is able to relate easily with other Spanish, Portuguese and Italians. Having people build a community definitely facilitates working together and exchanging views, but it requires either a good level of English or a diffused multilingualism in the group and certainly an open attitude.

For non-English speakers, tasks such as writing papers and applying for fellowships are harder. Amano pointed out that "*The dominance of English has created considerable bias in the scientific record*" [19]. A difference in perspectives is enriching to the scientific discourse, and a low competence in English – though it might still allow to be speakers at conferences - makes it harder to network, which is the main point of attending conferences, after all.

Moreover, submitting articles in English opens the path to core journals, the ones indexed in large databases, Scopus and WoS, and consequently to the highest evaluation, impact factor and worldwide visibility. The language issue is but one ring in a whole chain of research assessment and publication policies, regardless of the outlet: journals, proprietary databases and open access repositories, so an issue which might look *simply* language-related refers instead to the stabilization or to the rethinking of a whole system of values.

Cultural Context and Exchange. The physical and linguistic position of a digital collection is not irrelevant, suggests Castellucci [24]: ArxiV *"tastes"* of Los Alamos and New Mexico, its history can be read as part of the cultural context it developed into. Moving from the assumption that there is a *materiality* inherent in digital resources, one of the main concerns of policies for the development of Digital libraries nowadays regards the *decolonization* of electronic archives - in other words, a conscious effort in the selection of languages, collections, corpora as well as literary and aesthetic canons other than those mediated through English language [25]. *"English speakers have become the gatekeepers of science. By keeping those gates closed, we're missing out on a lot of perspectives and a lot of good research"* [19], says Vera Sheridan. Research needs to be led from different viewpoints, *"If you're a non-native speaker, you can bring a diversity of opinion and approach to the international community"* [19], says Tatsuya Amano.

Even the father of Cybernetics, Norbert Wiener, is extremely aware of the relevance of the cultural context, and often refers to the one he works within, the USA in the Fifties. A look at some quotes clarifies what that time and place *"tasted"* of: *"The education of the average American child of the upper middle class is such as to guard him solicitously against the awareness of death and doom."*; *"It is possible to believe in progress as a fact without believing in progress as an ethical principle; but in the catechism of many Americans, the one goes with the other"*; *"To the average American, progress means the winning of the West."* [16]. There would be much to say on these statements from an historical and social point of view, and it would be beyond our scope to go deeper, but it might be surmised at least that, at the time, the education of the average German or Japanese child was based on totally different experience. Moreover in Wiener we find the same *taste* of American society in the concept of *information* itself - *"The fate of information in the typically American world is to become something which can be bought or sold."* – and in the idea of research as Big science, when he says *"The skill by which the French and English do great amounts of work with apparatus which an American high-school teacher would scorn as a casual stick-and-string job, is not to be found among any but a vanishingly small minority of our young men."* [16]. Wiener tells us of a society where research is supported by large funds because it is a product for the market. In fact, he laments the lack of artistic creativity and proper training in the practice of science, the subservient attitude of research to the market, and feels that big laboratories are over-structured for a future where he does not *"foresee that the next generation will be able to furnish the colossal ideas on which colossal projects naturally rest."* [16]. Moreover he reflects the *"taste"* of a time when the scientist was male (*him*; *young men*), and *American* was synonymous with *from the USA*, when the perception in terms of *gender* and *post-colonial* had not settled yet – though even recently Isabel Allende was very surprised when an immigration clerk in the USA insisted that she should qualify herself as *coloured* and not *American* [26].

In a world of Big data we need all the different perspectives that we can use. Wiener defines himself as a "*scientific artist*" [16], because science is the language he chose to have his say, and he is most aware of the role of art and the humanities in the progress of human knowledge. We saw above that tasks and skills necessary for data analysis require creativity, since this is a completely new field we are still striving to understand. In a perspective of open, fair science the predominance of English should become less crucial, in order to prevent missing valuable publications and points of view only because the people expressing them do not master the language.

3   The Role of the Librarian and of the Humanist

Much boost to research is given by the possibility to access to raw data, pre-prints and publications in an open and fair way from wherever, and to be able to share views with researchers from different cultures. The contribution of specialists from different disciplinary backgrounds to perform specific tasks is beneficial to the work of a research team. Among them there is information curation and organization – something library and information specialists have been taking care of for a long time.

A digital library is defined by IFLA as "*an online collection of digital objects, of assured quality, [...] created or collected and managed according to [...] principles [...] and made accessible in a coherent and sustainable manner[which] forms an integral part of the services of a library*" [27]. The traditional mission of the librarian transposed into the digital environment implies collection curation, organization and access to materials for the specific communities served. The role of a librarian within an academic organization or a research team is exemplified by the experience of Luisella Goldschmidt-Clermont, who was for ten years Senior Scientific Information Officer at the European Organization for Nuclear Research (CERN) within the community of high-energy physicists [28]. She remarked that scientists, absorbed by their research duties, struggled to keep up with literature updates and with external communication of their results and suggested that some members on the research team should be specifically in charge of that. Differences are perceivable between scientist and humanist: Goldschmidt-Clermont observes that physicists are not keen on allocating more funding and staff to information management and communication. This might be a mark of the difference perceived between STEM and humanities scholars, especially in the digital world, where mathematicians and the like are at home, and where the humanists arrived later, as guests [24].

The competences of librarians and information specialists mediate between hard sciences and the humanities; LIS curricula combine the world of printed items with Information Science and Technology. It could not be otherwise, since the organization of documents passes through their translation into records, granular [29] representations of real materials, whatever their format. It was not by coincidence that CILIP, the

UK professional association, sprung in 2002 from the merger of the Library Association and the Institute of Information Scientists. Since the librarians' mission is to *"organize and present content in a way that allows an autonomous user to find the information s/he needs"* and *"to provide the best possible access for library users to information and ideas in any media or format."* and that *"This includes support for the principles of open access, open source, and open licenses."* [6], they would naturally be interested in any format of information. As a result, if the information goes digital, they need to become more proficient in IT.

After the digital revolution, being able to organize information in the best way has become crucial to the survival of science itself. Big data challenge libraries *"to adopt new service models to assist with the transformation of data into information"* […]. *"Today data science is seen as the blending of competencies in computer programming, software engineering and statistics, combined with a particular domain expertise"* [30]. The data librarian is supposed to be able to work closely with researchers, yet the tasks and skills of this professional figure are still being defined. Library associations and academia are behind in preparing standards for the job – the exception is CILIP, stating that data librarians are *"engaged in managing research data, using that data as a resource and supporting researchers in these activities*, and to that purpose they are likely *to be involved in developing or implementing an organization's Web data management plan, storing and managing data and determining retention and disposal periods"* [31]. Among qualifications, apart from a LIS degree, *"understanding of current technologies and standards such as institutional repositories, encoding standards (e.g. XML) and metadata"* are recommended.

Apparently, as in the case of the data scientists, specialists are already out there doing the job, but specific education is not ready. Moreover, tasks are all but defined. Recently, a research on *"What is a data librarian"* [32] analyzed job ads in the USA and found that the most required skill is research assistance, followed by a critical thinking/problem solving attitude. Apparently, the main task envisioned for the data librarian is instructional support, including copyright, intellectual property, licensing of data, embargoes, ethics and reuse, data literacy and privacy.

Data librarians are used at speaking *"multiple disciplinary languages"* [30], and therefore can play a role as connectors in a multicultural research environment; moreover, they are familiar with classification systems, which serve as multidisciplinary links, as Otlet [14] pointed out. Nevertheless, such a role in an international environment demands language competence. The right attitude, therefore, might be to raise awareness on the fact that English is a tool for communicating, while bearing in mind the value of vernacular, local literature. Librarians, who manage collections by standards, languages of their own, could help communicate internationally the products of research in local languages and the cultural diversity they represent. Moreover, learning a language is not about finding different labels for the same boxes, as in different contexts it is the boxes and their contents that change. Learning technical English and discussing the terminology for library services in another language *"enhances the librarians' perception about their role"* and helps them remain *"inventive and creative to match the transformations in the nature of information and society."* [33], states Fontanin, who has been teaching English to librarians for the past twenty years. Foreigners coming to the libraries might range from refugees to visiting researcher: the variety in meanings, contexts, social scenarios is as large as science, as diverse as society.

4 Attitude for Solutions

Access to multilingual, multi-register and multidisciplinary information fosters the development of a free science, but it is not always available. As Hibert [34] recently reasoned, in countries where funding is low and English proficiency not that high, Shadow Libraries [35] thrive, a bottom-up solution to the access to knowledge. Piracy according to some, resistance to others, they witness a critical issue in an apparently universal digital era: across embargoes, Internet blocks and expensive subscriptions, looking at the world from a non-Western perspective shows a not-so-fair landscape.

Probably the best approach is to start small, from practical solutions to single problems. Some examples are proposed by the interviewees on Nature [19]. First, English language should be taught at University level, specifically for those who are undergoing a research path. In addition, mentoring should become a habit: Vera Sheridan claims that writing experts are not enough to turn a PhD thesis into an article, as the process demands specific competence in the discipline. Extending the *embedded* approach – librarians and teachers working side by side to reach course goals - to larger research groups could prove beneficial.

International organizations should provide specific allocations to language support in the projects they finance. Shena Dharwadkar proposes that hiring locals to assist researchers in field research should be made a criterion to privilege project funding, and the same could be said for the mediation and dissemination of research in local languages with the help of libraries, data librarians and scientists.

5 Conclusion

All in all, though English is a very useful tool to exchange views in a global scientific community, a multilingual approach would not only facilitate conversations, but also envision different points of view. Learning a language is about experiencing a different worldview, it is a transformative experience, as is research.

In a research group diverse points of view enrich the final product: local perspectives, individual views, multidisciplinary approaches may open up new visions, therefore the role of women, of minority languages and cultures, of digital humanities contributes to creativity. Wiener was the father of cybernetics and defined himself as a scientific artist. Provided the art offered is aligned with the spirit of global science and with people's needs, provided it is striving to convey a message, it does not matter what language or alphabet is used to express it, be it text, visual, or else. An art installation by Dormino [36] used art to make a point on Web information: between 2015 and 2017, four chairs were placed in various locations. Three controversial figures - Edward Snowden, Julian Assange and Chelsea Manning - were standing on them, a fourth was left empty for whoever had got *"anything to say"*. It is another language, but it is effective.

We could close in the words of a scientist and a humanist. Albert Einstein stated: *"Man tries to make for himself in the fashion that suits him best a simplified and intelligible picture of the world; he then tries to some extent to substitute this cosmos of his for the world of experience, and thus to overcome it. This is what the painter, the poet, the speculative philosopher, and the natural scientists do, each in his own fashion. Each makes this cosmos and its construction the pivot of his emotional life, in order to find in this way peace and security which he cannot find in the narrow whirlpool of personal experience"*. Looking for answers requires a multi-faceted approach and a multitude of languages. This richness would be *lost in translation* - in the words of Roman Jakobson, founder of modern linguistics - if it were channeled through a single language code.

References

1. Berlin Declaration on Open Access to Knowledge in the Sciences and Humanities (2003). https://openaccess.mpg.de/Berlin-Declaration
2. Fontanin, M., Castellucci, P.: Water to the thirsty reflections on the ethical mission of libraries and open access. In: Manghi, P., Candela, L., Silvello, G. (eds.) IRCDL 2019. CCIS, vol. 988, pp. 61–71. Springer, Cham (2019). https://doi.org/10.1007/978-3-030-11226-4_5
3. Ross, A.: Real Love: In Pursuit of Cultural Justice. Routledge, London (1998)
4. United Nations: Universal Declaration of Human Rights (1948)
5. Shah, H.: How to involve citizen scientists to develop AI for Knowledge Exchange. Presented at the OAI11 – CERN-UNIGE Workshop on Innovations in Scholarly Communication, 19–21 June 2019
6. IFLA FAIFE <Freedom of Access to Information and Freedom of Expression>: IFLA Code of Ethics for Librarians and other Information Workers (2012)
7. The Joy of Stats. https://www.gapminder.org/videos/the-joy-of-stats/
8. Chan, L.: Contextualizing Openness: Situating Open Science. University of Ottawa Press, Ottawa (2019)
9. Budapest Open Access Initiative—Read the Budapest Open Access Initiative. https://www.budapestopenaccessinitiative.org/read
10. Cheney-Lippold, J.: We Are Data: Algorithms and the Making of Our Digital Selves. New York University Press, New York (2017)
11. Floridi, L.: The 4th Revolution: How the Infosphere is Reshaping Human Reality. Oxford University Press, Oxford (2014)
12. Davenport, T.H., Patil, D.J.: Data Scientist: The Sexiest Job of the 21st Century, HBR, October 2012. https://tinyurl.com/jb4lgum
13. Snow, C.P., Collini, S.: The Two Cultures. Cambridge University Press, Cambridge (2014)
14. Otlet, P.: Traité de documentation. Le livre sur le livre, théorie et pratique, par Paul Otlet, Bruxelles, Palais mondial (1934)
15. Pullum, G.: UQx Write101x English Grammar and Style - Interview with Geoffrey Pullum. https://tinyurl.com/sros83w
16. Wiener, N.: The Human use of Human Beings: Cybernetics and Society. Eyre and Spottiswoode, London (1950)

17. Commission of the European Communities: Accompanying document to the Communication from the Commission to the European Parliament, the Council, the European Economic and Social Committee and the Committee of the Regions Multilingualism: an asset for Europe and a shared commitment (2008). https://tinyurl.com/skd4gbq
18. Gordin, M.D.: Scientific Babel: How Science Was Done Before and After Global English. The University of Chicago Press, Chicago (2015)
19. Woolston, C., Osório, J.: When English is not your mother tongue. Nature **570**, 265 (2019). https://doi.org/10.1038/d41586-019-01797-0
20. Cheng, Y.: Let science be science again (2017). https://tinyurl.com/ug95gy9
21. FORCE11. https://www.force11.org/
22. Irawan, D.E.: Against all odds: we only see numbers. In: Indico (2019)
23. Walker, C.: Learn the local lingo to get ahead. Nature **534**, 425–427 (2016). https://doi.org/10.1038/nj7607-425a
24. Castellucci, P.: Carte del nuovo mondo: banche dati e open access. Il mulino, Bologna (2017)
25. Di Loreto, S., Morello, S.: Decolonizing the digital archive. In: 25th AISNA Biennial Conference - Gate(d)Ways. Enclosures, Breaches and Mobilities Across U.S. Boundaries and Beyond., Ragusa (Italy) (2019)
26. Allende, I.: Mi país inventado. Areté, Barcelona (2003)
27. IFLA – IFLA/UNESCO Manifesto for Digital Libraries. https://tinyurl.com/rmwbw5l
28. Goldschmidt-Clermont, L.: Communication patterns in high-energy physics. High Energy Physics Libraries Webzine, no. 6 (2002)
29. Zani, M.: Granularità: un percorso di analisi. DigItalia **2**, 60–128 (2006)
30. Klapwijk, W.: IFLA. Big Data Special Interest Group: A concept framework for data science in libraries (2018). https://tinyurl.com/vbg73c6
31. Data Librarians - CILIP: the library and information association. https://tinyurl.com/sue8nql
32. Khan, H.R., Du, Y.: What is a Data Librarian? Content Analysis of Job Advertisements for Data Librarians in the United States Academic Libraries (2017)
33. Fontanin, M.: The flexible Librarian: English @t the Circulation Desk. AIB, Roma (2017)
34. Hibert, M.: Ecologies of smart unstructuring: silicon regimes, alternatives in commons, and unparallel librarian. Presented at the IFLA Satellite Librarians and Information Professionals as (Pro)motors of Change, Zagreb, Croatia, 20 August 2019
35. Karaganis, J. (ed.): Shadow Libraries: Access to Knowledge in Global Higher Education. The MIT Press; International Development Research Centre, Cambridge; Ottawa (2018)
36. Dormino, D.D.: Anything to say? A monument to courage 2015–2017. https://tinyurl.com/tml22td

An Ontology and Knowledge Graph Infrastructure for Digital Library Knowledge Representation

Stefano Ferilli[1]([✉]) and Domenico Redavid[2]

[1] Department of Computer Science, University of Bari, Bari, Italy
stefano.ferilli@uniba.it
[2] R&D Department, Artificial Brain S.r.l., Bari, Italy
redavid@abrain.it

Abstract. New technologies for storing and handling knowledge provide unprecedented opportunities for enhanced fruition of digital libraries and archives. Going beyond document retrieval based on lexical content or metadata, using the context of documents, and/or of their content, may provide very new ways to put them in perspective and grasp a deeper understanding thereof, also for non-technical users.

Several components are needed to support this new perspective: suitable ontological resources to describe such variated knowledge, collaborative tools to collect the precious knowledge scattered across many scholars and practitioners spread all over the world, and to store it in a knowledge base, fruition tools to make the collected knowledge available to all interested stakeholders (scholars, researchers, but also common people).

This paper proposes the GraphBRAIN environment as a possible infrastructure. It is a general-purpose tool that allows its users to design and populate knowledge graphs, to collaboratively enrich them, and to exploit advanced fruition tools, consultation and analysis tools. Its functionality may also be provided as a set of Web services to end-user applications. An initial version of the ontology and knowledge graph for digital libraries and archives are also presented and discussed in the paper.

1 Introduction

While there has been a traditional focus on digital libraries and archives from the collection and consultation perspective, the current availability of new technologies for storing and handling knowledge provides unprecedented opportunities to handle further, high-level functionalities. One such functionality is an enhanced fruition that goes beyond 'simple' document retrieval based on lexical content or on the available metadata. For scholars and practitioners, but also for non-expert end users, a very relevant component, full of interesting information, may be the context of the document as a whole, and/or of its content, that allows to put it in perspective and grasp a deeper understanding thereof. For instance,

© Springer Nature Switzerland AG 2020
M. Ceci et al. (Eds.): IRCDL 2020, CCIS 1177, pp. 47–61, 2020.
https://doi.org/10.1007/978-3-030-39905-4_6

it might be interesting to know that a novel was first cited in a document that was found in a certain place of a certain country, and that a character in that novel was inspired to a real person, who was a friend of the author, who lived in a city, where an event took place that inspired him to write the novel. And, maybe, that the novel was used as the screenplay for a movie, which was shown for the first time in a certain theatre of a famous town, at the presence of some very important public persons. And so on.

Of course, collecting, storing and using such information is not trivial, for several reasons. First, the knowledge to be represented spans through a wide range that goes beyond the typical expertise of researchers and scholars, also involving amateurs, collectors, and enthusiasts. Also, the available knowledge may be scattered and spread across many persons, each perhaps knowing just part of the story, or specialized only on some aspects of it. Moreover, satisfactory usage of the available information might involve complex information patterns and aggregates, that might be domain-dependent and different for the different kinds of users involved. In short, a switch from data bases to knowledge bases is needed, so as to allow a shared understanding of the involved concepts, to improve the reuse of the available information, and to enable reasoning tasks on it that return additional higher-level, non-trivial information. Leveraging the enthusiasm of practitioners in this field, a possible solution would be to adopt a collaborative approach for the building and enrichment of the knowledge base. In a *wiki* approach, the motivation to share knowledge would be the possibility of using also the information contributed by other people.

However, a collaborative approach in which many people, with different expertise, culture, background and perspectives contribute small pieces that together make up the big picture, requires suitable schemes to represent and organize the knowledge in this field. From a traditional database perspective, these schemes are the table definitions. From the knowledge base perspective, these schemes are typically in the form of ontologies. Since this paper aims at merging both perspectives, we need a solution that may serve both as a database schema and as an ontology. Unfortunately, due to the very different traditional approach to data management in digital libraries and archives, the currently available resources, developed in the cultural heritage landscape, are unsuitable. Hence, a need for a new scheme, to be shared and reused by all the stakeholders involved in this area of interest, which is one of the contributions of this paper.

Handling the functionality described above requires an appropriate infrastructure, made up of advanced data representation and storage facilities, as well as of advanced information handling tools and algorithms. This paper proposes a solution based on the Web application **GraphBRAIN**, an on-line tool to collaboratively design, build and maintain knowledge bases. It was used to define a first version of the scheme/ontology describing the contextual information about digital libraries and archives, to serialize it in Web Ontology Language (OWL), and to build a first version of the knowledge graph.

This paper is organized as follows. The next section quickly recalls some related works. Then, after describing the features and interface of GraphBRAIN in the Sect. 3. Section 4 provides the ontology for the 'contextual' description of digital libraries and archives, and Sect. 5 briefly overviews its current content. Section 6 reports a sample case study and, finally, Sect. 7 concludes the paper and outlines future work issues.

2 Related Work

Concerning the ontology development functionality, several tools have been proposed in the literature, each one with specific targets as regards the construction, editing, annotation and merging of ontologies [1]. Among them, the most popular and mature tool is protégé[1], based on the OWL-API, which is fully compliant with the OWL specifications by W3C[2]. GraphBRAIN adopted the same OWL-API for its ontology export functionality, so that the generated ontologies are fully compliant with the standard and may be edited using protégé. We developed a specific ontology definition and handling tool for several reasons. First, it had to be embedded into GraphBRAIN's interface, so that the administrators could seamlessly and collaboratively build and refine the ontologies. Second, while existing tools are mainly aimed at defining formal ontologies starting from an RDF knowledge base model, our motivation was in the need to define a schema for the graph DB, and the translation in standard ontology format was a consequential objective in order to enable OWL reasoning capabilities.

On the methodological side, some works exist that analyze the possibilities of cooperation between ontologies and graph DBs. In [3] the potential of applying graph DBMSs to an ontological context in order to create essentially an ontological tensor, e.g. the algebraic counterparts of the combinatorial multi-layer graphs, is outlined, and its complexity is assessed. [9] discusses technical issues that might limit the impact of symbolic Knowledge Representation on the Knowledge Graph area, and summarizes some developments towards addressing them in various logics.

Another stream of related work is the development of ontologies and/or knowledge graphs. While standard ontologies used for describing resources in the library/archive domain do exist (e.g., the Dublin Core Metadata Initiative, or DCMI [8]), to the best of our knowledge, nothing exists for the specific objective of expanding its area of interest, from the strictly scholar approach to a broader, 'contextual' one that may be attractive also for non-specialized users. However, other resources are available for closely related topics. For instance, focusing on cultural heritage, and on the Italian landscape, **Cultural-ON** (Cultural ONtology) [11]. Very close to our perspective are also [10,14], concerning the development of a database relating movies to the places in which they were shot. Like GraphBRAIN, they adopt a collaborative approach, and aim at describing more than just the formal or technical aspects of filmography, also in a touristic perspective. These initiatives might be connected to GraphBRAIN to

---

[1] https://protege.stanford.edu.

[2] http://owlcs.github.io/owlapi.

enrich its knowledge base and provide a more effective and varied service to its users.

3   GraphBRAIN

GraphBRAIN[3] is a general-purpose knowledge base management system aimed at covering all stages and tasks in the lifecycle of a knowledge base, from knowledge acquisition, to knowledge organization, to (personalized) knowledge fruition and exploitation. The knowledge base is implemented as a graph database, using the Neo4j [13] DBMS. Nodes and arcs may have associated attribute-value maps; nodes (representing individuals) may be labelled with one or many labels (usually representing classes), while each arc (representing a relationship) may be labeled with one type only. No schema handling is provided for by Neo4j, meaning that the user is totally free to use any type and/or attribute name for any single node and arc. While ensuring great flexibility, this does not allow to associate a clear semantics to the graph items. For this reason, GraphBRAIN requires its users to work according to pre-specified data schemes, expressed in the form of ontologies. Thus, a characterizing feature of GraphBRAIN is its bringing to cooperation a database management system for efficiently handling, mining and browsing the individuals, with an ontology level that allows it to carry out formal reasoning and consistency or correctness checks on the individuals.

The administrators of the knowledge base may build and maintain the general and domain-specific ontologies by specifying the types of entities and relationships to be considered, each with its attributes and associated datatypes. The universal class is implicit, so the user must start the ontology description from the top-level classes, which are automatically considered as disjoint by the system. Each top-level class may be the root of a hierarchy of subclasses, for which no assumption about disjointness is made. Some classes and relationships may appear in different ontologies, possibly with different attributes, in order to reflect different perspectives on them. In particular, GraphBRAIN provides a top-level ontology, defining very general and highly reusable concepts (e.g., **Person, Place**) and relationships (e.g., **Person.wasIn.Place**). It plays a crucial role to interconnect the domain-specific ontologies, ensuring an overall connected knowledge graph. Indeed, there is a single, shared graph underlying all the domains. Thanks to the classes shared across different domains, this allows the system to reuse knowledge across domains, and thus to reach a wider range of outcomes for satisfying the user information needs. So, if an individual is used by different ontologies, it acts as a bridge among those ontologies, allowing the users of a domain to obtain additional information coming from other domains.

The ontologies are saved in an internal format, used as a schema for the graph database. The tool may also export them into standard Semantic Web formats, to make them publicly available for reuse. Currently, it can serialize them to Ontology Web Language (OWL)[4] format, with namespace prefix **lam,**

---

[3] A demo of the system can be found at http://193.204.187.73:8088/GraphBRAIN/.
[4] http://www.w3c.org/owl.

so that it can be published and exploited for ensuring semantic access to the knowledge base and make it interoperable with other resources. The tool models the particular case of different collection types by declaring some specific OWL classes and sub-properties. For example, object property **lam:belongsTo** has concept **lam:Collection** as the range, but several disjoint classes as domain (e.g., **lam:Person** and **lam:Document**). The tool defined one sub-property of **lam:belongsTo** for each of these domain classes. In this way, instead of having a generic property:

(**lam:Person** or **lam:Document**) **lam:belongsTo lam:Collection**

one may assert instances of either relationships:

lam:Person lam:personBelongsTo lam:PersonCollection
lam:Document lam:documentBelongsTo lam:DocumentCollection.

GraphBRAIN uses the ontologies to drive and support knowledge base creation and enrichment, plus all other functionalities, including a set of advanced tools for searching and browsing the knowledge base, and a set of mining, analysis and knowledge extraction tools that may be used interactively by end users or provided as services to other systems for obtaining selective and personalized access to the stored knowledge.

Information is fed into the knowledge base by interaction with users or by automatic knowledge extraction from documents and other kinds of resources (e.g., the Internet). The interactive interface, shown in Fig. 1, consists of two form-based tabs, one for entities (Fig. 1, bottom-left) and one for relationships (Fig. 1, bottom-right), allowing the user to insert/update/remove instances and their attribute values. The forms are automatically generated by the system from the internal format specification of the ontologies. For this reason, albeit GraphBRAIN may handle several ontologies, each specifying a different domain, the form-based interface for data management and querying requires the user to select one of the available domains in order to load the corresponding scheme/ontology to be used (Fig. 1, top-left). While the knowledge base content may be published as linked open data (LOD) [7], it is not available in its entirety as LOD. Indeed, it is accessible only through the querying and graph browsing facilities in the on-line interface, or through pre-defined tools exposed as services, that, based on their input parameters, return relevant portions of the graph serialized as RDF.

Additional functionality is also provided. First, users may manage (add, show, delete) attachments for each instance. In this way GraphBRAIN goes beyond knowledge management tools, becoming a full-fledged digital library, whose content is indirectly organized according to formal ontologies, and thus may foster interoperability with other systems. Second, users may add comments, or approve/disapprove, each entity or relationship instance, and even each single attribute value thereof. This can be used to ensure some kind of 'distributed' quality assurance on the content of the knowledge base, and to establish a trust mechanism for the users. Using the comments, the users may also provide useful suggestions to improve and extend the ontologies. Also, users are encouraged to provide high-quality knowledge, because using a combination of their number of contributions and trust they are assigned 'points' that they may spend in using advanced features provided by GraphBRAIN.

The same form-based interfaces can be used to query the knowledge base for instances of entities and relationships. The retrieved instances may be graphically displayed in another tab, as nodes and arcs in the graph (see Fig. 1, top-right). This allows the user to continue his search in a less structured way, by directly browsing the graph (by expanding or compressing node neighbors). This is useful to explore the available knowledge without a pre-defined goal in mind, but letting the data themselves drive the search. Thus, serendipity in information retrieval is supported, and the users may find unexpected information that is relevant to their information needs.

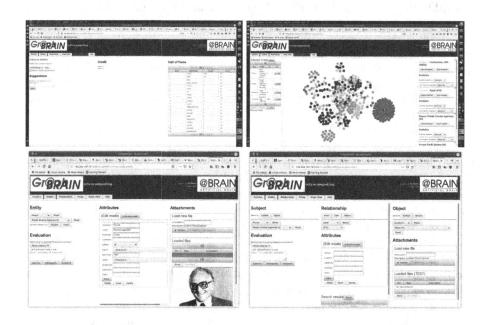

Fig. 1. GraphBRAIN interface for managing and consulting the knowledge base.

Moreover, several analysis, mining and information extraction functionalities are provided, such as:

- assess relevance of nodes and arcs in the graph, and extract the most relevant ones;
- extract a portion of the graph that is relevant to some specified starting points (nodes and/or arcs);
- extract frequent patterns and associated sub-graphs;
- predict possible links between nodes.

Some of the underlying algorithms are reused from the literature; others have been purposely extended to improve their ability to return personalized outcomes that may better satisfy the user's information needs. This would ensure that each user obtains tailored information, which is another novelty introduced by GraphBRAIN. For instance, since the graph is too large to be entirely displayed, when opening the graph tab, the neighborhood (computed by a modified version of the Spreading Activation procedure) of the most relevant nodes (based on PageRank, betweenness and harmonic centrality, etc.) is shown. If a user model is available, based on statistics collected about his previous interaction with the system, the starting nodes may be those more related to his interests, preferences, aims, background, etc. Of course, the displayed portion of the graph may also be the result of a specific user query.

4 Ontological Schema for the Knowledge Base

At the time of writing, the ontology for the 'contextual' description of digital libraries and archives includes 75 classes, 51 relationships and 75 attributes. Some are domain-specific, while some others are borrowed from other (general or domain-specific) ontologies already present in the system. The latter are crucial for allowing us to link domain-specific knowledge to contextual one and to knowledge belonging to other domains, providing information that usually would not be present in library- or archive-specific systems, but might be useful to better understand the library/archive items and to indirectly relate them to other library/archive items. In the following we will describe the main components of the ontology in an informal and intuitive style. For the sake of brevity, relationships and attributes will not be described. Of course, each class or relationship may have its own attributes, and inherits those of its super-classes (if any).

The top-level classes, and their immediate subclasses (if any), are the following (a short description is provided when not obvious).

- **Award**: any kind of recognition that can be awarded to, or record that can be marked by, persons, companies, devices, documents, or components. It has 3 subclasses:
  - **Education**: associated to (more or less formal) educational levels (e.g., B.Sc., M.Sc., PhD, etc., but also certifications, etc.).
  - **Prize**: awards formally granted (usually by some institution);
  - **Record**: the recognition of being the first or the best in doing something;
- **Collection**: any conceivable grouping of items. This ontology currently provides for 2 specific kinds of groupings, corresponding to subclasses:
  - **Persons** (e.g., families, teams, etc.).
  - **Documents** (e.g., series, archives, etc.).
- **Category**, with 2 subclasses:
  - **Concept**, useful to tag documents;
  - **Subject**, useful to categorize content.
- **Company**, currently used to represent both companies and institutions, corresponding to 2 subclasses of this class.

- **Document**, in its most general definition as "something that serves as evidence or proof". As such, it is not limited to printed documents (or documents that might in principle be printed, such as a PDF or word-processor file), but also includes audio-video recordings. It has currently 14 subclasses:
  - **Advertisement, AudioRecording, Book, Booklet, Card, Deed, Leaflet, Letter, Magazine, Manual, Movie, Picture, Postcard, Poster**
- **Event** (5 subclasses),
  - **Conference**: a meeting with mainly research or educational purposes.
  - **Fair**: a convention mainly oriented towards selling products and commerce.
  - **Show**: a convention mainly oriented towards showing new products.
  - **Lecture**
  - **Historical Event**: any significant event that should be recorded (e.g., the presentation of a book, etc.).
- **IntellectualWork**: the original result of an intellectual effort, relevant for methodological or practical purposes (9 subclasses)
  - **Algorithm** (e.g., Quicksort);
  - **Approach** (e.g., Step-Wise Refinement for algorithm design);
  - **Invention** (e.g., the Microprocessor);
  - **ProgrammingLanguage**
  - **Subject** (e.g., Information Theory, started by Shannon, or Graph Theory, started by Euler);
  - **Technology**
  - **Theorem**
  - **TheoreticalModel** (e.g., Turing's machine);
  - **WorkOfArt** (e.g., a novel).
- **Item**: a specific, identifiable specimen of a (mass-produced) object, in our case a **Document** (e.g., a signed or numbered copy of a book).
- **Package**: a specific packaging of documents (e.g., a set of books sold together);
- **Person**: reporting personal data about persons;
- **Place**: It is the root of a hierarchy currently made up of 27 subclasses, of which its direct subclasses are:
  - **Administrative, Building, Geographic, Mansion**
- **Software** with 19 subclasses, its direct ones being:
  - **Development, Educational, Embedded, OfficeAutomation, OperatingSystem, Videogame**

Domain-specific classes are **Award, Category, Company, Document, IntellectualWork**[5]. Classes borrowed from the general ontology are **Event, Person, Place, Collection**, and **Item** (the set of subclasses of **Collection** and

---

[5] Due to the pervasive use of documents in our lives, most elements in this ontology might be regarded as belonging to the general ontology. However, because of its specific focus, this ontology provides much more detailed and richer descriptions for them (in terms of subclasses, attributes and relationships).

Item is extended by defining additional domain-specific subclasses). Classes borrowed from other domain-specific ontologies are **Package** and **Software** (useful to represent digital media often packaged with books, magazines, etc.).

The most relevant relationships in the ontology are:

- **Person.developed.Document** (authors, editors, etc.),
- **Company.produced.Document** (publishers),
- **Document.belongsTo.Collection** (series, collections, etc.),
- **Company.produced.Collection,**
- **Company.wasIn.Place,**
- **Document.wasIn.Place,**
- **Document.concerns.Category.**

Also, other relationships were included to connect classes belonging to different partial ontologies, e.g.:

- **Software.packagedWith.Document, Document.requires.Software.**

5   Current Content of GraphBRAIN

A prototype of GraphBRAIN is currently in use as part of a larger ongoing project [5], in which GraphBRAIN will act as the knowledge base management platform underlying an integrated system under development, aimed at supporting all stakeholders involved in touristic activities (tourists, entrepreneurs and institutions). The library/archive domain-specific ontology perfectly fits this overall system, given the central role that documents play in the touristic perspective (e.g., books or movies describing or showing places or cultural heritage artifacts or collections, documents stored in certain places or institutions, etc.). Ontologies for the following domains are currently present in the system (ontology names are the same as the domain names):

general including very general concepts and relationships that are expected to be present in almost all domains;

tourism concerning history, cultural heritage items, points of interest, logistics and services, etc.;

food especially concerning the perspective of typical dishes and beverages from specific touristic regions;

computing concerning computing devices and their history[6] [6];

libraries&archives the ontology described in the previous section.

---

[6] It is included as a kind of cultural heritage, with the aim of integrating it with more traditional kinds of cultural heritage, both from a scholarly perspective and for fostering its fruition in a touristic perspective. E.g., a tourist interested in the history of computing, while in Bari, might be spotted the chance to visit the collection at the Department of Computer Science, in order to see a specimen of the Olivetti Programma 101 computer.

where 'general' may be considered as a top-level ontology, while the others are domain-specific ontologies purposely developed for the project. Albeit (partly or fully) reusing existing standard vocabularies, they also extend them for the project's specific needs. Table 1 reports overall structural statistics and a comparison among the three most populated ones.

Table 1. Statistics on some ontologies in GraphBRAIN

Ontology	Main classes	Subclasses	Attributes	Relationships	Attributes
Libraries&Archives	12	63	51	51	24
General	17	27	79	88	23
Computing	15	97	111	117	21

The available ontologies share some classes and relationships, by which knowledge items from different domains can be related to each other, extending in this way the available scope of search beyond the single perspectives. In particular, the *general* ontology acts as a hub to inter-link the other ontologies, and allow specific information from one domain to be connected to specific information from other domains. It has significant overlapping with the library/archive ontology described in the previous section, specifically as regards: **Category, Document, Person, Place, Series**.

Particularly interesting is class **Category**, aimed at hosting items from different taxonomies. Currently, it is filled with the WordNet lexical ontology [4,12] (under subclass **Concept** for its conceptual part, and under class **Word** for its lexical part) and with the standard part of the Dewey Decimal Classification (DDC) system [2] (under subclass **Subject**). The latter is fundamental for the library domain, because it provides labels to classify the documents. Also the former may play a significant role, allowing us to tag the documents with relevant concepts and words that are, in turn, related to each other, allowing to find non-trivial paths between documents. Specifically, words may be used for lexically tagging other items, while concepts may be used to semantically tag them. Note that the classes in these taxonomies are reified, becoming individuals in the knowledge graph. This allows to handle them within the graph, instead of formalizing thousands of classes in the ontology. So, the categories and words may be linked to individuals of other classes (e.g., documents, persons, places) and used as tags to express information about them (e.g., 'Alan Turing' might be linked with 'Computer Science', 'World War II', etc.).

The current content of the GraphBRAIN knowledge base is summarized in Table 2. For each ontology, the number of instances (*Inst*) and attributes (*Attr*), for both classes and relationships, is shown, along with the average number of attributes (*A/C*) and relationship instances (*R/C*) per class instance. Column *A/C+R/C* reports the average amount of information (i.e., the sum of number of attributes and number of relationships) associated to each class instance. Obviously, the vast majority of knowledge items is in the *general* ontology, including items automatically loaded from WordNet and the DDC taxonomy, plus

Table 2. Statistics on the current content of the GraphBRAIN knowledge base

Ontology	Classes			Relationships				
	Inst	Attr	A/C	Inst	Attr	A/R	R/C	A/C + R/C
Libraries&archives	9 902	31 615	3.19	13 649	10 614	0.78	1.38	4.57
General	333 020	1 744 116	5.24	488 639	39 186	0.08	1.47	6.71
Tourism	250	1173	4.69	318	54	0.17	1.27	5.96
Food	181	405	4.01	65	0	0.00	0.36	4.37
Computing	551	2 096	3.80	739	343	0.46	1.34	5.14
Total	343 904	1 779 405	5.17	503 410	50 197	0.10	1.46	6.63
Total knowledge items	2 123 309			553 607				

other items manually entered by the users. Next comes the *libraries&archives* ontology, also mostly automatically loaded from the records of a private collection, including 4.266 different books, mostly concerning general knowledge, linguistics, literature, history, folklore, and computer science. Then, with much less items, come the ontologies whose knowledge items were manually entered using the on-line collaborative interface: the *computing* ontology, which was the first domain-specific ontology built in GraphBRAIN, and the *tourism* and *food* ontologies, that are the most recently added (and thus the less populated).

There are usually (except for the *food* ontology) less class instances than relationship instances, indicating a quite connected graph, which is important for interlinking the knowledge and providing the users with information based on graph browsing. The R/C parameter reveals that the general subgraph is the most connected, followed by the libraries, food and computing subgraphs and finally by the tourism subgraph. As expected, the average number of attributes per instance is larger for class instances than for relationship instances. Indeed, relationships are by themselves information carriers. Comparing A/C and A/R, we see that the 'information density' is different between classes and relationships for the various domains. For classes, the richest information is in the general subgraph, while the poorest is in the libraries domain, suggesting the much information was missing in the records. For relationships, the richest domain is the library one, while the poorest is food. This shows that much relevant information in the library domain is in the relationships rather than in the attributes, which makes sense considering the strict interplay among several entities (documents, authors, publishers, places, categories, series).

6 Sample Case Study

Since the system is already on-line, no specific evaluation or validation is foreseen for it, except for the exploitation in the tourism-related project, that is indeed contributing in highlighting and fixing problems, refining the ontologies and feeding knowledge graph, and identifying the aspects of the approach to be extended and improved. Also, the on-line system allows any user to provide feedback, comments and suggestions, that will be carefully taken into account in the future versions of GraphBRAIN.

Instead, we provide in the following a sample case study. Due to space limitations, we can only provide very simple examples of use of GraphBRAIN, that
hopefully suggest its potential in supporting the users.

User *stefano* logs into the system, and selects the **libraries&archives** ontol-
ogy/schema. Then it moves to the Entities tab, and using the search facilities
selects the following instances (for the sake of readability, their distinguishing
attributes will be used instead of their graph id):

– Person:(Stefano Ferilli)
– Company:(Commodore)
– Company:(Apple)

He reads the available information (attribute values) for them, adds some missing
information and fixes some errors. This automatically raises his interaction score
in the 'hall of fame', and decreases the trust of the users who provided the
wrong information. Also, *stefano* sends these instances to the graph, and sends
(Commodore) to the Relationships tab, as the object.

Then, he moves to the Relationships tab, where Company:(Commodore) is
now selected as the object, and presses the Search button, that returns the list
of all relation instances (triples) having (Commodore) as the object instance.
Among these triples, he selects:

Person:(Chuck Peddle).wasIn.Company:(Commodore)

He reads the associated information, and decides to know more about (Chuck
Peddle). He sends it to the graph as well, and then sends it to the Entity tab.

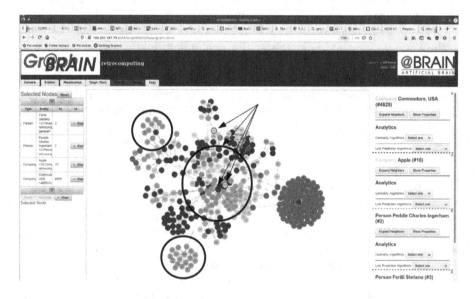

Fig. 2. Portion of GraphBRAIN's knowledge base.

He now turns to the Entity tab, where Person:(Chuck Peddle) is now selected. He reads the associated information, sees his picture in the attachments, and then moves to the Graph tab. There, he finds the list of instances he previously sent to this tab, and a portion of the graph (see Fig. 2) specifically selected starting from these instances and expanding them based on his preferences (e.g., he is more interested in entities **Company** and **Document**, and in relationships **wasIn** and **developed**), including[7]:

- Person:(Chuck Peddle).wasIn.Company:(Commodore)
- Person:(Chuck Peddle).wasIn.Company:(MOS Technology)
- Person:(Chuck Peddle).wasIn.Company:(Apple)
- Person:(Chuck Peddle).developed.Document:(6800 disclaimer)
- Person:(Stefano Ferilli).wasIn.Company:(UniBA)
- Person:(Stefano Ferilli).wasIn.Place:(Bari)
- Person:(Stefano Ferilli).wasIn.Event:(VCFI2019)
- Person:(Stefano Ferilli).developed.Document:(UAsCdB)
- Person:(Stefano Ferilli).developed.Document:(ACotE translation agreement)
- Document:(UAsCdB).wasIn.Collection:(Biblioteca F-Messito)
- Document:(ACotE translation agreement).wasIn.Collection:(Archivio Apulia Retrocomputing)
- Document:(UAsCdB).wasIn.Event:(VCFI2019)
- Document:(UAsCdB).concerns.Company:(Commodore)
- Document:(UAsCdB).concerns.Person:(Chuck Peddle)
- Company:(Apulia Retrocomputing).produced.Document:(UAsCdB)
- Company:(Apulia Retrocomputing).wasIn.Place:(Bari)
- Company:(Apulia Retrocomputing).owned.Collection:(Archivio Apulia Retrocomputing)

Note the occurrence of many instances of the entities and relationships in which *stefano* is more interested. Figure 2 shows the selected portion of the knowledge graph, where the starting nodes (instances) are indicated by arrows. Green nodes are documents, which allows *stefano* to easily spot further documents he might be interested in, obtained by indirect relationship with his initial interests. In particular, one can note potentially interesting aggregates of documents (indicated by circles in the figure).

stefano browses the graph (e.g., by looking at the owners of interesting documents and to the place where they can be found), and spots Event:(VCFI2019). He expands its neighbors, obtaining more information about it (e.g., its venue, other participants, and documents on show there). He asks for the centrality score of node Person:(Stefano Ferilli) based on the PageRank algorithm, obtaining 0.21375000000000002. He also asks for link prediction based on the Resource Allocation algorithm, obtaining 27 suggestions. Then he logs out the system.

This example shows how the proposed system can be used for describing and exploiting the contextual information of a specific digital library or archive, in ways that other traditional systems currently used by specialised users do not provide.

---

[7] For the sake of compactness, the book title 'Commodore - Un'azienda sulla cresta... del baratro' was reported as the acronym 'UAsCdB'.

7   Conclusions and Future Work

The current availability of new technologies for storing and handling knowledge provides unprecedented opportunities for enhanced fruition of digital libraries and archives, that goes beyond 'simple' document retrieval based on lexical content or metadata. For any kind of users, the context of the document as a whole, and/or of its content, may provide very interesting information, that allows to put it in perspective and grasp a deeper understanding thereof.

This new perspective requires, on one hand, suitable ontological resources to describe such variated knowledge, and, on the other, collaborative tools to collect the precious knowledge scattered across many scholars and practitioners spread all over the world, and to store it in a knowledge base, to make it available to all interested stakeholders (scholars, researchers, but also common people).

These solutions are provided through GraphBRAIN, a general-purpose tool developed to design and populate knowledge graphs, and to allow collaborative enrichment thereof, in addition to advanced fruition, consultation and analysis tools, that may be used as an intermediate layer to provide services to end-user applications aimed at personalized fruition of cultural heritage, also in a touristic perspective.

There are several directions for ongoing and future work. On the ontological side, we are currently extending the number and content of ontologies in GraphBRAIN, and specifically we are refining the ontology for digital libraries and archives, based on the feedback emerging from actual use of the system during the tourism-related project development or obtained by standard users of the on-line prototype. Concerning the knowledge base, we plan to contact pilot users and associations willing to contribute their knowledge. As to the platform, we are continuously improving the interface, also adding functionalities and features. The analysis and mining algorithms, in particular, will be extended and adapted for providing ever more advanced tools and services aimed at supporting researchers, scholars and other stakeholders in tailored fruition of the knowledge base.

References

1. Abburu, S., Babu, G.S.: Survey on ontology construction tools. Int. J. Sci. Eng. Res. **4**, 1748–1752 (2013)
2. Dewey, M.: A Classification and Subject Index for Cataloguing and Arranging the Books and Pamphlets of a Library. Amherst, Mass (1876)
3. Drakopoulos, G., Kanavos, A., Mylonas, P., Sioutas, S., Tsolis, D.: Towards a framework for tensor ontologies over neo4j: representations and operations. In: 8th International Conference on Information, Intelligence, Systems & Applications, IISA 2017, Larnaca, Cyprus, 27–30 August 2017, pp. 1–6. IEEE (2017)
4. Fellbaum, C. (ed.): WordNet: An Electronic Lexical Database. MIT Press, Cambridge (1998)

5. Ferilli, S., De Carolis, B., Buono, P., Di Mauro, N., Angelastro, S., Redavid, D.: Una piattaforma intelligente per la gestione integrata del settore turistico. In: Primo Convegno Nazionale CINI sull'Intelligenza Artificiale - Workshop on AI for Cultural Heritage, p. 2 (2019). http://www.ital-ia.it/submission/163/paper. (in Italian)
6. Ferilli, S., Redavid, D.: An ontology and a collaborative knowledge base for history of computing. In: Proceedings of the 1st International Workshop on Open Data and Ontologies for Cultural Heritage (ODOCH-2019), at the 31st International Conference on Advanced Information Systems Engineering, CAiSE 2016. Central Europe (CEUR) Workshop Proceedings, vol. 2375, pp. 49–60 (2019)
7. Heath, T., Bizer, C.: Linked Data: Evolving the Web into a Global Data Space. Synthesis Lectures on the Semantic Web. Morgan & Claypool Publishers, Williston (2011)
8. ISO/TC 46/SC 4 Technical Committee: Information and documentation - the Dublin core metadata element set - part 1: Core elements. Technical report ISO 15836–1:2017 (2017)
9. Krötzsch, M.: Ontologies for knowledge graphs? In: Artale, A., Glimm, B., Kontchakov, R. (eds.) Proceedings of the 30th International Workshop on Description Logics, Montpellier, France, 18–21 July 2017. CEUR Workshop Proceedings, vol. 1879. CEUR-WS.org (2017). http://ceur-ws.org/Vol-1879/invited2.pdf
10. Lavarone, G., Orio, N., Polato, F., Savino, S.: Modeling the concept of movie in a software architecture for film-induced tourism. In: Calvanese, D., De Nart, D., Tasso, C. (eds.) IRCDL 2015. CCIS, vol. 612, pp. 116–125. Springer, Cham (2016). https://doi.org/10.1007/978-3-319-41938-1_13
11. Lodi, G., et al.: Semantic web for cultural heritage valorisation. In: Hai-Jew, S. (ed.) Data Analytics in Digital Humanities. MSA, pp. 3–37. Springer, Cham (2017). https://doi.org/10.1007/978-3-319-54499-1_1
12. Miller, G.A.: WordNet: a lexical database for English. Commun. ACM **38**, 39–41 (1995)
13. Robinson, I., Webber, J., Eifrem, E.: Graph Databases, 2nd edn. O'Reilly Media, Newton (2015)
14. Zilio, D., Micheletti, A., Orio, N.: Crowdsourcing for film-induced tourism: an approach to geolocation. In: Grana, C., Baraldi, L. (eds.) IRCDL 2017. CCIS, vol. 733, pp. 108–116. Springer, Cham (2017). https://doi.org/10.1007/978-3-319-68130-6_9

Text-to-Image Synthesis Based on Machine Generated Captions

Marco Menardi[1], Alex Falcon[1], Saida S. Mohamed[1(✉)], Lorenzo Seidenari[2],
Giuseppe Serra[1], Alberto Del Bimbo[2], and Carlo Tasso[1]

[1] Artificial Intelligence Laboratory, University of Udine, Udine, Italy
{menardi.marco,falcon.alex,mahmoud.saidasaadmohamed}@spes.uniud.it,
{giuseppe.serra,carlo.tasso}@uniud.it
[2] Media Integration and Communication Center, University of Firenze,
Florence, Italy
{lorenzo.seidenari,alberto.delbimbo}@unifi.it

Abstract. Text-to-Image Synthesis refers to the process of automatic generation of a photo-realistic image starting from a given text and is revolutionizing many real-world applications. In order to perform such process it is necessary to exploit datasets containing captioned images, meaning that each image is associated with one (or more) captions describing it. Despite the abundance of uncaptioned images datasets, the number of captioned datasets is limited. To address this issue, in this paper we propose an approach capable of generating images starting from a given text using conditional generative adversarial network (GAN) trained on uncaptioned images dataset. In particular, uncaptioned images are fed to an Image Captioning Module to generate the descriptions. Then, the GAN Module is trained on both the input image and the "machine-generated" caption. To evaluate the results, the performance of our solution is compared with the results obtained by the unconditional GAN. For the experiments, we chose to use the uncaptioned dataset LSUN-bedroom. The results obtained in our study are preliminary but still promising.

Keywords: Generative Adversarial Networks (GANs) · StackGAN · Self-Critical Sequence Training (SCST) · Text-to-Image Synthesis

1 Introduction

Text-to-Image Synthesis, also called Conditional Image Generation, is a process that consists in generating a photo-realistic image given a textual description. It is a challenging task and it is revolutionizing many real-world applications. For example, starting from a Digital Library of adventure books it could be possible to enrich the reading experience with computer-generated images of the locations explored in the story, while a Digital Library of recipe books may be enriched with images representing the steps involved in a given recipe. In addition, such

M. Ceci et al. (Eds.): IRCDL 2020, CCIS 1177, pp. 62–74, 2020.
https://doi.org/10.1007/978-3-030-39905-4_7

images may be used to exploit Information Retrieval systems based on visual similarity. Due to its great potentiality and usefulness, it raised a lot of interest in the research fields of Computer Vision, Natural Language Processing, and Digital Libraries.

One of the main approaches used for the text-to-image task involves the use of Generative Adversarial Networks (GAN) [6]: starting from a given textual description, GANs can be conditioned on text [24,25,35] in order generate high-quality images that are highly related to the text meaning.

To condition a GAN on text, captioned images datasets are needed, meaning that one (or more) captions must be associated to each image. Despite the large amount of uncaptioned images datasets, the number of captioned datasets is limited. For example, LSUN [33] dataset, which consists in more than 59 million labeled images for each of 10 scene categories and 20 object categories [33]. The LSUN-bedroom dataset contains images from LSUN dataset tagged with the "bedroom" scene category. It contains around ∼3,000,000 images [33], but it does not contain the associated captions. This may lead to a difficulty in training a conditional GAN to generate bedroom images related to a given textual description, such as "a bedroom with blue walls, white furniture and a large bed". In this paper we propose an innovative, though quite simple approach to address this issue as shown in Fig. 1.

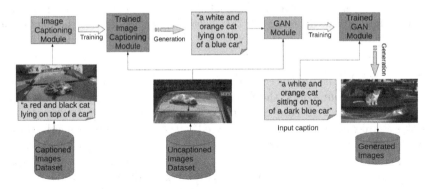

Fig. 1. Our pipeline: captioned images are used to train the Image Captioning Module; uncaptioned images are then captioned through the Trained Image Captioning Module and both the image and the generated captions are used to train the GAN Module; finally, the Trained GAN Module is used to generate an image based on an input caption.

First of all, a captioning system (that we call Image Captioning Module) is trained on a generic captioned dataset and used to generate a caption for the uncaptioned images. Then, the conditional GAN (that we call GAN Module) is trained on both the input image and the "machine-generated" caption. A high-level representation of the architecture is shown in Fig. 2. To evaluate the results, the performance of the GAN using "machine-generated" captions are compared with the results obtained by the unconditional GAN. To test and evaluate our pipeline, we are using the LSUN-bedroom [33] dataset.

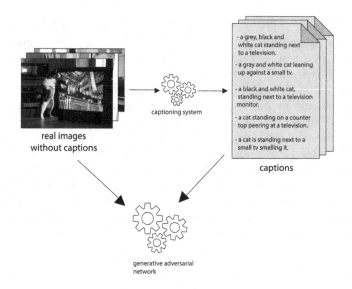

Fig. 2. Pipeline: images are fed to a captioning system that outputs its captions. The generated captions and the images are then given as input for training the conditional GAN.

The results obtained in the experiments are very preliminary yet very promising. According to our study, the GAN Module does not learn how to produce meaningful images, with respect to the caption meaning, and we hypothesize that this is due to the "machine-generated" captions we use to condition the GAN Module. The Image Captioning module is trained on the COCO dataset [17], which contains captioned images for many different classes of objects and intuitively this should lead the Image Captioning Module to learn how to produce captions for bedroom images as well. Despite being able to produce the desired captions, we notice that the "machine-generated" captions are often too similar and not detailed for different bedroom images. The last section of the paper proposes some approaches that can deal with these problems.

2   Related Work

In 2014, Goodfellow et al. introduced Generative Adversarial Networks (GAN) [6], a generative model framework that consists in training simultaneously two models: a generator network and a discriminator one. The generator network has the task of generating images as real as possible, while the discriminator network has to distinguish the generated images from the real ones. Generative models are trained to implicitly capture the statistical distribution of training data; once trained, they can synthesize novel data samples, which can be used for example in the tasks of semantic image editing [38] and data augmentation [1].

GANs can be trained to sample from a given data distribution, in such case a random vector is provided as input to the generator. Otherwise, as in the case of text-to-image synthesis, they can be trained conditionally, meaning that an additional variable is provided as input to control the generator output. In certain formulations, the discriminator observes the conditioning variable too, during training. In the literature, several possibilities were tested for the variables used to condition a GAN: attributes or class labels (e.g. [2,20]), images (e.g. for the tasks of photo editing [38] and domain transfer [11]).

Several methods have been developed to generate images conditioned on text. Mansimov et al. [18] built an AlignDRAW model trained to learn the correspondence between text and generated images. Reed et al. in [26] used PixelCNN to generate images using both text descriptions and object location constraints. Nguyen et al. [19] used an approximate Langevin sampling approach to generate images conditioned on text, but it required an inefficient iterative optimization process. In [25], Reed et al. successfully generated 64 × 64 images for birds and flowers conditioning on text descriptions. In their follow-up work [24], they were able to generate 128 × 128 images by using additional annotations on object part locations. Denton et al. in [5] proposed the Laplacian pyramid framework (LAPGANs), which is composed of a series of GANs. A residual image is conditioned at each level of the pyramid on the image of the previous stage to produce an image for the next stage. Also in [13], Kerras et al. use a similar approach by incrementally adding more layers in the generator and in the discriminator. [34] and [35] suggest the use of a so-called sketch-refinement process, where the images are first generated at low resolutions using a GAN conditioned over the textual description, and then refined with another GAN conditioned on both the image generated at the previous step and the input textual description. [9] and [15] infer a semantic label map by predicting bounding boxes and object shapes from the text, and then synthesize an image conditioned on the layout and the text description. A recent work by Qiao et al. [21] uses a three-step approach where it first computes word- and sentence-level embedding from the given textual description, then it uses the embeddings to generate images in a cascaded architecture, and finally starting from the image generated at the previous step it tries to regenerate the original textual description, in order to semantically align with it. Although several different state-of-the-art architectures may be chosen for the task, such as HDGAN [36] and AttGAN [32], in our pipeline we decided to use StackGAN-v2 [35] as the conditional GAN component, given the availability of its code on GitHub.

Recently, several impressive results [16,27,37] were obtained for the Image Captioning (or image-to-text) task, which deals with the generation of a caption describing the given image and the objects taking part to it. It is an important task that raises a lot of interest in the Computer Vision and Natural Language

Processing research fields. A recent and comprehensive survey about the task is provided by Hossain et al. in [10]. Some of the approaches used for this task involve the use of Encoder/Decoder networks and Reinforcement learning techniques.

The encoder/decoder paradigm for machine translation using recurrent neural networks (RNNs) [3] inspired [12, 30] to use a deep convolutional neural network to encode the input image, and a Long Short-Term Memory (LSTM) [8] RNN decoder to generate the output caption. Given the unavailability of labeled data, recent approaches to the image captioning task involve the use of reinforcement learning and unsupervised learning-based techniques. [37] and [16] use actor-critic reinforcement learning methods, where a "policy network" (the actor) is trained to predict the next word based on the current state, whereas a "value network" (the critic) is trained to estimate the reward of each generated word. These techniques overcome the need to sample from the policy (actors) action space, which can be enormous, at the expense of estimating future rewards. Another approach, used by Ranzato et al. in [22], consists in applying the REINFORCE algorithm [31]. A limitation of this algorithm consists in the requirement of a context-dependent normalization to tackle the high variance encountered when using mini-batches. The approach we are following uses Self-Critical Sequence Training (SCST) [27] which is a REINFORCE algorithm that utilizes the output of its own test-time inference algorithm to normalize the rewards it experiences: doing so, it does not need neither to estimate the reward signal nor the normalization.

3   Our Approach

We propose a pipeline whose goal is to generate images by conditioning on "machine-generated" captions. This is fundamental when image captions are not available for a specific domain of interest. Thus, the proposed solution involves the use of a generic captioned dataset, such as the COCO dataset, to make the Image Captioning Module capable of generating captions for a specific domain.

To do so, we want to explore the possibility of using an automatic system to generate textual captions for the images and use them for the training of a Generative Adversarial Network. For achieving our goal, we built a pipeline composed by an Image Captioning Module and a GAN Module, as shown in Fig. 1. First of all, the Image Captioning Module is trained over a generic captioned dataset to generate multiple captions for the input image. Then, real images are given as input to the Trained Image Captioning Module, which outputs multiple captions for each image. The generated captions together with the images are then fed to the GAN Module, which learns to generate images conditioned on the "machine-generated" captions. By feeding the GAN with multiple captions for each image, the GAN can better learn the correspondence between images and captions.

In the following sections, we detail the two modules used in our pipeline: the Image Captioning Module and the GAN Module.

3.1   Image Captioning Module

The goal of the Image Captioning Module is to generate a natural language description of an image. Good performance in this task are obtained by learning a model which is able to first understand the scene described in the image, the objects taking part to it and the relationships between them, and then to compose a natural language sentence describing the whole picture. Given the complexity of such a task, it is still an open challenge in the fields of Natural Language Processing and Computer Vision. The task of open domain captioning is a challenging task. It requires a fine-grained understanding of the whole entities, attributes and relationships in an image. In our pipeline, we are implementing our Image Captioning Module in a similar way as the one proposed in [27], meaning that we also use a captioning system based on FC models. It has been built using an optimization approach that is called Self-Critical Sequence Training (SCST).

Typical deep learning models used for the Image Captioning task are trained with the "teacher-forcing" technique, which consists in maximizing the likelihood of the next ground-truth word given the previous ground-truth word. This has been shown to generate some mismatches between the training and the inference phase, knows as "exposure bias". Moreover, the metrics used during the testing phase are non-differentiable (such as BLEU and CIDEr), meaning that the captioning model can not be trained to directly optimize them. To overcome these problems, Reinforcement Learning techniques such as the REINFORCE algorithm have been used. SCST is a variation and an improvement of the popular REINFORCE algorithm that, rather than estimating a baseline to normalize the rewards and reduce variance, utilizes the output of its own test-time inference algorithm to normalize the rewards it experiences. This means that it is forced to improve the performance of the model under the inference algorithm used at test time. Practically, SCST has much lower variance than REINFORCE and can be more effectively trained on mini-batches of samples using SGD. Moreover, it has been shown that SCST system has achieved state-of-the-art performance by optimizing their system using the test metrics of the MSCOCO task. Practically, it has been found that SCST has much lower variance, and can be more effectively trained on mini-batches of samples using SGD. Since the SCST baseline is based on the test-time estimate under the current model, SCST is forced to improve the performance of the model under the inference algorithm used at test time. In addition, this encourages training consistency like the maximum likelihood-based approaches except it optimized sequence metrics.

3.2   GAN Module

The GAN Module has the major role of learning to generate images by conditioning on the "machine-generated" captions. In particular, we are using StackGAN-v2 [35] as our GAN Module.

StackGAN-v2 consists of a multiple stage generation process, where high-resolution images are obtained by initially generating low-resolution images which are then refined in multiple steps. It consists in a single end-to-end network composed by multiple generators and discriminators in a tree-like structure. Different branches of the tree generate images of different resolutions: at branch i, the generator G_i learns the image distribution p_{G_i} at that scale, while the discriminator D_i estimates the probability of a sample being real. The framework of StackGAN-v2 has a tree-like structure, that takes as input the noise vector $z \sim p_{noise}$. The noise z is transformed in hidden feature layer by layer. The hidden features h_i for each generator G_i are calculated by a non-linear transformation

$$h_0 = F_0(z); \quad h_i = F_i(h_{i-1}, z), \tag{1}$$

where h_i represents hidden features for the ith branch, m is the total number of branches, and F_i are modeled as neural networks. The noise vector z is concatenated to the hidden features h_{i-1} as the inputs of F_i for calculating h_i. The generators produce samples at different scales $(s_0, s1, ..., s_{m-1})$ based on the hidden features at different layers $(h_0, h_1, ..., h_{m-1})$.

$$s_i = G_i(h_i), \quad i = 0, 1, ..., m-1, \tag{2}$$

where G_i is the generator for the ith branch. Since we are more interested in the conditional case, we are not reporting the loss function used by the generator and the discriminator in the unconditional setting, for which more details can be found in [35].

The discriminator D_i takes a real image x_i or a fake sample s_i as input and is trained to classify them as real or fake by minimizing the cross entropy loss:

$$\mathcal{L}_{D_i} = \underbrace{-\mathbb{E}_{x_i \sim p_{data_i}}[log D_i(x_i)] - \mathbb{E}_{x_i \sim p_{G_i}}[log(1 - D_i(s_i))]}_{\text{unconditional loss}}$$
$$\underbrace{-\mathbb{E}_{x_i \sim p_{data_i}}[log D_i(x_i, c)] - \mathbb{E}_{x_i \sim p_{G_i}}[log(1 - D_i(s_i, c))]}_{\text{conditional loss}} \tag{3}$$

where x_i is an image from the true image distribution p_{data_i} at the ith scale, s_i is from the model distribution p_{G_i} at the same scale. While StackGAN-v2 [35] follows the approach of Reed et al. [23] to pre-train a text encoder to extract visually-discriminative text embeddings of the given description, in our case we use Skip-Thought [14], that works at the sentence level, to generate the text embeddings (c in the Eqs. 3 and 4). Sentences that share semantic and syntactic properties are mapped to corresponding vector representations [14].

The multiple discriminators are trained in parallel each one for a different scale, while the generator is instead optimized to jointly approximate multi-scale image distributions $p_{data_0}, p_{data_1}, ..., p_{data_{m-1}}$ by minimizing the following loss function:

$$\mathcal{L}_G = \sum_{i=1}^{m} \mathcal{L}_{G_i}, \quad \mathcal{L}_{G_i} = \underbrace{-\mathbb{E}_{s_i \sim p_{G_i}}[log D_i(s_i)]}_{\text{unconditional loss}} \underbrace{-\mathbb{E}_{s_i \sim p_{G_i}}[log D_i(s_i, c)]}_{\text{conditional loss}} \tag{4}$$

where L_{G_i} is the loss function for approximating the image distribution at the ith scale. The unconditional loss is used to determine whether the image is real or fake, while the conditional loss is used to determine if the image and the condition match.

4   Experimental Results

In this section, we present the preliminary results of the experiments involving the proposed pipeline. The Image Captioning Module was trained on the COCO dataset [17], which contains 120, 000 generic images tagged with categories and captioned by five different sentences each.

The uncaptioned dataset that we considered is the LSUN [33] dataset, which consists in more than 59 million labeled images. From the LSUN dataset, we first select the ~3,000,000 images tagged with the "bedroom" scene category and from that set a subset of the first 120, 000 images is selected: 80, 000 are then used to train the GAN and 40, 000 as test set. Later on in this paper, the selection of the ~3,000,000 images tagged with the "bedroom" scene category is called "LSUN-bedroom".

A typical metric used to evaluate both the quality and the diversity of generated images is the Inception Score [28]. Unfortunately, the type of image of the LSUN dataset is very different from those used by ImageNet [4, 35], therefore it has been shown that the Inception Score is not a good indicator for the quality of generated images [35]. So we decided not to report the obtained scores.

We performed three experiments over the considered dataset.

The first experiment consists in training the GAN Module on the whole LSUN-bedroom dataset (~3,000,000 images). This is done because of two reasons: first, it serves as a baseline for the next experiment; second, we compare the results obtained by our computing facilities with the results obtained in [35], since with our graphics card we are limited to a lower batch size of 16. Figure 4 shows some examples of generated images, and it is possible to see that the quality of the generated images is similar to those shown in Fig. 3 [35].

Fig. 3. Examples of images generated by the StackGAN Module trained on the whole LSUN-bedroom dataset.

To reproduce the results reported in the paper, we used an NVIDIA GTX 1080 8 GB machine. It took us around one month to train the GAN Module on

Fig. 4. Examples of images generated by the GAN Module trained on the whole LSUN-bedroom dataset.

the whole LSUN dataset. Because of this, we decided to explore and understand how the GAN Module performs with less training images. In the second experiment, the training of the GAN Module without conditioning is done on a subset of LSUN-bedroom, consisting of 120,000 images. Some of the results obtained in this experiment are showed in Fig. 5. Although the quality of the generated images is slightly reduced, it is possible to see that the semantic content is still clear and defined.

Fig. 5. Examples of images generated by the GAN Module trained on a part of the LSUN-bedroom dataset.

Finally, to test our pipeline, we used the Image Captioning Module to generate captions for the images contained in the considered subset of the LSUN-bedroom dataset. Then, the GAN Module was trained on these same images and conditioned by the "machine-generated" captions. About the preliminary results that we obtained, some examples are shown in Fig. 6. We suspect the problem is due to the similarity of the "machine-generated" captions: the LSUN-bedroom dataset does not come with captions and thus the Image Captioning Module is trained on a generic dataset (COCO) and not for that specific dataset. Because of this, the Image Captioning Module is unable to produce detailed and varied captions for different bedroom images. In addition, Usually GANs used noise vector to generate images which always different from each other [6]. In our experiment, the noise vector is taken as input by the model and used to generate an image. Then, the captions are used to yield the embeddings, which are also used as noise by the generator. The fact that the noise is almost always the same could be the cause of the observed problem.

We found that the scores for the LSUN-bedroom dataset seem to not fully correlate with the quality of the generated images. As explained in [35], this may

(a) "this bedroom looks very
old-fashioned"

(b) "the bedroom has carpeted
floor and the walls are papered"

(c) "the room has rich colors and
overall looks very modern"

(d) "this small bedroom has matching
wooden and glass furniture"

Fig. 6. Examples of images generated by the GAN Module trained on a part of the LSUN-bedroom dataset and conditioned on "machine-generated" captions.

be due to the inception score being trained on the inception dataset, and thus it does not work well on datasets with specific types of images. Also, it has to be considered that different datasets get inception scores in different ranges. For this reason, inception scores must not be compared across different datasets.

5   Conclusion

We explored the problem of conditional image generation using Generative Adversarial Networks with machine-generated captions. For this task, we built a pipeline to first generate captions for uncaptioned datasets and then to use the "machine-generated" captions to condition a GAN. To test our pipeline, we run experiments on the LSUN-bedroom dataset, which is a subset of the LSUN dataset containing uncaptioned images of bedrooms, and then compare the generated images in the unconditional setting and in the conditional setting where "machine-generated" captions are used. The results observed in the experiments do not achieve success in the task of conditioning with "machine-generated" captions. So we identify, analyze, and propose possible solutions to the obstacles that need to be overcome.

The Image Captioning Module that we trained on the COCO dataset seems to generate captions too similar to each other. Moreover, The captions we generated lack details and contain some errors. This is probably related to the fact that more diverse and detailed captions are needed during training in order to achieve significant improvements. During a subsequent review of works on captioning, we found a work from Shetty et al. [29], that promises to generate more different captions, instead of variations of the same caption. This result is achieved by using GANs for image captioning instead of other traditional methods. An open question is whether with a bigger dataset the GAN could learn the image-captions correspondence, even when captions are very similar for each image. We believe improving the quality of the generated caption is the main challenge for our method. An hybrid approach could make our proposed method work by making humans write captions on a subset of the dataset, then use the obtained captions to train a captioning system. For generating human captions, crowdsourcing platforms like Amazon Mechanical Turk (AMT) could be used. We are currently working on this idea because it's likely that it will lead to improvements in the quality of generated bedroom images, given that AMT could make it possible to have high-quality and more diverse captions. Moreover, we are also considering the use of the Fréchet Inception distance [7] to evaluate the generated captions and images.

References

1. Bousmalis, K., Silberman, N., Dohan, D., Erhan, D., Krishnan, D.: Unsupervised pixel-level domain adaptation with generative adversarial networks. In: 2017 IEEE Conference on Computer Vision and Pattern Recognition (CVPR), pp. 95–104 (2016)
2. Chen, X., Duan, Y., Houthooft, R., Schulman, J., Sutskever, I., Abbeel, P.: Info-GAN: interpretable representation learning by information maximizing generative adversarial nets. Adv. Neural Inf. Process. Syst. 29(2016), 2172–2180 (2016)
3. Cho, K., et al.: Learning phrase representations using RNN encoder-decoder for statistical machine translation. In: Proceedings of the 2014 Conference on Empirical Methods in Natural Language Processing, EMNLP 2014, pp. 1724–1734 (2014)
4. Deng, J., Dong, W., Socher, R., Li, L.J., Li, K., Fei-Fei, L.: ImageNet: a large-scale hierarchical image database. In: 2009 IEEE Conference on Computer Vision and Pattern Recognition, pp. 248–255. IEEE (2009)
5. Denton, E.L., Chintala, S., Fergus, R., et al.: Deep generative image models using a Laplacian pyramid of adversarial networks. In: Advances in Neural Information Processing Systems, pp. 1486–1494 (2015)
6. Goodfellow, I., et al.: Generative adversarial nets. In: Ghahramani, Z., Welling, M., Cortes, C., Lawrence, N.D., Weinberger, K.Q. (eds.) Advances in Neural Information Processing Systems, vol. 27, pp. 2672–2680. Curran Associates, Inc. (2014)
7. Heusel, M., Ramsauer, H., Unterthiner, T., Nessler, B., Hochreiter, S.: GANs trained by a two time-scale update rule converge to a local Nash equilibrium-supplementary material
8. Hochreiter, S., Schmidhuber, J.: Long short-term memory. Neural Comput. 9(8), 1735–1780 (1997)
9. Hong, S., Yang, D., Choi, J., Lee, H.: Inferring semantic layout for hierarchical text-to-image synthesis. In: 2018 IEEE/CVF Conference on Computer Vision and Pattern Recognition, pp. 7986–7994 (2018)
10. Hossain, M., Sohel, F., Shiratuddin, M.F., Laga, H.: A comprehensive survey of deep learning for image captioning. ACM Comput. Surv. (CSUR) 51(6), 118 (2019)
11. Isola, P., Zhu, J., Zhou, T., Efros, A.A.: Image-to-image translation with conditional adversarial networks. In: 2017 IEEE Conference on Computer Vision and Pattern Recognition, CVPR 2017, pp. 5967–5976 (2017)

12. Karpathy, A., Fei-Fei, L.: Deep visual-semantic alignments for generating image descriptions, pp. 3128–3137 (2015)

13. Karras, T., Aila, T., Laine, S., Lehtinen, J.: Progressive growing of GANs for improved quality, stability, and variation. In: 6th International Conference on Learning Representations, ICLR 2018 (2018)

14. Kiros, R., Zhu, Y., Salakhutdinov, R., Zemel, R.S., Urtasun, R., Torralba, A., Fidler, S.: Skip-thought vectors. In: Advances in Neural Information Processing Systems 28: Annual Conference on Neural Information Processing Systems 2015, Montreal, Quebec, Canada, 7–12 December 2015, pp. 3294–3302 (2015). http://papers.nips.cc/paper/5950-skip-thought-vectors

15. Li, W., et al.: Object-driven text-to-image synthesis via adversarial training. CoRR abs/1902.10740 (2019), http://arxiv.org/abs/1902.10740

16. Zhang, L., Sung, F., Liu, F., Xiang, T., Gong, S., Yang, Y., Hospedales, T.M.: Actor-critic sequence training for image captioning (2017)

17. Lin, T.-Y., et al.: Microsoft COCO: common objects in context. In: Fleet, D., Pajdla, T., Schiele, B., Tuytelaars, T. (eds.) ECCV 2014. LNCS, vol. 8693, pp. 740–755. Springer, Cham (2014). https://doi.org/10.1007/978-3-319-10602-1_48

18. Mansimov, E., Parisotto, E., Ba, L.J., Salakhutdinov, R.: Generating images from captions with attention. In: 4th International Conference on Learning Representations, ICLR 2016, Conference Track Proceedings, San Juan, Puerto Rico, 2–4 May 2016 (2016). http://arxiv.org/abs/1511.02793

19. Nguyen, A., Clune, J., Bengio, Y., Dosovitskiy, A., Yosinski, J.: Plug & play generative networks: conditional iterative generation of images in latent space. In: 2017 IEEE Conference on Computer Vision and Pattern Recognition, CVPR 2017, pp. 3510–3520 (2017)

20. Odena, A., Olah, C., Shlens, J.: Conditional image synthesis with auxiliary classifier GANs. In: Proceedings of the 34th International Conference on Machine Learning, vol. 70, pp. 2642–2651. JMLR. org (2017)

21. Qiao, T., Zhang, J., Xu, D., Tao, D.: MirrorGAN: learning text-to-image generation by redescription. CoRR abs/1903.05854 (2019). http://arxiv.org/abs/1903.05854

22. Ranzato, M., Chopra, S., Auli, M., Zaremba, W.: Sequence level training with recurrent neural networks. In: 4th International Conference on Learning Representations, ICLR 2016 (2016)

23. Reed, S.E., Akata, Z., Lee, H., Schiele, B.: Learning deep representations of fine-grained visual descriptions. In: 2016 IEEE Conference on Computer Vision and Pattern Recognition, CVPR 2016, Las Vegas, NV, USA, 27–30 June 2016, pp. 49–58 (2016). https://doi.org/10.1109/CVPR.2016.13

24. Reed, S.E., Akata, Z., Mohan, S., Tenka, S., Schiele, B., Lee, H.: Learning what and where to draw. Adv. Neural Inf. Process. Syst. 29(2016), 217–225 (2016)

25. Reed, S.E., Akata, Z., Yan, X., Logeswaran, L., Schiele, B., Lee, H.: Generative adversarial text to image synthesis. In: Proceedings of the 33nd International Conference on Machine Learning, ICML 2016, pp. 1060–1069 (2016)

26. Reed, S.E., Oord, A.v.d., Kalchbrenner, N., Bapst, V., Botvinick, M.M., Freitas, N.d.: Generating Interpretable Images with Controllable Structure (2017). https://www.semanticscholar.org/paper/Generating-Interpretable-Images-with-Controllable-Reed-Oord/bd5c69fd9b34f481e03363f9d913c31af83547a5

27. Rennie, S.J., Marcheret, E., Mroueh, Y., Ross, J., Goel, V.: Self-critical sequence training for image captioning. In: 2017 IEEE Conference on Computer Vision and Pattern Recognition, CVPR 2017, pp. 1179–1195 (2017)

28. Salimans, T., Goodfellow, I.J., Zaremba, W., Cheung, V., Radford, A., Chen, X.: Improved techniques for training GANs. Adv. Neural Inf. Process. Syst. **29**(2016), 2226–2234 (2016)
29. Shetty, R., Rohrbach, M., Hendricks, L.A., Fritz, M., Schiele, B.: Speaking the same language: matching machine to human captions by adversarial training. In: IEEE International Conference on Computer Vision, ICCV 2017, pp. 4155–4164 (2017)
30. Vinyals, O., Toshev, A., Bengio, S., Erhan, D.: Show and tell: a neural image caption generator. In: IEEE Conference on Computer Vision and Pattern Recognition, CVPR 2015, pp. 3156–3164 (2015)
31. Williams, R.J.: Simple statistical gradient-following algorithms for connectionist reinforcement learning. Mach. Learn. **8**(3–4), 229–256 (1992). http://link.springer.com/10.1007/BF00992696
32. Xu, T., et al.: AttnGAN: fine-grained text to image generation with attentional generative adversarial networks. In: 2018 IEEE Conference on Computer Vision and Pattern Recognition, CVPR 2018, pp. 1316–1324 (2018)
33. Yu, F., Zhang, Y., Song, S., Seff, A., Xiao, J.: LSUN: Construction of a Large-scale Image Dataset using Deep Learning with Humans in the Loop. CoRR abs/1506.0 (2015). http://arxiv.org/abs/1506.03365
34. Zhang, H., et al.: StackGAN: text to photo-realistic image synthesis with stacked generative adversarial networks. In: Proceedings of the IEEE International Conference on Computer Vision (2017)
35. Zhang, H., et al.: StackGAN++: realistic image synthesis with stacked generative adversarial networks. IEEE Trans. Pattern Anal. Mach. Intell. **41**, 1947–1962 (2018)
36. Zhang, Z., Xie, Y., Yang, L.: Photographic text-to-image synthesis with a hierarchically-nested adversarial network. In: 2018 IEEE Conference on Computer Vision and Pattern Recognition, CVPR 2018, pp. 6199–6208 (2018)
37. Zhou, R., Xiaoyu, W., Ning, Z., Xutao, L., Li-Jia, L.: Deep reinforcement learning-based image captioning with embedding reward. In: Proceedings of the IEEE Conference on Computer Vision and Pattern Recognition, CVPR 2017, pp. 1151–1159 (2017)
38. Zhu, J.-Y., Krähenbühl, P., Shechtman, E., Efros, A.A.: Generative visual manipulation on the natural image manifold. In: Leibe, B., Matas, J., Sebe, N., Welling, M. (eds.) ECCV 2016. LNCS, vol. 9909, pp. 597–613. Springer, Cham (2016). https://doi.org/10.1007/978-3-319-46454-1_36

A Streamlined Pipeline to Enable the Semantic Exploration of a Bookstore

Miguel Ceriani$^{(\boxtimes)}$, Eleonora Bernasconi$^{(\boxtimes)}$, and Massimo Mecella$^{(\boxtimes)}$

Sapienza Università di Roma, Rome, Italy
{ceriani,bernasconi,mecella}@diag.uniroma1.it

Abstract. Searching in a library or book catalog is a recurrent task for researchers and common users alike. Thanks to semantic enrichment techniques, such as named-entity recognition and linking, texts may be automatically associated with entities in some reference knowledge graph(s). The association of a corpus of texts with a knowledge graph opens up the way to searching/exploring using novel paradigms. We present a pipeline that uses semantic enrichment and knowledge graph visualization techniques to enable the semantic exploration of an existing text corpus. The pipeline is meant to be ready for use and consists of existing free software tools and free software code contributed by us. We are developing and testing the pipeline on the field, by using it to access the catalog of a bookstore specialized in ancient Rome history.

Keywords: Semantic enrichment · Knowledge graph · Book catalog · Semantic web · Linked data · Pipeline

1 Introduction

Searching in a library or book catalog is a recurrent task for researchers and common users alike. The search tools, once cumbersome physical file cabinets organized by author, topic, etc., are now usually web-based interfaces that allow more search flexibility and are globally accessible from any web-connected device. Nevertheless, the adopted search paradigm is still mainly the same one, albeit with the important addition of free-text search.

In the last years, knowledge graphs gained broad adoption as a way of organizing and exploring a domain of knowledge. They organize information around concepts, which are connected to each other through semantic relationships. If these concepts are interpreted as topics, a knowledge graph is a rich way to organize a set of texts (or other media) by topic. The relationships between concepts (topics) are preserved and can be used to explore/search the corpus in ways that can go beyond the simple classification of media by topics.

This work is partly supported by the project *ARCA* (POR FESR Lazio 2014–2020 - Avviso pubblico "Creatività 2020", domanda prot. n. A0128-2017-17189) and by the *Centro di Eccellenza DTC Lazio* through the project *EcoDigit*.

© Springer Nature Switzerland AG 2020
M. Ceci et al. (Eds.): IRCDL 2020, CCIS 1177, pp. 75–81, 2020.
https://doi.org/10.1007/978-3-030-39905-4_8

We propose a lightweight system that takes advantage of existing technologies to organize a library or book catalog through a knowledge graph with little upfront effort. A visual user interface allows the user to search and explore the graph as a way to access the book corpus. The pipeline is being experimented on the book catalog of an editor specialized in ancient Rome history.

The rest of the paper is organized as follows. Section 2 analyses the related work, while Sects. 3 and 4 describe respectively the proposed system and used data models. Section 5 describes the implementation details and the concrete use case. Finally, Sect. 6 concludes and anticipates future work.

2   Related Work

There has been a large amount of work in literature about visual information seeking [6, 13]. Nevertheless, most of the work focus on how to explore and filter items classified by a homogeneous set of properties. For unstructured information like books, exploring and filtering by basic metadata (i.e., author, title, etc.) can be useful but it is often not sufficient. There has hence been recently a lot of research on how to attach semantics to unstructured data [11], through processes like *named-entity recognition and linking (NERL)* [9, 12].

Several software tools and research works deal with the issue of such semantic enrichments. Yewno Discover [2] is an integrated system that addresses similar challenges but does not offer flexibility, requiring the development of ad-hoc adjustments to build a specific pipeline. The GLOBDEF system [10] works with pluggable enhancement modules, which are dynamically activated to create on-the-fly pipelines for data enhancement, but it does not provide the management, integration, and visualization of the generated metadata. Apache Stanbol[1] is a set of components able to offer various services for semantic enrichment, visualization of knowledge graph and the management of metadata. It is extremely useful and can be integrated with our system, but on itself, it does not offer a ready to use pipeline. Multiple user interfaces for visualization and exploration of knowledge graphs have been researched [1,4,8], but the question on how to effectively use these extracted semantics is still open.

Although existing work deals with aspects of the pipeline proposed here, our system is novel in being designed from the ground up to offer knowledge graph-based access to an arbitrary corpus of texts. The mechanism of integration of semantic enrichment services, crucial for the adaptivity of the pipeline, is also novel, by being based on simple, actionable, semantic descriptions of the services. Finally, the user interface is novel in adopting visual linked data exploration as a means to search in a corpus of content, rather than just as an end in itself.

3   Scenario and System

In the considered scenario, the responsible of a catalog of books (e.g., an editor or a library) wants to facilitate the search and exploration of its corpus through

---

[1] https://stanbol.apache.org/.

a specialized knowledge graph. The knowledge graph needs to integrate existing metadata, concepts associated with texts through semantic enriching processes, and relationships between the concepts. Both *generic users* and *domain experts* will be able to interact with the knowledge graph via a visual user interface or via programmatic interfaces which will enable advanced queries, transformations, and integration with further data sources.

The proposed pipeline is shown in Fig. 1. In case of having access only to printed versions of some texts, those are first scanned and go through an OCR. The content of all the books is then stored in electronic form (e.g., PDFs), along with the relevant metadata, in a repository that supports the *linked data container* API, a standard RDF-based REST API [15]. This repository can be maintained by the catalog maintainers (e.g., editors or librarians) through a dedicated frontend application. It can also be directly connected with existing databases/systems for automatic content/metadata insertion/update.

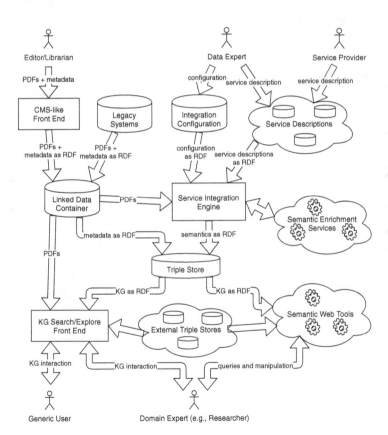

Fig. 1. The proposed pipeline

The content stored in that repository is analysed by some, possibly remote, semantic enrichment services (as NERL) that give as output some knowledge extracted from the content, possibly represented using existing models and knowledge graphs. To allow plugging diverse services, a component called *service integration engine* manages calling and integrating the desired web services based on a global *integration configuration*, which describes which services need to be called, and for each service a specific *service description*, which describes how to adapt it. While the integration configuration is maintained by experts for the specific pipeline, service descriptions are adapters of existing web services that could be developed by the maintainers of this pipeline as well as the service providers or third parties, favouring scalability of the system.

Both the metadata coming from the repository (linked data container) and the extracted knowledge coming from the service integration engine are stored in a triple store, where they can be accessed either through the front end or directly through a SPARQL endpoint. The front end offers a multi-paradigm user interface, in which the knowledge graph visual exploration is coupled with a tabular exposition of the metadata of texts in the corpus (Fig. 2 shows a mockup). Offering the data in RDF format through SPARQL, enables advanced and unanticipated use of the data, through semantic web standards and tools.

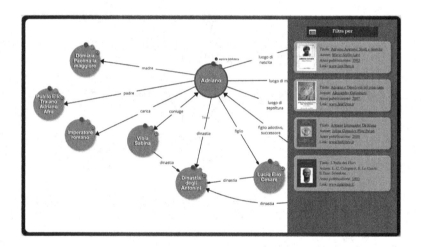

Fig. 2. A mockup of the user interface

4   Data Models

RDF [3], the basic data model for linked data, is used to represent all the data items in the pipeline, adopting specific vocabularies or ontologies for each type of managed data. The standard query language for RDF, SPARQL [5], is used as a basis to define views and mappings. The structure of the PDF repository is represented thanks to the *linked data platform* vocabulary [15]. Basic metadata about the books are represented through the *Dublin Core Metadata Element Set*[2].

For the description of external services and basic mapping of the inputs/outputs, the *actions* descriptors from the *schema.org*[3] vocabulary are used, as proposed in [14], augmented by the use of the SPARQL Generate language[4] [7] to define non trivial mappings of the output. The semantic annotations (output of the semantic enrichment services) are represented using the Web Annotations Vocabulary[5], which allows to associate properties to the annotation itself (e.g., reliability score) and to identify the exact portion(s) of text an annotation refers to. The annotations associate the text to concepts in some knowledge graph which may be topics (after named entity recognition and linking), moods (after sentiment analysis), etc. The knowledge graphs may adopt different data models.

5 Implementation and Case Study

We are in the phase of implementing the whole pipeline. For each step, there are existing solutions we adopted or new components that we are developing. For the triple store we are using Blazegraph[6], while for the content repository supporting LDP containers we use Fedora Commons[7]. The service integration engine is based on the SPARQL Generate engine[8], which maps the JSON output of each web service to RDF. The web front end is developed using the React framework[9] for modularity, using the JS library Ontodia[10] for the knowledge graph visual user interface. For books that do no exist natively in electronic format, the scanned pages go through the OCR of the software ABBYY FineReader Pro 15[11]. For semantic enrichment, we are using the external *entity extraction* (NERL) web service offered by the Dandelion API[12], which relates segments of the input text to resources in DBpedia, along with a confidence value. Nevertheless, given the flexibility of the service integration mechanism, the system is not tied to this specific service.

The practical case study considered is to implement the idea for "L'Erma di Bretschneider", an Italian editor with around two thousands publications. "L'Erma" specializes in ancient history, especially ancient Rome history, and it is well-known in the field. The system is being tested on a selected catalog of 198 books, each of them containing from around two hundreds to seven hundreds

---

[2] http://purl.org/dc/elements/1.1/.

[3] http://schema.org/.

[4] An extension of SPARQL designed to map JSON or XML content to RDF.

[5] http://www.w3.org/ns/oa.

[6] https://www.blazegraph.com/.

[7] https://duraspace.org/fedora/.

[8] https://github.com/sparql-generate/sparql-generate.

[9] https://reactjs.org/.

[10] https://www.ontodia.org/.

[11] https://www.abbyy.com/en-eu/finereader/.

[12] https://dandelion.eu/.

pages and measuring from around one megabyte to 180 megabytes as PDFs. The user interface to the knowledge graph will be publicly available, in order to support the exploration of the catalog of books. The expected users falls in two main categories: casual users willing to explore the catalogue and knowledge on ancient Rome history; expert users that do research in the field and need support to explore and find books relevant to their research topic.

6   Conclusions

This paper presented a concrete lightweight pipeline for enhancing access to a catalog of books through knowledge graph based exploration. The system is based on free software components and meant to be easily deployable for small-medium sized organizations that may not have the technical know-how and resources needed to build and maintain a specifically designed knowledge graph and software system. The development is still in progress but the design analysis and tests carried on so far indicate that the pipeline works without the need for custom coding and it appears useful to the target users. The presented case study will offer a context to thoroughly and formally evaluate the software. The evaluation will include a task oriented analysis as well as a holistic analysis of the impact of the tool on creative processes of research and personal enrichment.

References

1. Bikakis, N., Sellis, T.: Exploration and visualization in the web of big linked data: a survey of the state of the art. arXiv preprint. arXiv:1601.08059 (2016)
2. Bolina, M.: Yewno discover. Nord. J. Inf. Lit. High. Educ. **11**(1) (2019). https://doi.org/10.15845/noril.v11i1.2772
3. Cyganiak, R., Wood, D., Lanthaler, M.: RDF 1.1 concepts and abstract syntax. W3C REC 25 February 2014. http://www.w3.org/TR/2014/REC-rdf11-concepts-20140225/
4. Dadzie, A.S., Rowe, M.: Approaches to visualising linked data: a survey. Semant. Web **2**(2), 89–124 (2011)
5. Harris, S., et al.: SPARQL 1.1 query language. W3C REC 21 March 2013. http://www.w3.org/TR/2013/REC-sparql11-query-20130321/
6. Keim, D.A.: Information visualization and visual data mining. IEEE Trans. Visual. Comput. Graph. **8**(1), 1–8 (2002)
7. Lefrançois, M., Zimmermann, A., Bakerally, N.: A SPARQL extension for generating RDF from heterogeneous formats. In: Blomqvist, E., Maynard, D., Gangemi, A., Hoekstra, R., Hitzler, P., Hartig, O. (eds.) ESWC 2017. LNCS, vol. 10249, pp. 35–50. Springer, Cham (2017). https://doi.org/10.1007/978-3-319-58068-5_3
8. Marie, N., Gandon, F.: Survey of linked data based exploration systems (2014)
9. Nadeau, D., Sekine, S.: A survey of named entity recognition and classification. Lingvisticae Investigationes **30**(1), 3–26 (2007)
10. Nisheva-Pavlova, M., Alexandrov, A.: GLOBDEF: a framework for dynamic pipelines of semantic data enrichment tools. In: Garoufallou, E., Sartori, F., Siatri, R., Zervas, M. (eds.) MTSR 2018. CCIS, vol. 846, pp. 159–168. Springer, Cham (2019). https://doi.org/10.1007/978-3-030-14401-2_15

11. Ristoski, P., Paulheim, H.: Semantic web in data mining and knowledge discovery: a comprehensive survey. J. Web Semant. **36**, 1–22 (2016)
12. Shen, W., Wang, J., Han, J.: Entity linking with a knowledge base: issues, techniques, and solutions. IEEE Trans. Knowl. Data Eng. **27**(2), 443–460 (2014)
13. Shneiderman, B.: The eyes have it: a task by data type taxonomy for information visualizations. In: Proceedings of 1996 IEEE Symposium on Visual Languages, pp. 336–343 (1996)
14. Şimşek, U., Kärle, E., Fensel, D.: Machine readable web APIs with schema.org action annotations. In: Proceedings of SEMANTiCS 2018, pp. 255–261. Elsevier (2018)
15. Speicher, S., Arwe, J., Malhotra, A.: Linked data platform 1.0. W3C Recommendation 26 February 2015 (2015). http://www.w3.org/TR/2015/REC-ldp-20150226/

Re-implementing and Extending Relation Network for R-CBIR

Nicola Messina$^{(\boxtimes)}$, Giuseppe Amato⑩, and Fabrizio Falchi⑩

ISTI-CNR, Pisa, Italy
{nicola.messina,giuseppe.amato,fabrizio.falchi}@isti.cnr.it

Abstract. Relational reasoning is an emerging theme in Machine Learning in general and in Computer Vision in particular. Deep Mind has
recently proposed a module called Relation Network (RN) that has
shown impressive results on visual question answering tasks. Unfortunately, the implementation of the proposed approach was not public.
To reproduce their experiments and extend their approach in the context of Information Retrieval, we had to re-implement everything, testing
many parameters and conducting many experiments. Our implementation is now public on GitHub and it is already used by a large community of researchers. Furthermore, we recently presented a variant of
the relation network module that we called Aggregated Visual Features
RN (AVF-RN). This network can produce and aggregate at inference
time compact visual relationship-aware features for the Relational-CBIR
(R-CBIR) task. R-CBIR consists in retrieving images with given relationships among objects. In this paper, we discuss the details of our
Relation Network implementation and more experimental results than
the original paper. Relational reasoning is a very promising topic for
better understanding and retrieving inter-object relationships, especially
in digital libraries.

Keywords: Relation Network · Image retrieval · Deep Learning ·
Visual features

1 Introduction

In the growing area of Computer Vision (CV), state-of-the-art Deep Learning methods show impressive results in tasks such as classifying or recognizing
objects in images. Several recent studies, however, demonstrated the difficulties
of such architectures to intrinsically understand a complex scene to catch spatial,
temporal and abstract relationships among objects.

One of the most prominent fields of Deep Learning applied to CV within
which these ideas are being tested is Relational Visual Question Answering (R-
VQA). This task consists in answering to a question asked on a particular input
image. While in standard VQA the question usually concerns single objects
and their attributes, the R-VQA questions inquire about relationships between
multiple objects in the image.

M. Ceci et al. (Eds.): IRCDL 2020, CCIS 1177, pp. 82–92, 2020.
https://doi.org/10.1007/978-3-030-39905-4_9

R-VQA is considered a challenging task for current state-of-the-art deep learning models since it requires a range of different reasoning capabilities. In fact, in addition to finding and classifying objects inside the image or understanding the meaning of each word of the input question, it is necessary to understand what are the relationships connecting visual objects and it is required to link together learned textual and visual representations.

This work is about implementing and training the Relation Network architecture (RN) [17]. Our final goal was to extend the RN to extract visual relationship-aware features for a novel task that we called Relational Content-Based Image Retrieval (R-CBIR). The R-CBIR task consists in finding all the images in a dataset that contains objects in similar relationships with respect to the ones present in a given query image.

Specifically, in [13] and [14] we introduced some extensions to the original RN module, able to extract visual relationship-aware features for efficiently characterizing complex inter-object relationships. We trained our RN variants on the CLEVR R-VQA task and we demonstrated that the extracted visual features were suitable for the novel R-CBIR task.

The high-level relational understanding could become a fundamental building block in digital libraries, where multi-modal information has to be processed in smart and scalable ways. Furthermore, R-CBIR encourages the development of solutions able to produce efficient yet powerful relationships-aware features, capable of efficiently describing the large number of inter-object relationships present in a digital library. A digital library, in fact, is composed of a large amount of multi-modal objects: it contains both multimedia elements (images, audio, videos) and text. One interesting challenge in digital libraries is finding relationships either between cross-domain data (e.g., a newspaper article with the related video in the newscast) or between the individual objects that are contained in a single multimedia element (e.g., the spatial arrangement of furniture in a picture of a room). This is a must for constructing strong and high-level interconnections between inter- and intra-domain data, to efficiently collect and manage knowledge.

The first step was re-implementing the RN architecture and training it on the CLEVR dataset, using the same setup detailed in the original work [17]. This was a necessary step since the original code was not published. RN was originally proposed by Deep Mind, a company owned by Google and our code is the first public working implementation of RN[1] on the CLEVR dataset. Thus, it is already largely used.

We found different issues during the replication process. Hence, in this paper, we give many details about the problems we addressed during the implementation of the original version of RN. In the end, we were able to successfully train this architecture reaching an accuracy of 93,6% on the CLEVR R-VQA task.

---

[1] https://github.com/mesnico/RelationNetworks-CLEVR.

2 Related Work

R-VQA. R-VQA comes from the task of VQA (Visual Question Answering). Plain VQA consists in giving the correct answer to a question asked on a given picture, so it requires connecting together different entities coming from heterogeneous representations (text and visuals).

Some works [20,22] proposed approaches to standard VQA problems on datasets such as VQA [1], DAQUAR [11], COCO-QA [16].

Recently, there is the tendency to conceptually separate VQA and R-VQA. In R-VQA, in fact, images contain difficult inter-object relationships, and question are formulated in a way that it is impossible for deep architectures to answer correctly without having understood high-level interactions between the objects in the same image. Some datasets, such as CLEVR [5], RVQA [10], FigureQA [8], move the attention towards this new challenging task.

In this work, we address the R-VQA task by employing the CLEVR dataset. CLEVR is a synthetic dataset composed of 3D rendered scenes. It contains simple yet photorealistic 3D shapes, and it is suitable for testing out, in a fully controlled environment, the intrinsic relational abilities of deep neural networks.

On the CLEVR dataset, [17] and [15] proposed a novel architecture specialized to think in a relational way. They introduced a particular layer called Relation Network (RN), which is specialized in comparing pairs of objects. Objects representations are learned by means of a four-layer CNN, and the question embedding is generated through an LSTM. The overall architecture, composed of CNN, LSTM, and the RN, can be trained fully end-to-end, and it is able to reach superhuman performances. Other solutions [4,6] introduce compositional approaches able to explicitly model the reasoning process by dynamically building a reasoning graph that states which operations must be carried out and in which order to obtain the right answer.

To close the performance gap between interpretable architectures and high performing solutions, [12] proposed a set of visual-reasoning primitives that are able to perform complex reasoning tasks in an explicitly interpretable manner.

R-CBIR. On the R-CBIR task there was some experimentation using both CLEVR and real-world datasets. [7] introduced a CRF model able to ground relationships given in the form of a scene graph to test images for image retrieval purposes. However, this model is not able to produce a compact feature. They employed a simple dataset composed of 5000 images and annotated with objects and their relationships.

More recently, using the Visual Genome dataset, [21] implemented a large scale image retrieval system able to map textual triplets into visual ones (object-subject-relation inferred from the image) projecting them into a common space learned through a modified version of triplet-loss.

The works by [2,13,14] exploit the graph data associated with every image in order to produce ranking goodness metrics, such as nDCG and Spearman-Rho ranking correlation indexes. Their objective was evaluating the quality of the ranking produced for a given query, keeping into consideration the relational content of every scene. In particular, our previous works [13,14] analyzed two architectures for extracting relational data by exploiting knowledge acquired through R-VQA.

2.1   Original Setup

The overall architecture and the initial hyper-parameters we used in our code come from the original paper. Following, we briefly review this original setup.

The Relation Network (RN) [17] approached the task of R-VQA and obtained remarkable results on the CLEVR dataset. RN modules combine input objects forming all possible pairs and applies a common transformation to them, producing activations aimed to store information about possible relationships among input objects. For the specific task of R-VQA, authors used a four-layer CNN to learn visual object representations, that are then fed to the RN module and combined with the textual embedding of the question produced by an LSTM, conditioning the relationship information on the textual modality. The core of the RN module is given by the following:

$$r = \sum_{i,j} g_\theta(o_i, o_j, q) \,, \tag{1}$$

where g_θ is a parametric function whose parameters θ can be learned during the training phase. Specifically, it is a multi-layer perceptron (MLP) network. o_i and o_j are the objects forming the pair under consideration, and q is the question embedding vector obtained from the LSTM module. The answer is then predicted by a downstream network f_ϕ followed by a softmax layer that outputs probabilities for every answer:

$$a = softmax(f_\phi(r)) \,. \tag{2}$$

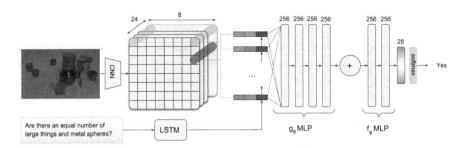

Fig. 1. Relation Network (RN) architecture.

During our implementation, we followed the guidelines and the hyper-parameters configuration by the authors. In particular, we setup the architecture as follows (Fig. 1 depicts the overall architecture):

- the CNN is composed of 4 convolutional layers each with 24 kernels, ReLU non-linearities and batch normalization;
- g_θ and f_ϕ are multilayer perceptrons. They are composed of 4 and 2 fully-connected layers of 256 neurons each. Every layer is followed by the ReLU non-linearity;
- a final linear layer with 28 units produces logits for a softmax layer over the answers vocabulary;
- dropout with 50% dropping probability is inserted after the penultimate layer of f_ϕ;
- the training is performed using the Adam optimizer, with a learning rate of $1e^{-4}$.

We took some decisions that probably brought our code to differ substantially from the original authors implementation. Concerning question processing, we built the dictionaries by sequentially scanning all the questions in the dataset. The zero index was used as padding during the embedding phase. We assumed uni-directional LSTM for question processing. Also, in the first place, we did not consider learning rate schedules nor dataset balancing procedures.

3   Preliminary Results

When training using the original configuration, we reached an accuracy plateau at around 53% on the validation set, while the authors claimed an accuracy of 95,5%.

We broke down the accuracy for the different question types, to have a better insight of what the network was learning. The validation accuracy curves are reported in Fig. 2.

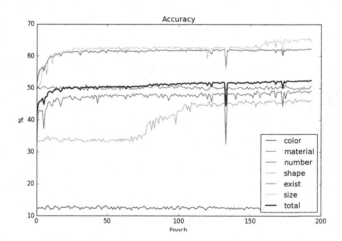

Fig. 2. Validation accuracy curve during the initial training.

This plot shows that the trained model was completely blind to the concepts of color and material since their accuracy was perfectly compatible with uniform random outcomes. However, even considering the other question types, the model was not performing as expected.

These results motivated us to concentrate on some implementation-level details that could help the network convergence.

In particular, we collected a list of some critical implementation details that may have played a role in the network training failure:

- **punctuation-level tokenization:** initially, we did not consider the punctuation as separate elements in the dictionary, so that sentences like *"There is a small cube behind the red object. What is its color?"* generated words like *"object."* and *"color?"*. Instead, one possibility was to break them down into four different entries: *"object"*, *"."*, *"color"*, and *"?"*.
- **training regularization:** in order to regularize training, we thought of adopting standard regularization procedures, like weight-decay and gradient clipping.
- **question inversion:** even if this trick applies to sentence translation models [19], it has been observed that feeding the LSTM with the reversed sentence often brings to an overall higher accuracy.
- **SGD optimizer:** the SGD optimizer is overall slower but asymptotically often performs slightly better than Adam.
- **answers balancing:** the answers distribution is not uniform in the CLEVR dataset. This could have caused problems during the training since less likely examples were penalized. One possible solution was trying to build batches in which all the answers were equally likely.
- **CNN pretraining:** to help the whole architecture to converge faster, we though of initializing the CNN parameters independently, by employing an easier non-relational task. In particular, we trained the CNN using a multi-label classification task, whose aim was to find out the attributes of all the objects inside the CLEVR scene. We aimed to bring the CNN parameters in a zone of the parameters space suitable for the downstream R-VQA task.
- **learning rate and batch size schedulers:** according to some detailed research on neural network parameters optimization, schedulers have a key role during training. We managed to try different schedulers to see if they could move the network parameters away from local minima.

4 Improvements

Following, we report our findings after experimenting with different variations of the original implementation.

Punctuation-Level Tokenization. First of all, we implemented the punctuation-level tokenization for processing the input questions. However, we immediately measured a strong drop in the validation accuracy, from 53% to 20%. This could be due to the fact that the network was effectively using the word-punctuation tokens (e.g. *"color?"*) for easily discerning the question type and better attending to the key question details.

Training Regularization. Gradient clipping and weight decay helped to stabilize the training. However, they did not change the accuracy in any significant way.

Question Inversion. We tried feeding the questions to the LSTM in reverse order. With these changes, accuracy moved from 53% to around 66%. It turned out that the question inversion was a key implementation detail.

To understand how the network outputs were distributed after these changes, we prepared the confusion matrix measured on the validation accuracy (Fig. 3).

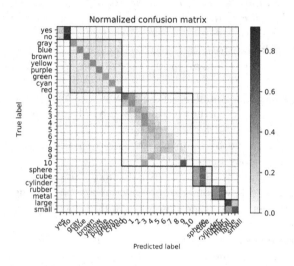

Fig. 3. Confusion matrix after question inversion.

In CLEVR scenario, there are 28 possible answers and they are clustered in 6 classes: *numbers, size, color, material, shape, exists.* In the confusion plot, there are 6 diagonal blocks corresponding to these classes. Empty entries outside the squared diagonal blocks show that answers falling outside their class were extremely unlikely. This was an important finding: the network was perfectly able to understand what kind of answer should be given in output (e.g. a binary yes/no answer rather than a color), but it was not able to figure out the correct label within that class.

SGD Optimizer. We tried training the network using the SGD optimizer, using the same learning rate employed with Adam ($1e^{-4}$). Unfortunately, the training process using SGD was too slow to collect some useful insights. In particular, during the first 50 epochs the architecture remained completely unable to solve the *number* and the *color* classes. Also, the model trained with SGD was not able to understand the 6 different question types, while with Adam this happened already during the first 5–7 epochs.

CNN Pretraining. Although the CNN pretraining sped up the overall convergence during the first epochs, it did not improve the overall validation accuracy. This made us formulate the hypothesis that the problem could be not in the perception module, but rather in the reasoning one, probably in the core of the relation network. In fact, the multi-label classification task reached a mean average precision of 0.99, meaning that the CNN was perfectly able to attend to all the object attributes. The multi-label classification task was trained using 5000 and 750 training and validation images respectively.

Answers Balancing. We wrote a custom batch sampler to ensure a uniform distribution among the answers. In this scenario, we obtained a better accuracy distribution among the different answer classes, w.r.t. the initial validation curves in Fig. 2. In particular, we observed that the model was no more color blind. However, once converged, the overall mean accuracy remained the same as in the initial experiment.

Schedulers. Initially, we tried standard learning rate schedulers, such as CosineAnnealing [9], Exponential, Step-Exponential, and ReduceOnPlateau. Unfortunately, none of them resulted in an accuracy boost, even trying different hyper-parameters such as the step size (in epochs) and the step multiplier.

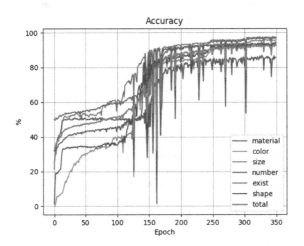

Fig. 4. Validation accuracy - increasing learning rate policy.

Accuracy started growing when we adopted the findings by [18], which suggested increasing the batch size instead of decreasing the learning rate. Our policy consisted in doubling the batch size every 45 training epochs, starting from 32 up to a maximum of 640. We experimented on the *state description* version of the dataset, in which the scene is already encoded in a tensor form suitable for the relation network so that the perception pipeline (the CNN module) is temporarily kept apart. During this experiment, the learning rate remained fixed. With this batch size scheduling policy, we obtained an accuracy of 85%.

The best result, however, was reached using a warm-up learning rate scheduling policy similar to the one used in [3]. In particular, we doubled the learning rate every 20 epochs, from $1e^{-6}$ to $1e^{-4}$. When experimenting on the *state description* version of CLEVR, we were able to reach an accuracy of 97,9%. We repeated the same experiment on the full CLEVR, training end-to-end from pixels and words to answers, and we finally obtained an accuracy of 93,6%. This value is fully compatible with the accuracy claimed by the authors of 95,5%. Validation curves from this training setup are reported in Fig. 4.

The final confusion matrix in Fig. 5 highlights the answers for which there are still problems. Overall, the only remaining issues reside in the *number* class. In fact, the network has still some difficulties when the objective for a particular question is counting many object instances (the number *9* is almost never output as answer).

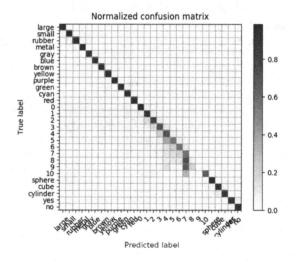

Fig. 5. Final confusion matrix.

5   Conclusions

In this work, we re-implemented the Relation Network architecture [17]. After a few experimentations, we were not able to reach the accuracy claimed by the authors for the R-VQA task on the CLEVR dataset. For this reason, we conducted multiple experiments testing different architectural and implementation tweaks to make the network converge to the claimed accuracy values. In the end, we discovered that the learning rate warm-up scheduling policy was the main missing component. We were able to reach an accuracy of 93,6%, perfectly compatible with the one reached by the Deep Mind team.

We used these results to develop some extensions of the original Relation Network, capable of producing relationships-aware visual features for the novel task of R-CBIR. We noticed that slight modifications to the original architecture to achieve our R-CBIR objectives did not affect the network convergence when using the described learning rate scheduling policy. In particular, in [13] the two-stage RN (2S-RN) reached almost the same accuracy as the original architecture.

Instead, the introduction of the in-network visual aggregation layer in the Aggregated Visual Features RN (AVF-RN) architecture [14] made the performance drop to around 65%. This was due to the strong visual features compression needed. However, we demonstrated that AVF-RN was still able to produce state-of-the-art relationships-aware visual features suitable for R-CBIR.

References

1. Antol, S., et al.: VQA: visual question answering. In: Proceedings of the IEEE International Conference on Computer Vision, pp. 2425–2433 (2015)
2. Belilovsky, E., Blaschko, M.B., Kiros, J.R., Urtasun, R., Zemel, R.: Joint embeddings of scene graphs and images. ICLR (2017)
3. Goyal, P., et al.: Accurate, large minibatch SGD: training imageNet in 1 hour. http://arxiv.org/abs/1706.02677 (2017)
4. Hu, R., Andreas, J., Rohrbach, M., Darrell, T., Saenko, K.: Learning to reason: end-to-end module networks for visual question answering. In: The IEEE International Conference on Computer Vision (ICCV) (October 2017)
5. Johnson, J., Hariharan, B., van der Maaten, L., Fei-Fei, L., Zitnick, C.L., Girshick, R.: CLEVR: a diagnostic dataset for compositional language and elementary visual reasoning (2017)
6. Johnson, J., et al.: Inferring and executing programs for visual reasoning. In: The IEEE International Conference on Computer Vision (ICCV) (October 2017)
7. Johnson, J., et al.: Image retrieval using scene graphs. In: Proceedings of the IEEE Conference on Computer Vision and Pattern Recognition, pp. 3668–3678 (2015)
8. Kahou, S.E., Atkinson, A., Michalski, V., Kádár, Á., Trischler, A., Bengio, Y.: FigureQA: an annotated figure dataset for visual reasoning. CoRR abs/1710.07300 (2017). http://arxiv.org/abs/1710.07300
9. Loshchilov, I., Hutter, F.: SGDR: stochastic gradient descent with warm restarts. In: ICLR (2017)
10. Lu, P., Ji, L., Zhang, W., Duan, N., Zhou, M., Wang, J.: R-VQA: learning visual relation facts with semantic attention for visual question answering. In: SIGKDD 2018 (2018)
11. Malinowski, M., Fritz, M.: A multi-world approach to question answering about real-world scenes based on uncertain input. In: Ghahramani, Z., Welling, M., Cortes, C., Lawrence, N., Weinberger, K. (eds.) Advances in Neural Information Processing Systems 27, pp. 1682–1690. Curran Associates, Inc. (2014)
12. Mascharka, D., Tran, P., Soklaski, R., Majumdar, A.: Transparency by design: closing the gap between performance and interpretability in visual reasoning. In: The IEEE Conference on Computer Vision and Pattern Recognition (CVPR) (June 2018)

13. Messina, N., Amato, G., Carrara, F., Falchi, F., Gennaro, C.: Learning relationship-aware visual features. In: Leal-Taixé, L., Roth, S. (eds.) ECCV 2018. LNCS, vol. 11132, pp. 486–501. Springer, Cham (2019). https://doi.org/10.1007/978-3-030-11018-5_40

14. Messina, N., Amato, G., Carrara, F., Falchi, F., Gennaro, C.: Learning visual features for relational CBIR. Int. J. Multimedia Inf. Retr. 1–12 (2019). https://doi.org/10.1007/s13735-019-00178-7

15. Raposo, D., Santoro, A., Barrett, D.G.T., Pascanu, R., Lillicrap, T., Battaglia, P.W.: Discovering objects and their relations from entangled scene representations. In: 5th International Conference on Learning Representations, ICLR 2017, Toulon, France, April 24–26, 2017, Workshop Track Proceedings (2017). https://openreview.net/forum?id=rkrjrvmKl

16. Ren, M., Kiros, R., Zemel, R.: Exploring models and data for image question answering. In: Cortes, C., Lawrence, N.D., Lee, D.D., Sugiyama, M., Garnett, R. (eds.) Advances in Neural Information Processing Systems 28, pp. 2953–2961. Curran Associates, Inc. (2015)

17. Santoro, A., et al.: A simple neural network module for relational reasoning. In: Guyon, I., et al. (eds.) Advances in Neural Information Processing Systems 30, pp. 4967–4976. Curran Associates, Inc. (2017)

18. Smith, S., Kindermans, P.J., Ying, C., Le, Q.V.: Don't decay the learning rate, increase the batch size (2018). https://openreview.net/pdf?id=B1Yy1BxCZ

19. Sutskever, I., Vinyals, O., Le, Q.V.: Sequence to sequence learning with neural networks. In: Ghahramani, Z., Welling, M., Cortes, C., Lawrence, N.D., Weinberger, K.Q. (eds.) Advances in Neural Information Processing Systems 27, pp. 3104–3112. Curran Associates, Inc. (2014). http://papers.nips.cc/paper/5346-sequence-to-sequence-learning-with-neural-networks.pdf

20. Yang, Z., He, X., Gao, J., Deng, L., Smola, A.: Stacked attention networks for image question answering. In: The IEEE Conference on Computer Vision and Pattern Recognition (CVPR) (June 2016)

21. Zhang, J., Kalantidis, Y., Rohrbach, M., Paluri, M., Elgammal, A., Elhoseiny, M.: Large-scale visual relationship understanding. In: Proceedings of the AAAI Conference on Artificial Intelligence, vol. 33, pp. 9185–9194 (2019)

22. Zhou, B., Tian, Y., Sukhbaatar, S., Szlam, A., Fergus, R.: Simple baseline for visual question answering. CoRR abs/1512.02167 (2015). http://arxiv.org/abs/1512.02167

Actual Researcher Contribution (ARC) Versus the Perceived Contribution to the Scientific Body of Knowledge

Mohanad Halaweh$^{(\boxtimes)}$

Al Falah University, Dubai, UAE
Mohanad.halaweh@afu.ac.ae

Abstract. The aim of this paper is to propose a new quantitative metric that can be used to measure the total actual researcher contribution (ARC) to a body of knowledge. The proposed ARC metric is a fair measure that is needed to address the abuse of research collaboration and issues arising from honorary authorship, which both lead to the inflation of the total number of published articles by a researcher. This inflation can provide misleading information about a researcher's expertise and competence based on their perceived contribution. Research ranking agencies, database indexes, universities, and other decision makers can rely on the ARC metric to rank and evaluate university and researcher contributions to a body of knowledge and thus make more informed decisions and allocate research resources more efficiently.

Keywords: Actual researcher contribution · Publishing · Contribution · Metrics · Research collaboration · Honorary author

1 Introduction and Background

Writing and publishing academic research papers is one of the key activities that faculty members perform while working in the higher education environment. In fact, publications are one of the key areas considered when evaluating a faculty member's contribution to the scientific body of knowledge. They play an important role in the decision making for the hiring, funding, rewarding, or promoting of a faculty member. Research and publications are an important factor for evaluating an instructor's prestige, promotion, and pay (Borry, Schotsmans and Dierickx 2006 Mitcheson, Collings, and Siebers 2011). Increases in salary are dependent on the quantity and quality of the research papers produced by an instructor (Bergen and Bressler 2017). Furthermore, publishing in peer-reviewed journals is considered as prestigious because it provides proof of academic competence, and it is thus considered a key criterion for the ranking of top research universities and has become one of the main criteria for university accreditation by local and international agencies (Bergen and Bressler 2017). Therefore, it is essential for a faculty member to have many and high-quality publications. This sometimes pressures instructors to concentrate more on research rather than on teaching or other responsibilities (Bergen and Bressler 2017). More importantly, this pressure might encourage the publication of scientifically insignificant papers or raise

© Springer Nature Switzerland AG 2020
M. Ceci et al. (Eds.): IRCDL 2020, CCIS 1177, pp. 93–102, 2020.
https://doi.org/10.1007/978-3-030-39905-4_10

issues of gifted, guest, or honorary authorship (Bergen and Bressler 2017; Fong and Wilhite 2017; Kaushik 2013) where faculty members are listed as article authors even when they have not contributed significantly to the research. A critical need to publish research has created authorship abuse. This is evidenced by the many empirical studies that have provided surveys of past co-authors indicating that their names had been included on articles in which they did nothing or made only a minor contribution to the research work (Al-Herz, Haider, Al-Bahhar and Sadeq 2014; Bavdekar 2012; Borry et al. 2006; Seeman and House 2010). For example, Seeman and House (2010) surveyed 600 faculty members in the United States and found that 25% of them discovered their names listed on research papers only after they had already been submitted to a journal. Another survey study conducted by Al-Herz et al. (2014) also showed that 33.4% of 1246 corresponding authors admitted that they had added authors who did not deserve authorship credit. Empirical research has also shown that academic articles with more than five authors are more likely to have "honorary authors" than those with fewer than three authors (Bavdekar 2012). Undoubtedly, honorary authorship is a misrepresentation that leads to the perception of an extensive intellectual contribution that was not actually made by an author, making the publication record a less reliable measure of research productivity (Bergen and Bressler 2017). There are three reasons why honorary authorship should be considered as an unethical practice (Bergen and Bressler 2017):

- A publication credit that is not genuinely earned may falsely represent an individual's expertise.
- Due to the gift authorship, the credited individual is perceived as being more skilled than colleagues who have not been published or published fewer times. This gives the individual an unfair advantage professionally over their colleagues when applying for jobs or promotion.
- Such individuals are also falsely perceived to have a higher level of competence and may be expected to accomplish tasks that are outside the range of their expertise.

Honorary authorship occurs for many reasons. For example, in some countries, cultural norms cause writers to show respect to department heads, senior researchers, or PhD supervisors or advisors by including their names on papers despite their not being involved. In other cases, scholars will sometimes perceive that adding more guest or honorary authors, especially if they have a reputation in the field, will increase the likelihood of a paper being accepted. Then sometimes, senior faculty members will help junior faculty members achieve tenure by adding their names to research papers (Bergen and Bressler 2017). In other cases, authors might cultivate a mutual relationship where they add an honorary author to their own paper with an agreement that the beneficiary will return the favour on their own paper in the future (Feeser and Simon 2008; Marusic, Bosnjak and Jeroncic 2011). In addition, at some universities, there is a research policy (i.e. cash-per-publication policies) that financially rewards faculty members who publish papers that included the university name. Some guest or honorary authors might abuse these policies by making agreements with friends or colleagues from other universities. If the friends include the guest author's name on their work, the guest author will share the reward money with them, so it becomes a win-win relationship. In all of the above cases, there is an increase in the number of faculty member publications without actually making real contribution to the body of knowledge. In fact, research collaboration has increased the number of publications for authors and the number of authors for each paper, which further opens the opportunity for honorary authorship. This leads to the question of what constitutes an author and what is an author's role, which has not yet been standardized across fields and is still unclear for many (Bergen and Bressler 2017; Papatheodorou, Trikalinos and Ioannidis 2008). Nevertheless, various scientific associations have indicated that an author needs to have provided substantial or significant contributions to the conception or design of a study, formulated its problems or hypothesis, analysed and/or interpreted its data, drafted the work, or revised it critically, and they be held accountable for all of the work's accuracy and integrity (International Committee of Medical Journal Editors (ICMJE) 2018; the Council of Science Editors (CSE) 2016; Publication Manual of the American Psychological Association 2001). Those who have only provided funding, general supervision, general administrative support, writing assistance, editing, or proofreading should not be considered as contributing authors but may be given acknowledgment in the article (ICMJE 2018).

Indeed, research collaboration raises the issue of the allocation of credit for scientific work (Ackerman and Brânzei 2014). Two specific problems emerge: first, exploiting the rational for collaboration by adding guest or honorary authors who make no or trivial contributions to a research paper and this may not be known by the research community, and second, problems caused by the order of author names on a research paper (even for those who have made actual contributions). In this paper, we do not address the problems of research collaboration as there are many, but our focus is on the issue of authorship and the actual contributions and allocation of credit for authors. For example, counting an article as one paper for each co-author is too generous and unfair (Mesnard 2017) when compared to a paper written by only one author. In fact, there is no commonly accepted metric for assessing the actual contribution of an author to a particular article, and the standards for determining the order of author names vary from one field to another (Efthyvoulou 2008; Lake 2010). In certain fields, researchers use alphabetical ordering, but this favours those whose last names start with letters that appear earlier in the alphabet. It is also common to assume that the more established authors deserve more credit even though their names appear last in the list (Efthyvoulou 2008; Einav and Yariv 2006). Others list the authors' names according to their contribution in descending order where (the sequence determines the contribution) the first/leading author name indicates the author who has made the greatest contribution (Tscharntke et al. 2007). Nevertheless, if the second or last author listed is a well-known scholar, then there might be a perception in the research community that this author should receive more credit than the others despite the fact that others have made greater contributions. Sometimes research collaborators who work on big research project agree to rotate the first author on all resulted research papers regardless of their actual contributions (Ackerman and Brânzei 2014). Hence, the interpretation of author sequence seem like "a lottery" as one does not really know for sure if being the first or last author reflects whether the overall contribution was the most or least important (Tscharntke et al. 2007). As an alternative solution, some journals have a policy that requires authors to declare their contributions in a checklist form (i.e. a contribution statement, for an example, see the Author Contribution Form from the

European Endodontic Journal (2020) at http://eurendodj.com/author_contribution.pdf). However, these contribution statements are sometimes primarily descriptive and very subjective. In this regard, the American Mathematical Society (2004) has indicted that "Determining which person contributed which ideas is often meaningless because the ideas grow from complex discussions among all partners... mathematicians traditionally list authors on joint papers in alphabetical order." This means that the authors have all made equal contributions, but again, those whose names are listed first will benefit, especially if the paper is written by a large number of authors. Dance (2012) has also pointed out that the credit allocation for collaborative works today is highly subjective, open to abuse, and often determined by the research centre's politics or seniority rather than by actual effort or contribution. Recent studies (for examples, see Boyer et al. 2017; Mesnard 2017) have proposed metrics or indexes that quantify the actual contribution to each paper or per author, but these proposed metrics have a major limitation in that they depend mainly on data, such as contributions percentages and other variable values, provided by the authors themselves when submitting the paper to a journal, which are unavailable for articles and authors published in the past, so the metrics cannot be universal and generalized to evaluate the actual contributions made by all past authors. Kaushik (2013) also proposed a quantitative metric (formulae that calculates the total contribution per author) that basically gives weight to each paper written by an author depending on the position of the author's name. For example, more weight (1 point) is given if the author is the first or corresponding author, while half a point is given to the authors who appear later in the list of authors. Although this measure can be used to calculate the total contribution of past and future authors, it is still subjective in assigning weight because it is unknown if the first author is actually is the lead author or made the greatest contribution or if the authors' names are sorted in alphabetically. In this case, the first author will perhaps gain an undeserved 1 point advantage over others. Furthermore, giving more weight to the corresponding author is also questionable. It is unknown to the research community or evaluation committees if the corresponding author really made the greatest contribution. In summary, as we have seen, no previous study has provided a fair generic and objective measure to calculate the total actual contribution made by a researcher, which is what this paper aims to propose.

2 Proposed Metric (ARC)

The proposed metric was developed with the following assumptions in mind:

1. There is a logical assumption that when a group of scholars have decided to collaborate on a research project, they understand from the start that each one of them will make a major contribution without which the work will be incomplete and unable or difficult to complete. Thus, the collaboration is seen as teamwork where one cannot claim to have contributed more than others, and it becomes a subjective matter as to which part is the most difficult and important, especially when research tasks are interdependent. For example, in a study, the person who gathers or provides the data might claim that this is the most important element, while another

might claim that analysing the data is the most crucial part. A third person might say that conceptualizing the basis of the paper is the most important element and without it, the paper would be impossible to publish. Therefore, it remains a subjective matter as to which task is the most important. In fact, performing research collaboratively is teamwork, like a football team working together in order to achieve the common goals of scoring and wining that cannot be claimed by only one player. In addition, we cannot always evaluate the exact level of contribution in terms of time and effort for each individual performing the research tasks. For example, a collaborator who is an expert at quantitative data analysis might be perceived to have a made great expenditure of time and effort by an inexperienced contributor who has no idea what is required to perform the data analysis. In addition, the arrangements made between the contributors are unknown to the research community. Therefore, it is better to consider of the all contributors as equal. If certain authors have agreed to add honorary authors to their paper, then it should then be their choice and responsibility for reducing their own credit and share of the contribution as their accumulated points will be fewer when more author names are added to the paper. The advantage of this is that the honorary authors will get a percentage share (in any instance, it will be ≤ 0.5 assuming at least one honorary co-author name was added to a genuine author name) rather than a 100% authorship contribution for each paper carrying the honorary author name, thus this reduces free rider scores.

2. Most importantly, there is need for a universal generic metric that measures the actual total contribution of an individual author for past and future published research, not only for a particular paper, but collectively. Existing metrics have not developed a standard measure that tells us the total actual contributions per author including past articles. As we have unknown data (except when past authors did declare a contribution percentage) for millions of articles published in the past (in 2009, the estimated total scholarly research articles passed 50 million since the first journal articles appeared in 1665 (Jinha 2010), the fairer measure would be to consider the contribution of the collaborators as equal so that the measure can be applicable for future and past articles. The data showing the amount of input by each collaborator has sometimes been provided by the authors of past articles because of a request by the journal or provided voluntarily, but these are limited cases, and in some other instances, they were descriptive statements not quantitative measurable data.

3. For the reasons mentioned previously regarding the unethical and misleading information on the total number of publications produced by faculty members (perceived contribution through an honorary gift or having a minimal contribution), the number of publications should not be used as an criteria for promotions, hiring, or increases in salary. Rather, using the actual total contribution collectively for all articles would be a fairer measure. Although it might not be completely accurate, it is the best way to reflect actual contributions and minimize free rider scores. It is unfair to consider one paper written by one author the same as one written by two or n authors. Simply put, more credit should be given to a paper by a single author as more time and effort has been allocated than if two or more authors were collaborating. If two collaborate, the contribution share is reduced to half as the effort is

reduced by half. Furthermore, the work of authors who have published 10 papers as the fourth author should not be treated as equal to an author who has published 10 papers as a single author or with one co-author.

The following provides a clear definition for ARC:

Actual Researcher Contribution (ARC) is the total of the percentages of the contribution shares accumulated from each published paper that carries an author's name. The percentage share for each paper is calculated based on the assumption that all authors have made an equal contribution for the reasons mentioned above (i.e. teamwork, interdependent research work, need for an objective and not subjective metric, fair and applicable for past and future articles).

Perceived Contribution (PC) is the total number of published papers that carry the author's name regardless of the order in which the name appears or the exact level of contribution made by each author, including an honorary contribution.

ARC can be calculated using the following formula:

$$ARC \; for \; Author \; X = \sum_{n=1}^{T} \frac{1}{Pn \; \# \; of \; Authors} \tag{1}$$

P: Published refereed paper
T: Total number of papers that carry the author name

$$ARC \; for \; University \; X = \frac{\sum_{n=1}^{T} ARCn}{\# \; of \; affiliated \; Authors} \tag{2}$$

T: Total number of published authors affiliated with university X

Sharing credit among co-authors by percentage or by dividing by n ("1/n rule") is fairer, though it may be considered harsh (Mesnard 2017). However, knowing the percentage of one paper does not provide much information unless it is aggregated with the entire author's other publications, which is a new perspective addressed by this paper. The ARC value allows for comparisons between the total contributions of authors and universities.

Let us assume that we have three authors (A, B, C) who have published the number of papers shown in Table 1 and supposing that they have all published good papers with the same level of quality. According to PC, authors A and B are considered as the best as each has published three papers. However, ARC provides the actual contribution made in all papers collectively per author. Given the number of published papers carrying a particular author name and the number of authors who worked on each article, it can be found that authors B and C have made greater contributions than author A. In addition, both of them (B and C) have same level of ARC despite that author B's name has appeared on three papers, while author C's name has appeared on only two.

$$ARC\ for\ Author\ A = \frac{1}{3} + \frac{1}{2} + \frac{1}{3} = 1.16$$

$$ARC\ for\ Author\ B = \frac{1}{2} + \frac{1}{2} + \frac{1}{1} = 2$$

$$ARC\ for\ Author\ C = \frac{1}{1} + \frac{1}{1} = 2$$

Table 1. Calculating ARC

	# of Published papers	PC	# of authors for each paper (P)	Percentage of paper contribution	ARC	Rank as per ARC
Author A	3	3	P1: 3 authors P2: 2 authors P3: 3 authors	0.33 0.50 0.33	1.16	2
Author B	3	3	P1: 2 authors P2 2 authors P3:1 author	0.50 0.50 1	2	1
Author C	2	2	P1: 1 author P2: 1 author	1 1	2	1

3 Discussion and Implications

ARC reflects the actual aggregated contributions of an author as an alternative to the perceived contributions that focuses on counting the papers that carry the author name, which can be misleading or reflect unfairly on the competency and capability of authors and their contributions to the body of knowledge. Therefore, university administrators and the directors of research institutions should use this metric to make more effective and efficient decisions for allocating research resources and funding and for promotions and salary increases, and do so according to actual contributions made without giving credit to a person that does not deserve it.

We suggest that this metric be used as a standard practice for all journals, where authors should be asked to include the percentage of their contribution on the title page beside their names and affiliations (self-reported percentage). If a group of collaborators who have worked on a research project have decided not to include this percentage, they will by default be considered to have made an equal contribution.

ARC can also be used to calculate the total actual research contributions for each university by aggregating all ARC values for its researchers (past, present, and future), so it can be used for ranking a university's contribution to the body of knowledge. From the above example, if we assume that the three authors are all working at one university, then the ARC for that university will be 5.16 (1.16 + 2 + 2, the sum of the

ARC values for all of the published authors affiliated with the university). However, because the size of the universities (number of researchers/faculty members) is different from one to another (range from tens to thousands), the comparison and ranking becomes unfair (with regards the actual total contribution to the body of knowledge) as a large university might get a higher score than a small school. Therefore, we suggest adjusting that by dividing the value of $\sum_{n=1}^{T} ARCn$ by the number of affiliated authors (see above formula 2) in order to get the ratio of total actual contributions to the total number of university's authors, which provides a fair measure for rankings and comparisons with other universities. Back to the above example the ARC for the above university (has 3 three authors) should be 1.72 (5.16/3), taking into consideration the size of the university (i.e. only total number of authors not total number of the university's staff).

Adopting this ARC metric will make authors more responsible and accountable when working on a collaborative research project as they will know that adding gift or honorary authors to the paper will decrease their contribution percentage share for that paper, and thus, their ARC score will be lower, which will discourage accepting honorary authors.

Research ranking agencies and databases such as Scopus and Google Scholar can adopt this metric as the required data (i.e. the total number of papers that carry the author's name and the total number of co-authors for each paper) is available, and so it is easy to calculate for the past and future research of an author. This universal standard metric can also be used for comparing faculty member competence. Other measures, such as the total number of published papers or h-index, fail to address the issue of honorary authors, which is unfair. Honorary authorship leads to more publications being attributed to an author and more self-citations that increase when many authors are added to paper, so there will be more chances for manipulating and inflating the h-index value as well. ARC can give more reliable data about researcher productivity than the h-index.

We also suggest using ARC-5, which uses a time window of the previous five years to calculate ARC for authors and universities to avoid concerns regarding unfair comparisons between senior and junior researchers and scientists or newer and older universities. Thus, ARC-5 can inform research communities how active a researcher or university has been in the last five years in regard actual contributions to the literature.

As a limitation of ARC, it does not consider the quality of a paper when calculating the percentage share. For example, assume that author A has published two papers with a second author, and the first paper has been published in a highly ranked journal indexed by Scopus and the second has not yet been indexed or has been published in a low ranked journal. The contribution percentage share (0.50) from the first paper is considered as equivalent to the second paper (0.50). However, the issue of quality can be tackled depending on the database or agency doing the ranking. For example, Scopus might calculate ARC only based on the prestigious journals that are listed in Scopus database. However, this might create inconsistent values if used along with Google Scholar, which might consider any author published paper regardless of journal rank or quality. In fact, this inconsistency is the same as with the h-index or total citation values, which are also not identical in Google Scholar and Scopus.

4 Conclusion

ARC is fair, universal, and standard metric that can be used to measure the actual intellectual contributions made by authors and universities. ARC can be calculated and used for any discipline, at any time, and for both past and new publications without any restrictions. The development of such a metric is very important as existing metrics are either inaccurate, unfair, or impractical and difficult to implement for academic and research universities and ranking agencies. ARC is easy to calculate because it relies on data that is readily available. It is easy to calculate, but it is also a powerful metric that can provide a great deal of information and assist in ranking and comparing between authors and universities to allow the more efficient use of research resources. It also discourages honorary authorship and provides the ability to give fair credit to collaborative authors and universities. In the case of unethical activities through guest or honorary authorships, ARC does not allow these authors to receive more than a percentage of the share of the contribution to a particular paper as it does not provide 100% authorship for each co-authored paper. Thus, it provides a more reliable measure for the total research contribution of a particular author or university.

References

Al-Herz, W., Haider, H., Al-Bahhar, M., Sadeq, A.: Honorary authorship in biomedical journals: how common is it and why does it exist? J. Med. Ethics **40**(5), 346–348 (2014)

Ackerman, M., Brânzei, S.: The authorship dilemma: alphabetical or contribution? In: Lomuscio, A., Scerri, P., Bazzan, A., Huhns, M. (eds.) Proceedings of the 13th International Conference on Autonomous Agents and Multiagent Systems (AAMAS 2014), Paris, France, 5–9 May 2014 (2014)

American Mathematical Society: The Culture of Research and Scholarship in Mathematics: Joint Research and Its Publication (2004). http://www.ams.org/profession/leaders/culture/CultureStatement04.pdf. Accessed 2 Sept 2017

American Psychological Association: Publication Manual of the American Psychological Association, 5th edn. American Psychological Association, Washington (2001)

Bergen, C.V., Bressler, M.: Academe's unspoken ethical dilemma: author inflation in higher education. Res. High. Educ. J. **31**, 1–17 (2017)

Borry, P., Schotsmans, P., Dierickx, K.: Author, contributor or just a singer? A quantitative analysis of authorship trends in the field of bioethics. Bioethics **20**(4), 213–220 (2006)

Boyer, S., Ikeda, T., Lefort, M., Malumbres-Olarte, J., Schmidt, J.: Research integrity and peer review, percentage-based author contribution index: a universal measure of author contribution to scientific articles. Res. Integrity Peer Rev. **2**, 18 (2017)

Bavdekar, S.B.: Authorship issues. Lung India **29**(1), 76–80 (2012)

Dance, A.: Who's on first? Nature **489**, 591–593 (2012)

European Journal Of Endodontic. Author Contribution Form (2018). http://eurendodj.com/author_contribution.pdf. Accessed 6 Jan 2020

Efthyvoulou, G.: Alphabet economics: the link between names and reputation. J. Soc.-Econ. **37** (3), 1266–1285 (2008)

Einav, L., Yariv, L.: What's in a surname? The effects of surname initials on academic success. J. Econ. Perspect. **20**(1), 175–187 (2006)

Feeser, V.R., Simon, J.R.: The ethical assignment of authorship in scientific publications: issues and guidelines. Acad. Emer. Med. **15**, 963–969 (2008)

Fong, E.A., Wilhite, A.W.: Authorship and citation manipulation in academic research. PLoS One **12**(12), e0187394 (2017)

Jinha, A.: Article 50 million: an estimate of the number of scholarly articles in existence. Learn. Publish. **23**(3), 258–263 (2010)

International Committee of Medical Journal Editors. Defining the Role of Authors and Contributors (2018). http://www.icmje.org/recommendations/browse/roles-and-responsibiliti es/defining-the-role-of-authors-and-contributors.html. Accessed 2 Sept 2017

Kaushik, R.: The "Authorship Index" - a simple way to measure an author's contribution to literature. Int. J. Res. Med. Sci. **1**(1), 1–3 (2013)

Lake, D.A.: Who's on first? Listing authors by relative contribution trumps the alphabet. Polit. Sci. Polit. **43**(47), 43–47 (2010)

Marusic, A., Bosnjak, L., Jeroncic, A.: A systematic review of research on the meaning, ethics and practices of authorship across scholarly disciplines. PLoS One **6**(9), e23477 (2011)

Mesnard, L.D.: Attributing credit to coauthors in academic publishing: The 1/n rule, parallelization, and team bonuses. Eur. J. Oper. Res. **260**(2), 778–788 (2017)

Mitcheson, H., Collings, S., Siebers, R.W.: Authorship issues at a New Zealand academic institution. Int. J. Occup. Environ. Med. **2**(3), 166–171 (2011)

Papatheodorou, S.I., Trikalinos, T.A., Ioannidis, J.P.A.: Inflated numbers of authors over time have not been just due to increasing research complexity. J. Clin. Epidemiol. **61**(6), 546–551 (2008)

Seeman, J.I., House, M.C.: Influences on authorship issues: An evaluation of receiving, not receiving, and rejecting credit. Accountability Res. **17**(4), 176–197 (2010)

The Council of Science Editors: 2.2 Authorship and Authorship Responsibilities (2016). http:// www.councilscienceeditors.org/resource-library/editorial-policies/white-paper-onpublication-ethics/2-2-authorship-and-authorship-responsibilities/. Accessed 2 Sept 2017

Tscharntke, T., Hochberg, M.E., Rand, T.A., Resh, V.H., Krauss, J.: Author sequence and credit for contributions in multiauthored publications. PLoS Biol. **5**(1), e18 (2007)

Cultural Heritage

Towards a Tool for Visual Link Retrieval and Knowledge Discovery in Painting Datasets

Giovanna Castellano and Gennaro Vessio[✉]

Dipartimento di Informatica, Università degli Studi di Bari, Bari, Italy
{giovanna.castellano,gennaro.vessio}@uniba.it

Abstract. This paper presents a preliminary investigation aimed at developing a tool for visual link retrieval and knowledge discovery in painting datasets. The proposed framework is based on a deep convolutional network to perform feature extraction and on a fully-unsupervised nearest neighbor approach to retrieve *visual links* among digitized paintings. Moreover, the proposed method makes it possible to study influences among artists by means of graph analysis. The tool is intended to help art historians better understand visual arts.

Keywords: Cultural heritage · Deep learning · Computer Vision · Visual link retrieval · Knowledge discovery · Paintings

1 Introduction

The cultural heritage, in particular visual arts, have invaluable importance for the cultural, historic and economic growth of our societies. One of the building blocks of most analysis in visual arts is to find similarity relationships, i.e. link retrieval, among paintings of different artists and genres. These relationships can help art historians discover and better understand influences and changes from an artistic movement to another. Traditionally, this kind of analysis is done manually by inspecting large collections of human annotated photos. Unfortunately, manually searching over thousands of pictures, spanned across different epochs and painting schools, is a very time consuming and expensive process.

In the last years, large-scale digitization efforts have been made, leading to a growing availability of digitized fine art collections (e.g., WikiArt[1] and the MET collection[2]). This has opened new opportunities for computer science researchers to assist the art community with automatic tools to further understand visual arts. Automated painting analysis, in fact, is becoming increasingly important for several tasks, ranging from object detection [5] to artistic style classification [15]. The purpose of our research is to develop an automatic tool to be used to retrieve *visual links* within large digitized collections of paintings by using simple

---

[1] https://www.wikiart.org.

[2] https://www.metmuseum.org/art/collection.

© Springer Nature Switzerland AG 2020
M. Ceci et al. (Eds.): IRCDL 2020, CCIS 1177, pp. 105–110, 2020.
https://doi.org/10.1007/978-3-030-39905-4_11

image queries. Relying only on visual patterns makes the approach desirable when difficult to collect textual metadata are either scarce or unavailable.

The ability to recognize artistic styles and similarities in fine art paintings inherently falls within the domain of human perception. Understanding semantic attributes of a painting, such as content and meaning, in fact, originates from the composition of the shape, colour and texture features visually perceived by the human expert. Recent breakthroughs in Computer Vision, particularly in Convolutional Neural Networks (CNNs), proved to be very effective to tackle the problem of learning meaningful representations from the low-level colour and texture features (e.g., [3,14]). For this reason, the proposed tool is mainly based on visual attributes automatically learned by a well-known CNN architecture, i.e. VGG. The resulting high dimensional representation is then embedded in a more compact feature space through the use of Principal Component Analysis (PCA). Finally, similarities among paintings, i.e. visual links, are obtained through a distance measure in a completely unsupervised nearest neighbor fashion. The proposed method not only provides the nearest neighbors for each query image, i.e. those images more similarly linked to the input query, but it also allows the user to study historical patterns by means of graph analysis.

2 Proposed Method

The method we propose is partly inspired by the research presented in [11] and [12]. In both works, a deep learning-based approach is followed to retrieve common visual patterns shared among paintings and to discover near duplicate patterns in large collection of artworks, respectively. In both cases, the authors used a supervised approach in which the labels to be predicted are manually provided by human experts. Conversely, our method works in a fully unsupervised fashion, making the laborious acquisition of annotations unnecessary.

An overall scheme of the proposed framework is depicted in Fig. 1. The method assumes to have a large collection of digitized paintings of different artists and genres, as those nowadays collected in several museum Websites. The goal is to transform the raw pixel images into a new, numerical feature space in which to search for similarities among paintings. In order to obtain meaningful representations of visual attributes of paintings, we used *transfer learning* from a pre-trained deep Convolutional Neural Network. This practice is common and it is now usually preferred over classic approaches based on hand-crafted features in several perceptual domains. For example, it has been recently applied to the problem of Parkinsonian handwriting classification [7].

The input to our system is thus represented by a 224×224 three-channels painting image, normalized within the range $[0, 1]$: this is the typical input expected by the CNN we used. In fact, each input image is propagated through a VGG16 architecture [13], pre-trained on the very large ImageNet dataset [6]. The main assumption is that if the original dataset is large and general enough, then the weights learned by the network on this set of data can be used to new, even completely different image datasets. VGG16 is a well-known CNN architecture

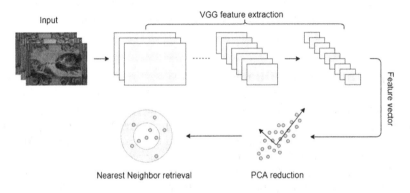

Fig. 1. Workflow of the proposed method.

which adopts 3×3 convolution and 2×2 max pooling throughout the network. All hidden layers are equipped with the ReLU activation function. To achieve transfer learning, we used the common practice to ignore the fully-connected layers stacked on top of the convolutional base and to extract the output features from the last convolutional layer. The network is able to construct a hierarchy of visual features, starting from simple edges and shapes at the earlier layers to higher-level concepts at the later layers. This approach is thus apt to obtain useful, semantic representations for the problem at hand.

Once the features extracted by the deep network are flattened, they have still too high dimensionality (i.e., $25,088$ dimensions) to make the use of distance measures feasible. For this reason, we need to transform this high dimensional feature space into a more compact low dimensional representation given by the application of PCA. Dimensionality reduction techniques are tailored to this goal (e.g., [2]); PCA, in particular, minimizes the mean ℓ_2 distance between data points and their linear projections [8]. For instance, the first two principal components span the plane that is *closest*, in terms of average distance, to the data points provided as input. In our case, to achieve a good compromise between representation power and dimensionality, the original $25,088$ dimensional feature space is projected onto a reduced space of 50 features.

The final search for visual links among paintings is performed in the reduced feature space in a fully unsupervised nearest neighbor fashion. In other words, for each query point q the methods returns the k data points *closest* to q. "Closeness" implies a metric that, as in PCA, corresponds to the usual ℓ_2 distance: $\sqrt{\sum_{i=1}^{N} (q_i - p_i)^2}$, being q_i and p_i the query point and each other data point, respectively, with N their dimensionality. In our case, we set k to 3, i.e. for each query, the three most similar paintings are provided by the system. Clearly, when searching for a particular artist's query, the other paintings from the same artist are excluded from the research, otherwise obvious, self links are likely to be retrieved. As previously stated, relying on a completely unsupervised approach makes the proposed method simple and practical, as it excludes the necessity to acquire labels of visual links or similarities of local parts of paintings, which are very difficult to collect.

3   Experimental Evaluation

We preliminarily investigated the effectiveness of the proposed method on a dataset collecting paintings of 50 very popular painters. More precisely, we used data provided by the Kaggle platform,[3] scraped from an art challenge Website.[4] Artists belong to very different epochs and painting schools, ranging from Giotto di Bondone and Renaissance painters such as Leonardo da Vinci and Michelangelo, to Modern Art exponents, including Pablo Picasso, Salvador Dalí, and so on. Painting images are non-uniformly distributed among painters for a total of 8,446 images of different sizes.

Experiments were run on an Intel Core i5 equipped with the NVIDIA GeForce MX110, with dedicated memory of 2 GB. As deep learning framework, we used TensorFlow 2.0 and the Keras API. It is worth to note that we did not perform an execution time analysis. In fact, one advantage of the proposed method is that its most expensive part, i.e. the VGG-based feature extraction, can be done completely offline, thus making the visual link retrieval, i.e. the search over the reduced feature space, only dependent on the collection size.

Some image queries together with their corresponding three output neighbors are provided in Fig. 2. In the first row, we asked for paintings visually linked with the Romanticist "Fort Vimieux" by William Turner, depicting a classic red sunset of the author. It can be seen that the system was able to retrieve paintings similar in their content. In the second row, we searched for paintings visually linked with the Impressionist "Confluence of the Seine and the Loing" by Alfred Sisley. It can be noticed that the given neighbors, i.e. two artworks by Camille Pissarro and a work by Claude Monet, share the same painting style. Finally, the third sample query was the more classic "Virgin and Child with Six Angels and the Baptist" by the Renaissance artist Sandro Botticelli. As it was expected, the visual features provided by the deep network were able to retrieve paintings similar in composition (holy family) and shape (tondo).

Finally, it is worth remarking that by collecting the nearest neighbors of all painters' artworks and by retaining only the most occurring linked painters, the proposed approach makes it possible to build a graph, possibly showing influences among artists. In other words, also historical knowledge discovery can be done. As depicted in Fig. 3, three connected components can be observed together with some *hubs*, represented by very influencing painters, such as Vincent Van Gogh and Edgar Degas. As expected, painters belonging to the same school appear to be close to each other.

---

[3] https://www.kaggle.com/ikarus777/best-artworks-of-all-time.
[4] http://artchallenge.ru.

Fig. 2. Sample queries (on the left) and corresponding output neighbors (on the right).

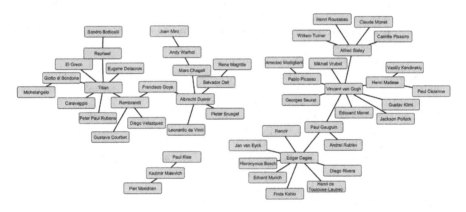

Fig. 3. Famous painters graph.

4   Conclusion and Future Work

In this paper, we have presented our preliminary research aimed at developing a tool for finding visually linked paintings among large digitized collections. The tool is based on a deep convolutional neural network as a feature extractor and on a fully-unsupervised nearest neighbor approach as image retrieval system. The proposed method provides the users with a very simple approach, as it requires only a sample image as a query; moreover, it does not need very difficult to collect human annotated labels. The proposed method may be helpful not only to historians for studying school paintings' evolution across centuries, but also to practitioners, for navigating through very large painting databases, as well as to forgery experts, for detecting suspicious plagiarism. Automatized tools can play a crucial role in managing large digitized collections and their use is receiving a lot of attention in the field of cultural heritage, for example also in the document layout analysis domain [4].

As future work, we plan to develop an easy-to-use user interface and to involve art historians to evaluate the effectiveness of the system. Finally, also a more refined graph analysis needs further work. Network analysis, in fact, is a powerful framework to study network systems and their interactions and several successful applications have been reported in the literature (e.g., [1,9,10]).

References

1. Carli, R., Dotoli, M., Cianci, E.: An optimization tool for energy efficiency of street lighting systems in smart cities. IFAC-PapersOnLine **50**(1), 14460–14464 (2017)
2. Casalino, G., Gillis, N.: Sequential dimensionality reduction for extracting localized features. Pattern Recogn. **63**, 15–29 (2017)
3. Cetinic, E., Lipic, T., Grgic, S.: Fine-tuning convolutional neural networks for fine art classification. Expert Syst. Appl. **114**, 107–118 (2018)
4. Corbelli, A., Baraldi, L., Balducci, F., Grana, C., Cucchiara, R.: Layout analysis and content classification in digitized books. In: Agosti, M., Bertini, M., Ferilli, S., Marinai, S., Orio, N. (eds.) IRCDL 2016. CCIS, vol. 701, pp. 153–165. Springer, Cham (2017). https://doi.org/10.1007/978-3-319-56300-8_14
5. Crowley, E.J., Zisserman, A.: In search of art. In: Agapito, L., Bronstein, M.M., Rother, C. (eds.) ECCV 2014. LNCS, vol. 8925, pp. 54–70. Springer, Cham (2015). https://doi.org/10.1007/978-3-319-16178-5_4
6. Deng, J., Dong, W., Socher, R., Li, L.J., Li, K., Fei-Fei, L.: ImageNet: a large-scale hierarchical image database. In: 2009 IEEE Conference on Computer Vision and Pattern Recognition, pp. 248–255. IEEE (2009)
7. Diaz, M., Ferrer, M.A., Impedovo, D., Pirlo, G., Vessio, G.: Dynamically enhanced static handwriting representation for Parkinson's disease detection. Pattern Recogn. Lett. **128**, 204–210 (2019)
8. James, G., Witten, D., Hastie, T., Tibshirani, R.: An Introduction to Statistical Learning, vol. 112. Springer, Heidelberg (2013)
9. Lella, E., Amoroso, N., Lombardi, A., Maggipinto, T., Tangaro, S., Bellotti, R.: Communicability disruption in Alzheimer's disease connectivity networks. J. Comp. Netw. **7**(1), 83–100 (2018)
10. Piccinni, G., Avitabile, G., Coviello, G.: An improved technique based on Zadoff-Chu sequences for distance measurements. In: 2016 IEEE Radio and Antenna Days of the Indian Ocean (RADIO), pp. 1–2. IEEE (2016)
11. Seguin, B., Striolo, C., diLenardo, I., Kaplan, F.: Visual link retrieval in a database of paintings. In: Hua, G., Jégou, H. (eds.) ECCV 2016. LNCS, vol. 9913, pp. 753–767. Springer, Cham (2016). https://doi.org/10.1007/978-3-319-46604-0_52
12. Shen, X., Efros, A.A., Mathieu, A.: Discovering visual patterns in art collections with spatially-consistent feature learning. arXiv preprint arXiv:1903.02678 (2019)
13. Simonyan, K., Zisserman, A.: Very deep convolutional networks for large-scale image recognition. arXiv preprint arXiv:1409.1556 (2014)
14. Tan, W.R., Chan, C.S., Aguirre, H.E., Tanaka, K.: Ceci n'est pas une pipe: a deep convolutional network for fine-art paintings classification. In: 2016 IEEE International Conference on Image Processing (ICIP), pp. 3703–3707. IEEE (2016)
15. Van Noord, N., Hendriks, E., Postma, E.: Toward discovery of the artist's style: learning to recognize artists by their artworks. IEEE Sign. Process. Mag. **32**(4), 46–54 (2015)

Identifying, Classifying and Searching Graphic Symbols in the NOTAE System

Maria Boccuzzi[1], Tiziana Catarci[2], Luca Deodati[3], Andrea Fantoli[3],
Antonella Ghignoli[1], Francesco Leotta[2(✉)], Massimo Mecella[2], Anna Monte[1],
and Nina Sietis[1]

[1] Dipartimento di Storia Antropologia Religioni Arte Spettacolo,
Sapienza Università di Roma, Rome, Italy
{maria.boccuzzi,antonella.ghignoli,anna.monte,nina.sietis}@uniroma1.it
[2] Dipartimento di Ingegneria Informatica, Automatica e Gestionale,
Sapienza Università di Roma, Rome, Italy
{catarci,leotta,mecella}@diag.uniroma1.it
[3] Facoltà di Ingegneria dell'Informazione, Informatica e Statistica,
Sapienza Università di Roma, Rome, Italy
{fantoli.1467336,deodati.1488696}@studenti.uniroma1.it

Abstract. The use of *graphic symbols* in documentary records from the
5th to the 9th century has so far received scant attention. What we
mean by graphic symbols are graphic signs (including alphabetical ones)
drawn as a visual unit in a written text and representing something
other or something more than a word of that text. The Project NOTAE
represents the first attempt to investigate these graphic entities as a historical phenomenon from Late Antiquity to early medieval Europe in any
written sources containing texts generated for pragmatic purposes (con-
tracts, petitions, official and private letters, lists etc.). Identifying and
classifying graphic symbols on such documents is a task that requires
experience and knowledge of the field, but software applications may
come in help by learning to recognize symbols from previously annotated documents and suggesting experts potential symbols and likely
classification in newly acquired documents to be validated, thus easing
the task. This contribution introduces the NOTAE system that, in addition to the aforementioned task, provides non expert users with tools to
explore the documents annotated by experts.

Keywords: Graphic symbols · Paleography · Image processing ·
Clustering

This work is supported by the ERC grant *NOTAE: NOT A writtEn word but graphic
symbols*, funded by the European Union's Horizon 2020 research and innovation programme (grant agreement no. 786572, Advanced Grant 2017, PI Antonella Ghignoli).
See also http://www.notae-project.eu.

The original version of this chapter was revised: The original version of the chapter 12
was previously published non-open access. It has now been changed to open access
under a CC BY 4.0 license and the copyright holder has been updated to 'The
Author(s).' The book has also been updated with the change. The correction to this
chapter is available at https://doi.org/10.1007/978-3-030-39905-4_19

M. Ceci et al. (Eds.): IRCDL 2020, CCIS 1177, pp. 111–122, 2020.
https://doi.org/10.1007/978-3-030-39905-4_12

1   Introduction

With the gradual introduction of signature and the increasing use of papyrus from the 4th century, the presence of *graphic symbols* became widespread in legal documents as it already was in other written records, and continued in post-Roman kingdoms as part of the same historical process of reception of the late antique documentary practice. The sources of this practice - records written both in greek and latin, on diverse supports as papyrus, wooden tablet, slate, parchment - are expression of the so called "pragmatic literacy", defined in [8] as the "literacy of one who has to read or write in the course of transacting any kind of business".

A new approach to studying documents meant as complex systems of written texts and graphic devices was introduced in the 1990s by Rück [10,12]: morphology, semantics, syntax, pragmatic function and changes over time of the symbolic elements of a document were explicated involving results and concepts of other disciplines, e.g., archaeology, numismatics, semiotics, anthropology. The well-studied subjects in the new field of Diplomatics promoted by Rück have been however the striking graphic features of the charters issued by rulers and elites or written by public notaries of high medieval Europe (10th–12th century), and the few comparative analyses have so far been conducted mainly on high and late medieval western sources. Recent years have seen a renewed interest in the graphic aspects of early medieval written sources, and some works have shown also the connection between Late Antiquity and early Middle Ages; they have dealt, however, only with some specific signs (crosses, christograms and monograms) selected in advance as graphic signs of identity, faith, and power, disseminated in diverse media, but not in documentary records. The project NOTAE represents therefore the first attempt to conduct a research on graphic symbols in documentary records from Late Antiquity to early medieval Europe from a novel perspective: in the long historical period in question, drawing symbols had a major social impact, because, provided it was done in one's own hand, it placed on the same footing professional scribes, basic literates and illiterates. For illiterates, it certainly meant, both in the late Roman state (a Greek-Latin graphic and linguistic community) and in the post-Roman kingdoms (as long as Latin functioned as language of vertical communication) a way of taking an active part in the writing process. A thorough investigation of this 'other side' of the written world can therefore provide precious insights about the spread of literacy as a whole.

In this novel perspective graphic symbols are meant as graphic entities (composed by graphic signs, including alphabetical ones or signs of abbreviation [11]) drawn as a visual unit in a written text and representing something other or something more than a word of that text. The message they carry on is to be discovered, because there is no intrinsic prior relationship between the message-bearing graphic entity and the information it conveys. Examples of frequently employed graphic symbols are shown in Fig. 1.

Identifying and classifying graphic symbols on documents is a task that requires experience and knowledge of the field; specific software applications may support this task, by learning to recognize symbols from previously annotated documents and suggesting experts potential symbols and

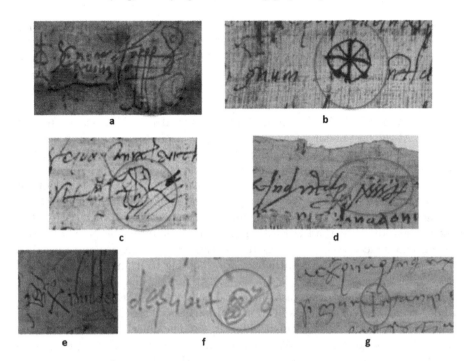

Fig. 1. Examples of graphic symbols. *(a)* graphic symbol in a complex structure at the end of the autograph subscription of a greek notary. *(b)* autograph symbol (greek cross and diagonal cross crossing each other) of an illiterate seller. *(c)* graphic symbol in a complex structure at the end of the autograph subscription of a witness. *(d)* staurogram and $\chi\mu\gamma$-group at the end of the final datation written by a notary. *(e)* autograph diagonal cross (or letter χ) of an illiterate man. *(f)* graphic symbol in complex structure at the end of the autograph subscription of a bishop. *(g)* autograph greek cross of an illiterate clerk.

likely classification in newly acquired documents to be validated. This contribution introduces the NOTAE system that, in addition to the aforementioned task, provides non expert users with tools to explore the documents annotated by experts. The system is part of the NOTAE project [5], which broadly studies the employment of graphic symbols in documents, in relation to historical and geographical contexts.

The paper is organized as it follows. Section 2 relates this work in the wider area of digital paleography and digital humanities. Section 3 initially describes the approach with a bird-eye view, and then specifically describes each component of the system. Section 4 finally concludes the paper also describing the ongoing validation and future research directions.

2   Related Works

Paleography is the study of ancient and historical handwriting. Included in this discipline, it is the practice of deciphering, reading, and dating historical manuscripts, and the cultural context of writing.

The approach proposed in this paper falls into the category of computing systems applied to paleography [6], which are part of the digital paleography [3] area belonging to the wider field of digital humanities [1]. Digital humanities represent a field of study that raised a growing interest from the research community and funding agencies as witnessed by the number of project recently funded at national and European level (e.g., D-Scribes[1], NEPTIS [7], etc.).

In the field of digital paleography, our task is to identify and classify graphic symbols. At the best of our knowledge, this represents a completely new research area. This task is much different from handwritten text recognition, which is the goal of many recent works such as [4] and of research projects like the above mentioned D-Scribe, whose aim is to make papyrologists able to look for similar, or identical, handwritings to a given papyrus and for typical samples of writing for a given period. Anyway, symbols have indeed several characteristics making them different than words. For example, it is impossible to employ row spacing and spaces between words to identify them, being usually placed in casual position with respect to the text, overlapping to it and covering several lines.

Commonly to many other tasks in digital humanities, a prior step for graphic symbols identification and classification is preprocessing the digital reproduction of the documents and, in particular, binarizing it. The binarization of documents is a particularly hot topic as witnessed by the availability of challenges such as DIBCO [9]. In the case of the NOTAE system, the binarization is particularly difficult as physical supports varies both in terms of material (e.g., papyrus, slate) and preservation conditions.

3 Proposed Approach

Figure 2 depicts the approach proposed in this paper. Documents considered in the NOTAE project are available either in museums' showcases or, more and more frequently, through digital reproductions in public web repositories and aggregators[2]. An expert who wants to identify and study graphic symbols in a specific document, usually inspects its digital reproduction together with associated bibliography. Visual inspection is, generally, an hard task, especially if executed on several documents in a working session, due to the state of conservation of the document, the color of the background, and the possible overlapping between graphic symbols and normal text.

The NOTAE system simplifies the work of experts in the NOTAE project by providing a Web app that assists them by providing useful functions to ease their job by leveraging on previously acquired annotations.

When a NOTAE expert, also referred to as curator, is studying a document, s/he can upload a digital reproduction (see step (1) in Fig. 2), taken from a public repository, in the NOTAE Curator Web app. The Web app communicates with the intelligent core of the NOTAE system, the Symbol Engine, through the Classification API. The Symbol Engine is a python service which exploits

---

[1] See https://d-scribes.philhist.unibas.ch.

[2] See, for example, https://papyri.info/.

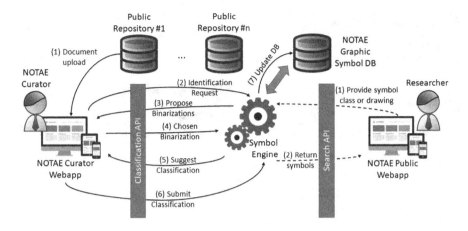

Fig. 2. The proposed approach.

OpenCV [2] for image processing tasks. Once a document has been uploaded, the curator Web app shows five different possible binarizations of the document (steps (2) and (3), see Sect. 3.1. At this point, the curator chooses the binarization version that preserves more the original content (step (4)). Once a binarization has been selected, the Symbol Engine returns a picture containing all the graphic symbols contained in the document (step (5), see Sect. 3.2).

The symbols identified by the Symbol Engine are not supposed to be perfect, as the main goal is to provide experts with potential symbols, leaving to them and to their expertise the burden of classifying symbols. As a consequence, curators send a feedback about identified and classified symbols (step (6, see Sect. 3.3). As a last step, expert classification of symbols is stored inside the NOTAE Graphic Symbol DataBase (step (7)).

The NOTAE Graphic Symbols DataBase stores information about graphic symbols contained in the documents within the scope of the project. Documents are referenced by using identifiers that are globally recognized in the research community. Information does not only include their presence in a specific document, but also additional details such as comments about their usage. In the NOTAE system, one of the goal of the NOTAE Graphic Symbols DB is to be used as a reference to detect symbols in newly uploaded documents. At the bootstrap, this database is empty and, as a consequence, the very first identification tasks simply provide no results to the expert user. With experts continuously introducing new classifications of symbols, the database is progressively populated (step (7)) with graphic symbols, and this allows to increasingly refine the identification and classification skills of the Symbol Engine.

Beyond providing a mean to identify and automatically classify symbols in documents, the Symbol Engine also serves as a search engine. The final users of this engine are researchers (this category includes the NOTAE curators themselves), who will access through the NOTAE Public Web app This one employs a specifically designed API, called Search API, to navigate the content of the

Fig. 3. Color clusters obtained from selected documents. (Color figure online)

NOTAE Graphic Symbol DB by performing the research activity using symbols category or event drawing (see Sect. 3.4).

3.1 Binarization

As previously stated, the binarization of documents of interest for NOTAE curators is hard due to issues related to the nature of the physical supports and their conservation status. A standard way to binarize an image is to choose a threshold and to convert every pixel of the image to 1 if a specific combination of the components of the color of the pixel is above/below the threshold, to 0 otherwise. The choice of the threshold depends on the specific document and is not possible to find a one-fits-all solution. As the approach followed by the NOTAE system consists in involving the curators in a man-in-the-loop process, we decided to follow an approach that leaves the choice of the threshold to the curator. Instead of allowing him to choose any value though, we applied an approach that computes five possible thresholds based on the employment of K-means. It is a centroid-based clustering algorithm that, given a set of points in a coordinate space, the RGB color space in our case, groups them into K sets, where the parameter K is given as an input to the algorithm according to some distance function, usually the euclidean distance. The output of the algorithm is a set of K centroids providing the center of each group in the coordinate space. These centroids will be in our case specific colors. Figure 3 shows the result of the execution of K-means with K set to 4 on four different documents. Colors are ordered from left to right according to an increasing red component.

Once the clustering step has been executed, the five thresholds are computed as *(i)* the red component of the first color extracted which is different from black, *(ii)* the red component of the second color extracted which is different from black, *(iii)* the average value between the first two threshold values, *(iv)* the average between the first and third thresholds, and *(v)* the average between the second and third thresholds.

Once the thresholds have been determined, we move on to the effective removal of the background and generation of the binary images. To this aim, we compare the red component of every pixel in the image to a specific threshold. If the value is above the threshold we turn the pixel to white, leaving the value unchanged otherwise. At this point a very simple filtering, i.e., erosion, is

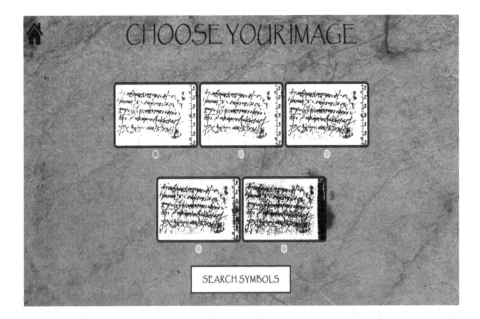

Fig. 4. The proposed binarization options.

applied to bring to the foreground the marginal components of the writing. At this point, we turn every pixel different from 1 into 0. As shown in Fig. 4, the obtained results are five different versions of the document, among which the curator will choose the best one for detecting symbols.

One issue with binarization is that digital reproductions of documents in public repository are usually at very high resolution. This makes the above described process very slow, as clustering must be applied to millions of pixels. To limit the binarization time, we decided to resize the original image, working with a small-sized version of the document and the original-sized version. The small-sized version is obtained by downsizing the original reproduction to 10% of its size. This version is employed for clustering and choosing the threshold. The original-sized version is instead used for actual binarization, which is instead a quick task.

3.2 Symbol Identification and Classification

Once the curator has chosen the best binarization of the document, the NOTAE Symbol Engine can identify symbols. In order to perform this task, we apply template matching. This is a method for searching and finding the location of a template image in a larger image. It simply slides the template image over the input image and compares the template with the current part of the original image. Several comparison methods are possible. Template matching returns a grayscale image, where each pixel denotes how much the neighborhood of that pixel matches the template. Template matching is performed using all different symbols available in the NOTAE System DB.

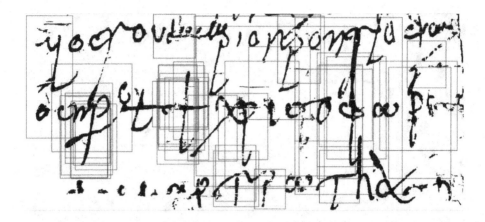

Fig. 5. Results of symbol identification without clustering.

As the size in terms of pixels of the symbols in the NOTAE System DB depends on the original document, applying template match to a single version of a document would likely return several false negatives. As a consequence, we apply template matching to several different scales of the document, keeping track of the best match, and after looping over all scales, we take the global best match as our matched region. At each step, we collect the coordinates of each match for each template used, and we use these coordinates to draw different rectangles on the image.

The result on an example document is shown in Fig. 5. As can be easily understood, the obtained result is not satisfying, as it contains too many rectangles and too many false positives. To solve this issue, we used DBSCAN - Density-Based Spatial Clustering of Applications with Noise.

DBSCAN, differently from K-means employed for binarization, finds clusters of similar density, thus allowing to obtain clusters of any shapes. We fed all the centers of the symbols identified at the previous steps into DBSCAN. DBSCAN takes as input two parameters $min\_samples$ and ϵ, the first one representing the minimum number of points that form a cluster, and the second one representing the maximum distance between two samples for one point to be considered as in the neighborhood of the other. DBSCAN also returns points that were not included in any clusters. Then, iterating on the previously populated array of coordinates we have checked if the corresponding center was part of one of the clusters obtained thanks to the aforementioned function, and if this happens the user will see that rectangles on the image related to the papyrus.

As shown in Fig. 6, in this way the search for symbols returns the most plausible ones. Clearly, the more symbol templates the NOTAE System DB contains, the more accurate the search will be. This fits very well with a system intended to operate with a human-in-the-loop approach, as curators can provide feedback about the performed identification, making the system smarter and smarter.

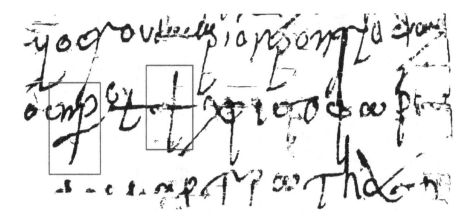

Fig. 6. Results of symbol identification with DBSCAN clustering.

As in the case of binarization, the bottleneck of this method is certainly the dimension of the digital reproduction of the document. Thus, the search of the symbols is performed on a version of the document scaled to 20% of the size. The result is instead shown on the original-sized version of the document.

Noteworthy, the very same mechanism employed for graphic symbol identification can be employed for symbol classification. As discussed, the identification of symbols is performed by looking for all symbols available in the database inside the digital reproduction of the document. For each symbol in the symbol database, a classification, provided by the experts as described in Sect. 3.3, is available reporting the type of symbol. By computing the type with the majority of occurrences in a DBSCAN cluster, the system assigns a class to each identified symbol. This class will be then confirmed or refused by the experts.

3.3   Manual Symbol Classification

Identification and classification results are shown to the expert using the window shown in Fig. 7, where identified symbols are marked with red boxes. This window provides the user with different functionalities.

In particular, given an identified and classified symbol, the expert can tell the system whether a box really contains a symbol and if the classification was correct, suggesting the system a different classification. Symbols validated by the expert are marked with a green box.

The curator can also select, using drag and drop, an area of the document where a symbol is present but nothing has been detected by the system. At this point, the symbol engine returns, for the given selection, the most likely classification that can be confirmed or corrected by the expert.

Noteworthy, the involvement of the expert in the process is deep. The system is initially dumb and becomes smarter and smarter thanks to the corrections and the labelling performed by the user. This allows us to overcome the lack of labelled datasets in the field of graphic symbols.

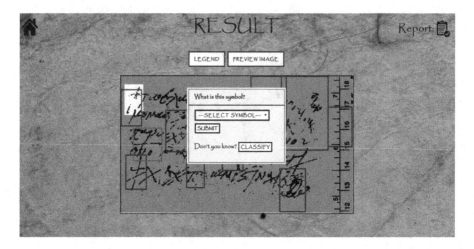

Fig. 7. The manual classification window. (Color figure onine)

3.4 Searching Symbols

Experts are not the only users of the NOTAE system. The aim of the NOTAE project is to provide researchers in the area of paleography with a useful tool to explore the world of graphic symbols and their usage. This consideration involves the necessity for implementing advanced query interfaces for search and analysis.

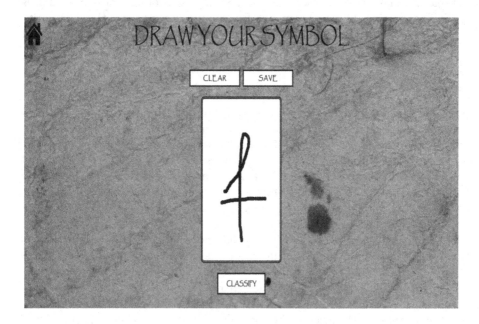

Fig. 8. The manual drawing input window.

At the current state, two search mechanisms have been implemented: search by type and search by drawing. *Search-by-type* is implemented as a simple query inside the database of symbols. In this case, the Symbol Engine retrieves from the database all the symbols labeled from expert users with the required category (notably, not using any image processing technique but simply by taking into account the classifying labels previously assigned).

The *search-by-drawing* mechanism is instead intended for less expert users. In this case, the user can draw through the window shown in Fig. 8 a symbol, maybe casually seen in a document, and search for it inside the symbol database. This feature allows the user to draw a symbol, with the trackpad or with the mouse on a canvas and to receive from the system the classification of what has been drawn. This classification is implemented likewise the identification and classification mechanism seen in Sect. 3.2. Here, instead of matching available symbols within an entire document, the comparison is performed against the user drawing.

4   Concluding Remarks

In this paper, we have presented the NOTAE system as the component of the NOTAE project in charge of automatically identify and classify graphic symbols in Late Antique and Medieval documents. The contribution, in particular, introduced all the different components of the system.

At the actual stage, the system is in use to the NOTAE project members who are conducting the evaluation of the system. In particular three experts are involved in evaluating the ability of the system at *(i)* identifying symbols in documents with respect to the amount of documents already labelled, *(ii)* classifying identified symbols, *(iii)* searching symbols by manual drawings. Evaluation will be also performed against the DIBCO challenge [9] in order to globally assess the performance of binarization.

The public Web app will be made available in the following months from the web site of the NOTAE project: www.notae-project.eu.

The current version of the system suffers from some limitations including the fact that negative feedbacks from experts, i.e., the fact that an expert mark an identified symbol as a false positive or wrongly classified, are not taken into account in the identification and classification process. A future research step will consist in including these negative feedbacks in the classification task, e.g., by including negative matching scores. Additionally, as the identification and classification process involves the comparison of all symbols in the database, this task is supposed to become slower and slower while the size of the symbol database grows.

Other future research directions include the possibility to automatically analyze symbols category by *(i)* highlighting geometric shapes patterns, i.e., recognizing the component shapes and their arrangement in graphic symbols categories, *(ii)* produce heat maps of the positions of graphic symbols categories, and *(iii)* define visual analytic tools to correlate the employment of symbols with the historical and geographical context.

References

1. Berry, D.M.: Introduction: understanding the digital humanities. In: Berry, D.M. (ed.) Understanding Digital Humanities, pp. 1–20. Palgrave Macmillan UK, London (2012). https://doi.org/10.1057/9780230371934_1
2. Bradski, G., Kaehler, A.: Learning OpenCV: Computer Vision with the OpenCV Library. O'Reilly Media, Inc., Newton (2008)
3. Ciula, A.: Digital palaeography: using the digital representation of medieval script to support palaeographic analysis. Digit. Medievalist 1 (2005)
4. Firmani, D., Maiorino, M., Merialdo, P., Nieddu, E.: Towards knowledge discovery from the vatican secret archives. In codice ratio - episode 1: machine transcription of the manuscripts. In: Proceedings of the 24th ACM SIGKDD International Conference on Knowledge Discovery & Data Mining, KDD 2018, London, UK, 19–23 August 2018, pp. 263–272 (2018)
5. Ghignoli, A.: The notae project: a research between east and west, late antiquity and early middle ages. Comp. Orient. Manuscript Stud. Bullettin **5/1**, 27–41 (2019)
6. Hassner, T., Rehbein, M., Stokes, P.A., Wolf, L.: Computation and palaeography: potentials and limits. Kodikologie und Paläographie im Digitalen Zeitalter 3: Codicology and Palaeography in the Digital Age **3**, 1 (2015)
7. Mecella, M., Leotta, F., Marrella, A., Palucci, F., Seri, C., Catarci, T.: Encouraging persons to visit cultural sites through mini-games. EAI Endorsed Trans. Serious Games **4**(14), e3 (2018)
8. Parkes, M.B.: Scribes, Scripts and Readers: Studies in the Communication, Presentation and Dissemination of Medieval Texts. Hambledon Press, London/Rio Grande (1991)
9. Pratikakis, I., Gatos, B., Ntirogiannis, K.: H-DIBCO 2010-handwritten document image binarization competition. In: 2010 12th International Conference on Frontiers in Handwriting Recognition, pp. 727–732. IEEE (2010)
10. Rück, P.: Graphische Symbole in mittelalterlichen Urkunden: Beiträge zur diplomatischen Semiotik, vol. 3. Jan Thorbecke Verlag (1996)
11. Sietis, N.: Abbreviations in Greek documentary texts. a case study of significant paleography. In: Conference on Novel Perspectives on Communication Practices in Antiquity, pp. 2–5 (2019)
12. Worm, P.: Ein neues bild von der urkunde: Peter rück und seine schüler. Archiv für Diplomatik **52**(JG), 335–352 (2006)

TindArt, an Experiment on User Profiling for Museum Applications

Daniel Zilio, Nicola Orio[✉], and Camilla Toniolo

Department of Cultural Heritage, University of Padua,
Piazza Capitaniato, 7, 35139 Padua, Italy
daniel.zilio@phd.unipd.it, nicola.orio@unipd.it,
camilla.toniolo@studenti.unipd.it

Abstract. In this paper an Android application called TindArt is presented. It has been developed to investigate a way to profile the user in cultural contexts, through the application of Recommender Systems for museum visits in the future. The purpose of the research also includes the study of the User Experience with TindArt to understand how it could be used in a real museum context. Two pilot studies are also presented.

Keywords: Recommender System · User profiling · User experience · Mobile application · Museum · Cultural heritage

1 Introduction

One of the most important institutions of our society are *museums*. Since the foundation of the first museum more than 2500 years ago, this entity gave a fundamental contribution to the preservation, conservation and communication of the Cultural Heritage. Thanks to museums we can enjoy artworks, find ruins of the human and natural past and many other examples of items that are the bearer of human knowledge. There is an uncountable number of museums in the world, Italy alone hosts nearly five thousand museums covering all the aspects of culture – from archaeology, to art, from music to industrial heritage. In 2017, Italian museums attracted 57.8 millions of tourists which increase to 73.2 millions if archaeological sites are included)[1].

Despite this richness and the fact that Italy is one of the most important tourist destination in the world, there is no Italian museum inside the top ten visited museums[2]. There are a number of reasons to explain this apparent contradiction. Probably the main reason is that museums are not so attractive for

---

[1] ISTAT, I musei, le aree archeologiche e i monumenti in Italia. Anno 2017, https://www.istat.it/it/files//2019/01/Report-Musei_2017_con_loghi.pdf.

[2] Global Attractions Attendance Report, Themed Entertainment Association (TEA) and the Economics practice at AECOM, 2018, https://www.aecom.com/content/wp-content/uploads/2019/05/Theme-Index-2018-5-1.pdf.

© Springer Nature Switzerland AG 2020
M. Ceci et al. (Eds.): IRCDL 2020, CCIS 1177, pp. 123–134, 2020.
https://doi.org/10.1007/978-3-030-39905-4_13

tourists and citizens because they are seen like boring places[3]. It is related to the generalized problem of transmission of the *cultural message*, which may become specially crucial for art and archaeological museums. Museums plays a double role, enabling both the study and the dissemination of cultural heritage, and in many cases they are not able to communicate with all the variety of their potential users. For instance, a panel with a very long technical text is particularly useful for scholars and experts but may be difficult to understand for normal visitors without a training in the subject.

To tackle these problems, the aim of this paper is to propose a methodology and an experiment to connect visitors preferences with museums items. The approach is based on the creation of personalised museum visits, and its starting point is the problem of user profiling from a cultural standpoint. The general idea is to use *Recommender Systems* (RSs) to adapt the presentation and the enjoyment of museum items to the visitor, while maintaining the quality and the depth of the content that is communicated. The approach regards both the itinerary that touches the most relevant items for the user and the manner in which the cultural message is transmitted to visitors.

The research work presented in this paper is part of a larger project on the design and development of a RS and represents the initial step on collecting user choices and preferences. To this end, we developed a tool for Android to collect users preference in a fun way. The app, called *TindArt* because it mimics the interaction of a famous dating application, presents a sequence of pictures of artworks and asks users to express their preference with a binary choice between *"like"* and *"nope"*. TindArt is a stand-alone application but it can also be embedded in a larger software application, for instance the one that visitors use while in line before entering a museum. The items included in TindArt were gathered during a pilot study, which allowed us to obtain a first sample of user preferences regarding art works. We present an analysis of the initial results on user usage and preferences.

2   Related Works

As discussed in the previous section, the application of RSs to enrich the visitor's experience is still far from being widely applied to real case scenarios. User profiling, collaborative filtering, content-based analysis are essential components of modern content-delivery platforms. It is a common experience to receive recommendations about books by Amazon [6], music by Spotify, or videos by Netflix – just to mention the most prominent players in the respective areas – but the access to cultural heritage is still mediated through the traditional approach: written guides, panels, audio-guides, panels.

Yet there are a number of researchers that are addressing the problem of enriching the visitor experience in museums, exhibitions and archaeological sites.

---

[3] European Report CULTURAL ACCESS AND PARTICIPATION, 2013: http://ec.europa.eu/commfrontoffice/publicopinion/archives/ebs/ebs_399_en.pdf.

For instance, a mobile application to personalize museum guides have been proposed in [8] with the aim to improve visitors' experience. Education is the main aspect of the work presented in [5], which is aimed at attracting new visitors [11] a goal shared by most of the institutions involved in this kind of projects.

A key component of many approaches to recommendations regards the recollection of visitors' preferences and tastes. A number of approaches have been tested: from direct interaction with visitors [2] to indirect feedback [1] during the development of a narrative, to the use of virtual characters that interact with the visitor [9]. Evaluation is a key aspect in the development of any automatic system, and it has been the subject of a number of research papers like [4], which directly collected users data during an exhibition and evaluated the effectiveness of the system on this dataset, and [7] that addressed the impact on novel tools on user experience. User experience and satisfaction has been addressed also by [12] and [10]. One interesting aspect in recommending visit paths [3] in a museum is given by the number of constraints that have to be taken into account, including the lengths of the visit, the effect of fatigue, the mandatory items that everybody has to be see in any museum.

3   The Project

The aim of the proposed project is to design and develop a RS to be used in a real museum context. Let us imagine a visitor who is waiting in a (perhaps long) queue at the entrance of an art museum. In order to kill time, the visitor is very likely to resort to his/her smartphone looking for some entertainment. TindArt could be the app he/she decides to play with. The simple interaction, discussed in Sect. 3.2, is designed to record visitor preferences expressed by simple gestures while providing some entertainment with a slide show of art works. The gathered information can be exploited to provide users with personalized visits, either by classifying the user interest in a group of predefined visit routes or by simply suggesting potentially interesting items while the user freely visits the museum.

The set of images that are displayed by TindArt has been gathered during a pilot study that involved a group of students. We analyzed their choices to investigate the presence of common patterns that could be used to cluster user in groups with similar interests. The results of the pilot study are presented in Sect. 3.1. After collecting and normalizing the images, we involved a group of test users, monitoring their interaction with the application. The initial outcomes are described in Sect. 3.2.

3.1   Pilot Study

The pilot study has been carried out involving 61 undergraduate students attending the course in *History and Conservation of the Artistic and Musical Heritage* of the University of Padua. Their assignment was to choose five artworks from the *Heilbrunn Timeline of Art History*[4], the online archive of the Metropolitan

---

[4] https://www.metmuseum.org/toah/.

Museum of New York which contains images and bibliographical records of hundreds of artworks. In particular, records are well structured and include a rich set of tags that describe the content in detail. Students were asked to choose freely the artworks according to their interest, with the only requirement that the chosen element were classified as *Painting* (the digital collection contains also images of sculptures, photographs, furniture, and furnishing). Once chosen the artworks, the participants had to download the corresponding digital image and copy the metadata, which were both uploaded to a web-based platform. After this step, 305 annotated images were available.

3.1.1   Pre-processing

The majority of participants accurately followed the assignment, although we needed to carry out some cleaning. A small subsets of uploaded artworks did not met the constraint and were chosen from others categories like *Prints, Photographs, Drawings* and so on. Moreover, some students misspelled the website URL and chose the artworks from the official site of Metropolitan Museum[5] instead of the *Heilbrunn Timeline of Art History*. After manually aligning the metadata, we maintained all the elements because they were all part of a larger category of bi-dimensional artistic representations.

We added two extra fields to the metadata, using as a reference the information provided by the above cited *Heilbrunn Timeline of Art History* combined with *WikiArt*[6].

– Artistic movement.
– Artistic genre.

The classification in artistic movement and genre was carried out in different steps. Starting from 35 artistic movements and 25 artistic genres, we merged similar categories obtaining respectively 21 and 11 classes. Grouping allowed as to improve the overlap between student choices, and was carried out through a process of generalization; for instance the artistic movements Informal Art and Dadaism were put together in Abstract Art group.

3.1.2   Results

As a first step, we analyzed the consistency of individual participants in selecting the artworks, that is how they were distributed across the artistic movement and artistic genre classes. Afterwards, we investigated the possibility to cluster participants according to their artistic preferences.

3.1.2.1 Consistency of Participants
Our interest was to find out whether participants consistently chose artworks from a limited group of artistic movements and genres or they had wider interests. From Table 1, which reports the two trends, it can be seen that the majority

---

[5] https://www.metmuseum.org/art/collection/.
[6] www.wikiart.com.

Table 1. Distribution of participants according to the amount of chosen artistic movement or genre

Amount of different choices	Artistic movement	Artistic genre
1	3	1
2	6	10
3	13	26
4	23	19
5	16	5

of participants chose artworks belonging to four different artistic movements and that only 15% chose artworks belonging to one or two movements. As regards the artistic genre, the majority of students chose artworks belonging to three or four different genres.

3.1.2.2 Grouping Participants
Our goal was to check the possibility to profile participants by assigning them to a limited number of groups. The main assumption is that participants chose the artwork according to their *artistic taste*. In this paper our intention is not to investigate the intrinsic meaning of what *artistic taste* could be, but to investigate the possibility to grouping users starting from their preferences in an artistic context. We carried out a *cluster analysis* according to either the artistic movement or the artistic genres. Similarity between participants was computed using the cosine distance. Results of cluster analysis are shown in Figs. 1 and 2. As it can be seen from the two dendrograms, there are three main clusters for the artistic movement and four clusters for the artistic genre, showing that participants can in principle be profiled according to their choices. Clearly this initial positive result should be confirmed by experiments with a larger set of participants.

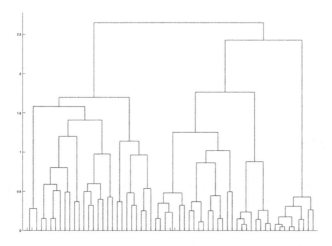

Fig. 1. Cluster analysis of students by the similarity of chosen artistic movements

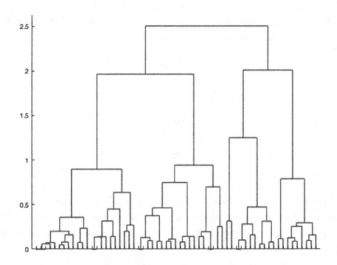

Fig. 2. Cluster analysis of students by the similarity of chosen genres

Still using the cosine distance as a measure of similarity, we carried out multidimensional scaling in order to highlight how participants can be organized on a bi-dimensional space. Results of multidimensional scaling are shown in Fig. 3 and in Fig. 4 for artistic movement and genre respectively. Even if in this case the representation is quite sparse, a number of small groups (highlighted in the two figures) can be seen. Extending multidimensional scaling to a third dimension did not improve the results.

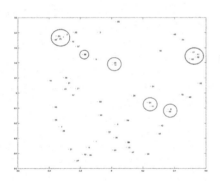

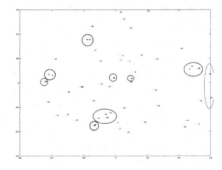

Fig. 3. MDS by movement   **Fig. 4.** MDS by genre

Results obtained in these first preliminary experiments show that there can be some common trends in the choices made by the participants, and thus users can be profiled according to their choices.

3.2 TindArt

As stated in Sect. 1 there are two motivations for the development of the mobile application TindArt. The first is to create a tool that can be used to profile users from a cultural point of view and the second is to study the interaction and user experience with an app that can be used in a museum *pre-visit*. It is important for our research to investigate both if this approach is a suitable method to obtain a user profile aimed at providing effective recommendations, and if it is appealing for users in a real setting.

3.2.1 How TindArt Works

TindArt is developed for Android devices and it can be downloaded in beta version from Google Play[7]. The application mimics the dating app Tinder[8] in the way it uses the *swipe* gesture to express preferences according to the swipe direction. As it is well known, swipe represents a linear motion of fingers over a screen in order to move onto the next page, choose something, and so on. This gesture is used in Tinder to express preferences about persons appearance, while it is used in TindArt to express preferences about artworks. Our choice is motivated by the idea of giving the user an intuitive and fan tool so he/she can immediately learn how it works. In opposition to Tinder, that shows several information about the people, in our App we show the user only the name of the artwork, in order to make the choice more spontaneous possible and not linked to other aspects (such as if an artist is more famous than others). After download, the user creates an account using his/her email[9] and so a session is created. In the main screen (see Fig. 5) there are four buttons and one that is implicit:

- Logout: it is used to disconnect from actual session;
- Guida: a small tutorial of the application;
- Progetto: it shows information about the project;
- Inizia: it starts the artworks evaluation;
- PERSONAL INFORMATION (implicit): it's the logo in the centre of the upper task bar and now it is only used for the preliminary study described in Sect. 3.3.

Figure 6 shows the main screen of the application. The application randomly shows an artwork from a set of artworks, taken from collections of The Heilbrunn Timeline of Art History and The Metropolitan Museum of New York as described in Sect. 3.1, and the user can only rate it positively or negatively. There are two ways to express a preference:

- using the green button for *LIKE* or the red button for *NOPE*;
- using swipe gesture, left to right for *LIKE*, right to left for *NOPE*.

---

[7] https://play.google.com/store/apps/details?id=tindar_evo.meeple.tindart.

[8] https://play.google.com/store/apps/details?id=com.tinder.

[9] The user account management is relegated to Google Firebase, https://firebase. google.com/.

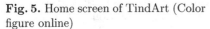

Fig. 5. Home screen of TindArt (Color figure online)

Fig. 6. Main screen of TindArt (Color figure online)

There is also a button in the high right corner named `Chat`, but it is reserved for future experiments. A rating session can be stopped anytime by the user and it is possible in a second time to restart it. An artwork can be rated more than once. The total number of artworks are not known by the user and when he/she completes all of them an appropriated screen is shown. Unlike Tinder, the swipe gesture is not visually simulated, so when a user expresses a choice it is immediately recorded and a visible feedback is shown.

3.2.2 Shown Items

The items have been selected starting from a subset of the artworks provided by the 61 students who participated to the pilot experiment. We kept only paintings, removed duplicate items and images with low quality on a standard mobile phone. The final number of artworks that are presented by TindArt is 352.

3.2.3 User Experience with TindArt

An important issue of the research is to understand if an application like TindArt could be used in a real museum context and, at the same time, could investigate the user behaviour when interacting with this tool. To this end, a set of variables are stored into a database during the application use.

These variables are reported for every single rated artwork:

- *Swipe*: a boolean flag that represents if user rated using buttons or swipe gesture.
- *Date*: the information about date could be used to analyse the number of votes that a user gives in a specific period of time. It also could be a measure of how many times a user uses the app, representing a evidence of the reliability of a choice.
- *Time of choice*: the timing spent by user for a single vote.

– *Resolution of smartphone*: We included this passive information to investigate if different devices could influence the user's choice.

The number of artworks on which a user gives his preferences before dismissing the application is another information that will be considered in a future release.

3.3   Initial Study with TindArt

Once collected the set of artworks, we tested whether the user preferences could be collected using the smartphone app TindArt. Data were gathered from a fixed period of time since after the application release on Play Store. Although still in beta version, the app can be installed and used freely by anyone with a Google Play account under the Play Store testing policy[10].

We asked a second group of undergraduate students, attending the course in *Design and Management of Cultural Tourism* of the University of Padova, to use the app. There was no particular assignment, because students were free to express their choice for any number of artworks. The interaction is straightforward and did not require any explanation to the students.

The experiment lasted for about one month. During this period 54 users downloaded and tested the app, for an amount of 9882 choices. By inspecting their Gmail accounts, we estimate that about 60% of users were students of the mentioned course, while the remaining are *common* people that found and tried the application. We were not interested in demographic or personal data because the main goal was to obtain an initial set of preferences to analyse. Thus users could start playing with the application without providing any personal data or filling any questionnaire. It has to be noted that we proposed TindArt to students just to promote the application and to obtain potential feedback easily. Yet students of *Design and Management of Cultural Tourism* are a good representative of potential users of this kind of application in a museum context.

3.3.1   Pre-processing

It is likely that some of the interactions were just random or interfered with other activities on the smartphone. So we decided to remove choices that were either too fast or too slow. The following thresholds were applied to the *time of choice t*:

$$t_{min} = 0.5\,\text{s}$$

$$t_{max} = 20\,\text{s}$$

We assumed that choices outside this interval had no significance and could be removed because either completely random ($t_{min} < 0.5\,\text{s}$) or distracted by other activities ($t_{max} > 20\,\text{s}$). We removed about 7% of the choices, obtaining 9196 preferences that were analyzed.

---

[10] https://developers.google.com/actions/deploy/release-environments.

3.3.2   Analysis of the Interaction

After applying the threshold, the average time for a choice was:

$$t_{mean} = 2.39\,\text{s}$$

with variance $t_{var} = 3.68\,\text{s}$. In Fig. 7 we reported the histogram of time choices, which has the shape of an F-distribution.

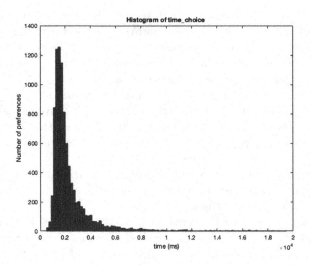

Fig. 7. Histogram of time choice

Swipe was used for 26.6% of preferences, thus there was a clear preference for using the buttons. About 50% of users used the swipe for less than 10% of the preferences, only the about 19% for more than 70%. This result was somehow surprising because swipe seemed to be more engaging than pressing buttons. We intend to investigate if this trend is maintained also in future experiments. The mean time of choice using swipe was:

$$t\_mean\_swipe = 2.64\,\text{s}$$

whilst with buttons the average time was lower:

$$t\_mean\_button = 2.30\,\text{s}$$

The overall number of *LIKE*, considering swipe and buttons, was 4615 (50.2%), the overall amount of *NOPE* was 4581 (49.8%). Using swipe the number of *LIKE* and *NOPE* were, respectively:

$$N_{like\_swipe} = 1349\ (55.1\%)$$

$$N_{nope\_swipe} = 1101\ (44.9\%)$$

Using buttons they were:

$$N_{like\_button} = 3266 \ (48.4\%)$$

$$N_{nope\_button} = 3480 \ (51.6\%)$$

An item has been rated on average 26.1 times, the minimum is 16, the maximum 34. Figure 8 shows the histogram about the number of items rated, while Fig. 9 shows the trend of choices from the most appreciated item to the least one. It is interesting to see trend is linear and do not follow the typical power-law that is seen on user preferences.

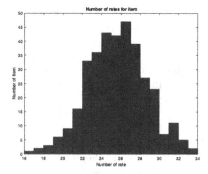 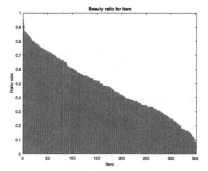

Fig. 8. Histogram of items rated   **Fig. 9.** Trend of the choices

4   Conclusions and Future Work

In this paper we described the preliminary results of a larger project about the design and development of a recommender system for the tourism area, in particular for museum visits. We ran an experiment to gather a collection of images, taking advantage of the experiment by testing the possibility to profile users according to their choices on artistic movements and genres.

An application, called TindArt, which collects information about user cultural preferences has been presented. The information obtained from the first analysis of user experience shows that it could be a useful tool to gathered information about user in a *pre-visits* museum scenario. For the user profiling we conducted a pilot study without using the application, but focusing on the problem to cluster user using a small collection of preferences about artworks. The results indicate that this can be a viable approach, but a deeper analysis on the different ways to use the metadata associated to the items have to be done. The next step is to increase the dataset of the choices made by users with TindArt and proceed with their analysis in order to create a system that allows us to cluster and profile users. When we will complete this step the aim will be to use this information gathered to create different kinds of visits for a real museum case.

References

1. Antoniou, A., et al.: Capturing the visitor profile for a personalized mobile museum experience: an indirect approach (2016). http://eprints.gla.ac.uk/143234/
2. Aroyo, L., Brussee, R., Rutledge, L., Gorgels, P., Stash, N., Wang, Y.: Personalized museum experience: the rijksmuseum use case. In: Museums and the Web 2007, San Francisco, USA, 11–14 April 2007. http://www.archimuse.com/mw2007/papers/aroyo/aroyo.html
3. Berre, D.L., Marquis, P., Roussel, S.: Planning personalised museum visits. In: Proceedings of the Twenty-Third International Conference on Automated Planning and Scheduling, ICAPS 2013, Rome, Italy, 10–14 June 2013 (2013). http://www.aaai.org/ocs/index.php/ICAPS/ICAPS13/paper/view/6025
4. Keller, I., Viennet, E.: Recommender systems for museums: evaluation on a real dataset. In: Fifth International Conference on Advances in Information Mining and Management, July 2015
5. Kuflik, T., Sagy, O., Lanir, J., Wecker, A., Mogilevsky, O.: A different kind of experience: using a smart mobile guide for education and aging research at the Hecht museum. In: Museums and the Web 2013 (2013). https://mw2013.museumsandtheweb.com/paper/hecht-smart-mobile-guide/
6. Linden, G., Smith, B., York, J.: Amazon.com recommendations. Item-to-item collaborative filtering. IEEE Internet Comput. **7**(1), 76–80 (2003)
7. Loboda, O., Nyhan, J., Mahony, S., Romano, D.: Towards evaluating the impact of recommender systems on visitor experience in physical museums, September 2018
8. Lykourentzou, I., et al.: Improving museum visitors' quality of experience through intelligent recommendations: a visiting style-based approach, July 2013
9. Oliviero Stock, M.Z.: PEACH - Intelligent Interfaces for Museum Visits. Cognitive Technologies, 1st edn. Springer, Heidelberg (2007). https://doi.org/10.1007/3-540-68755-6
10. Rossi, S., Barile, F., Galdi, C., Russo, L.: Recommendation in museums: paths, sequences, and group satisfaction maximization. Multimedia Tools Appl. **76**(24), 26031–26055 (2017). https://doi.org/10.1007/s11042-017-4869-5
11. Tan, E., Oinonen, K.: Personalising content presentation in museum exhibitions - a case study. In: International Conference on Virtual Systems and MultiMedia, pp. 232–238, September 2009. https://doi.org/10.1109/VSMM.2009.42
12. Tesoriero, R., Gallud, J.A., Lozano, M.D., Penichet, V.M.R.: Enhancing visitors' experience in art museums using mobile technologies. Inf. Syst. Front. **16**(2), 303–327 (2014). https://doi.org/10.1007/s10796-012-9345-1

Recognition of Concordances for Indexing in Digital Libraries

Simone Marinai$^{(\boxtimes)}$, Samuele Capobianco, Zahra Ziran, Andrea Giuntini, and Pierluigi Mansueto

University of Florence, Firenze, Italy
{simone.marinai,samuele.capobianco,zahra.ziran}@unifi.it,
{andrea.giuntini,pierluigi.mansueto}@stud.unifi.it

Abstract. We describe a system for the automatic transcription of books with concordances. Even if the recognition of printed text with OCR tools is nearly solved for high quality documents, the recognition of structured text, where dictionaries and other linguistic tools can be of little help, is still a difficult task. In this work, we propose to use several techniques for correcting the imperfect text recognized by the OCR software by taking into account both physical features of the documents and the redundancy of information implicit in concordances.

1 Introduction

One of the primary aims of digital libraries is to collect and organize information which can be accessed all over the world. Clearly digital information requires less space than paper based information reducing the library costs. Another obvious advantage is the reduction of the access time to the information. Digitization is also a way to preserve historical documents from the damage and wearing effect of time. Having digitized documents it is clearly possible to use automatic techniques to analyze and extract structured information.

When a word list is an index to a limited body of writing, with references to each passage, it is called a concordance [9]. In general, constructing concordances has been very difficult and time consuming. The term concordance originally applied just for indexing the Bible. Its root (i.e., concord) means unity and the term seemingly arose out of the school of thought that the unity of Bible should be reflected in consistency between the old and new Testaments and could be demonstrated by concordances. The 1960s and 1970s saw another uprising of concordance made possible by the ease with which indexes could be constructed with the use of computers. Concordances then came into being for all types of literature, from Charlotte Bronte to Dylan Thomas. More recently, it has become possible to accomplish this task effectively by the use of Optical Character Recognition [12].

In this work we deal with one digitized volume which is stretched from the *Concordances of the writings of S. Antonio M. Zaccaria* [1], which consists of the verbal concordances that refer to the holy volumes *Letters*, *Sermons* and

M. Ceci et al. (Eds.): IRCDL 2020, CCIS 1177, pp. 135–147, 2020.
https://doi.org/10.1007/978-3-030-39905-4_14

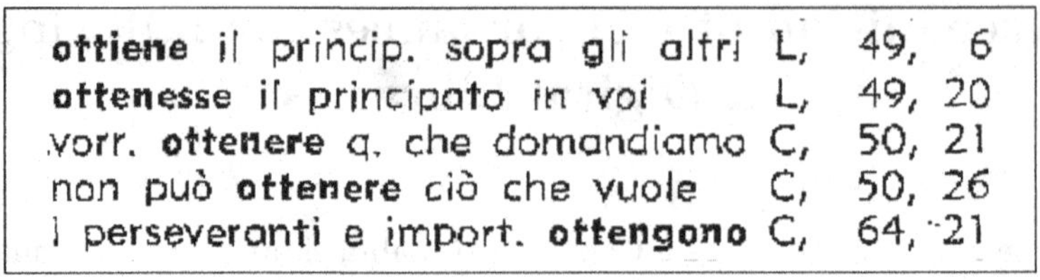

ottiene il princip. sopra gli altri	L,	49,	6
ottenesse il principato in voi	L,	49,	20
vorr. ottenere q. che domandiamo	C,	50,	21
non può ottenere ciò che vuole	C,	50,	26
i perseveranti e import. ottengono	C,	64,	21

Fig. 1. Example of concordances in *Concordances of the writings of S. Antonio M. Zaccaria.*

Constitutions. The document is 442 scanned pages long and each one has a regular structure containing a given number of entries of the concordances. To better illustrate the concordances in general and in particular for this volume we describe in the following the example shown in Fig. 1 that is extracted from one page. As we can notice, the five lines correspond to five occurrences of the verb "**ottenere**" or different verb tenses. For each occurrence (printed in bold), the text line in the left shows its context (the words around the given occurrence). On the right part we can find the position of the occurrence; this part can be considered as an inverted index for this information: the first column corresponds to the book (L: *Letters*, S: *Sermons*, C: *Constitutions*), the first number to the page, and the last to the textline in the page.

By closely inspecting the example, we can notice some features of the problem that can help understand the motivations for designing the tool described in this work and some of its main peculiarities. First of all the scanning resolution is rather low and therefore a state-of-the-art Optical Character Recognition (OCR) tool leads to some errors. These errors are particularly difficult to detect and to correct especially in the case of numbers in the right part of the page. However, one important peculiarity of concordances (printing the context of the indexed word) can help us since in most cases the same textline is indexed several times and we can exploit this feature in the recognition as detailed in Sect. 2.

1.1 Previous Work

Page segmentation is performed on document images to extract homogeneous components from one page image. Physical layout analysis is a combination of page segmentation and classification. Important applications of layout analysis are text-line or word segmentation from printed documents. Several techniques have been presented to address text line segmentation on historical handwritten documents [2,5], however, one widely adopted solution to detect textlines in printed documents relies on projection profiles [3]. State of the art text recognition is on the other hand achieved with optical character recognition (OCR) tools like Tesseract [10] which includes line finding, features/classification methods, and an adaptive classifier.

Automatic table of content (ToC) recognition is another related task in document image analysis research. One example is [7] where the authors propose a

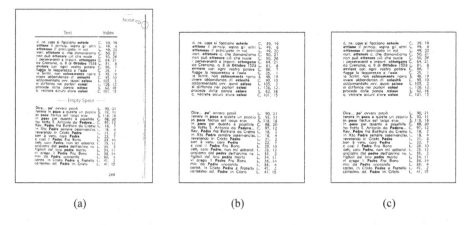

Fig. 2. One example page (a), the resulting image after cropping and noise removal (b), and after skew correction (c).

tool to recognize and extract ToC from PDF making navigation of book content easier. In order to extract the ToC from printed documents, one solution has been proposed in [6] to support the indexing of documents in a digital library.

In this work we describe a system designed to extract information from one digitized book of concordances. To improve the results achieved by a standard OCR tool we integrate specific methods to extract and recognize specific features of the document (e.g. bold words) and take into account the mutual relationships of context textlines for different entries of concordances.

2   The Proposed Method

To better illustrate the proposed method we show in Fig. 2(a) one example page where we highlight the main components of the structure: the text, indices, and some features of pages, like empty spaces between paragraphs, and noise in the page border. After cleaning the page with suitable pre-processing (Fig. 2(b)) the page is also slightly skewed and is rotated (Fig. 2(c)) to make the subsequent OCR process easier.

2.1   Pre-processing

The aim of pre-processing is to improve the quality of document images in order to produce an enhanced page for further analysis [4]. The pre-processing is automatically performed on each page and is composed by four main steps.

Initial Crop. The first naive process is to crop the input image with a specific dimension. The aim is to remove the noise occurring in some page edges and mainly due to the document scanning. Among other items it is important to remove the page number (on the bottom-right of Fig. 2(a)) that could harm the de-skew and segmentation. The final size for each page is 1400×1660. The crop is approximately 200 px wide and 600 px high. The initial image crop is made with a standard projection profile based method. The cropped image is shown in Fig. 2(b).

Noise Reduction. Noise reduction is a filtering transformation, which leads to the removal of most noise. First of all the image is converted in binary [8] and connected components are computed together with their total area. Then, small dotted regions (corresponding to noise) are filtered out.

Skew Correction. Skew correction is a geometrical transformation, which leads to an improvement for the OCR phase. Firstly, the image is projected vertically to get an histogram of the pixels. This process is repeated for various angles. The best angle leads to the maximum sum of the squared differences between consecutive histogram values. Once we obtain this angle, the image is then rotated, as shown in Fig. 2.

Blank Spaces Removal. Blank spaces that may occur between paragraphs are removed to allow the location of a single text block in the page. The result is shown in Fig. 3(a).

2.2 Text Block Finding

Text blocks are located by using standard techniques that take into account their regular shape. To find a text block in a page, we need the following steps:

1. **Canny edge detector:** that uses a multi-stage algorithm to detect edges in images (the colors are inverted by its execution);
2. **Rank filter:** which is needed to remove the borders. It essentially replaces a pixel value with the median of the ones to its left and right. A border pixel is then easily noticed by their new value;
3. **Removal of possible noise:** finding the contours in the border of the image (contours with a large bounding box) and cleaning everything outside them.

Finally, we look for a crop that is maximizes the number of white pixels inside it and is as small as possible. A standard way to solve this problem is to optimize the *F1 score*, which is the harmonic mean of *Precision* and *Recall* [11].

This is the pipeline used to improve the pages before segmenting the textlines and performing the recognition of text and indexes in each page.

Texline Segmentation. To extract textlines we first convert the image in black and white and its colors are inverted. Then, we compute the mean vector of all rows. For each element of the vector, a comparison between a threshold and

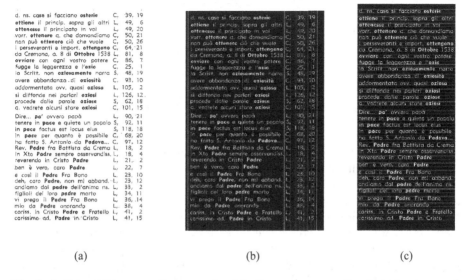

(a)   (b)   (c)

Fig. 3. Left to right, page after removing blank spaces, separation between text and index, identification of texlines.

both the considered item and the next one is made. To perform the textline segmentation we look for the upper and lower border of each text line. We have an *upper* line when the considered item is lower or equal than the threshold and the next one is greater than this threshold; there is a *lower* line when the opposite situation occurs. To illustrate the output of this process, we show the segmentation lines in Fig. 3(c) where *upper* and *lower* lines are drawn in green and white respectively. Even if in this Figure we show the segmentation only for the text part of each page, it is made also for the index part.

2.3   Text Recognition

Text recognition is performed by using `Tesseract` that is an `OCR` engine with support for Unicode and the ability to recognize more than 100 languages out of the box. It is an open source project developed over the past 20+ years at HP and Google and it can be trained to recognize other languages. In this work we mostly used the `Tesseract` version 4.00, except for the index identification where we used the 3.04 version because of implementation reasons. Before using `Tesseract`, we divide the image into two different parts: the text and the index as shown in Fig. 3(b) where the separation is marked with a white line.

In a preliminary implementation of the system we attempted to use the layout analysis algorithms implemented in `Tesseract` to recognize the whole page. Unfortunately, this approach does not provide satisfactory results especially for the index part of the page. To recognize the page content we therefore need to first identify and segment each textline in the main text and then segment each index entry.

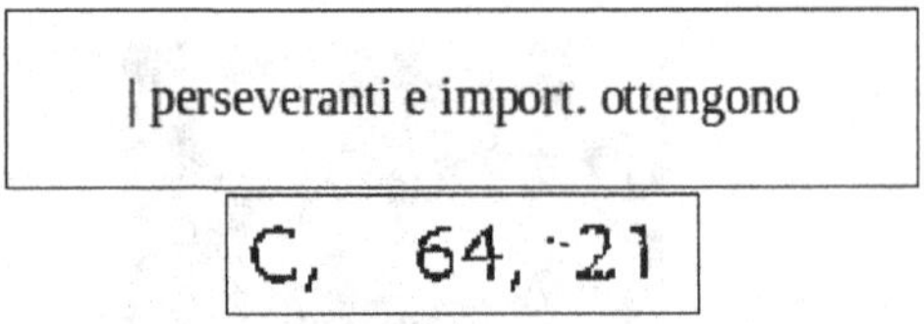

| perseveranti e import. ottengono

C,   64, ·21

Fig. 4. Example of textline (top) and the corresponding index (bottom).

Main Text. The text extraction is simpler than the extraction of the index. We first compute the distance between closer horizontal *upper* and *lower*, lines. If this distance is above a specific threshold, we hypothesize the presence of a text line. To better identify the text areas we need to enlarge the textline area before recognizing it with the OCR. In particular, for the first and last lines we increase the *upper* and decrease the *lower* positions by 10 pixels, respectively. For the other textlines, these values are modified growing the area half of the difference between the previous horizontal *lower* and the actual horizontal *upper* for the upper side, and half of the difference between the next horizontal *upper* and the actual horizontal *lower* for the bottom side.

To make the OCR task easier, we copy the detected text in a new empty image, leaving out some edge pixels for each side. Furthermore, we apply a morphological **dilation** to make the text thicker, using a cross-shaped kernel and apply **Gaussian blur** to smooth the image.

Finally, using Tesseract, we convert the image to string. As an additional control, we check if the text length is above a certain threshold because it may happen that some lines are not real text lines, but just noise. A text line sample is shown in Fig. 4 with the respective result extracted by the Tesseract OCR engine.

Index. As mentioned in the introduction, in the concordances the index refers to three values, separated by commas. We first have a letter describing the referenced book and three values are possible in this case: [L, S, C] (*Letters, Sermons* and *Constitutions*); the page number $\sim [0, 200]$; and the line number $\sim [0, 60]$. The identification method for index lines is analogous to the one used in the text extraction. For better recognition, also in this case the index is copied into a new image, larger than the original one. Since the index structure is regular, we make a vertical segmentation for separating each element of the index: this leads to a better accuracy than performing the OCR in the whole line.

For each element, to avoid OCR errors due to the mis-identification of commas as letters or numbers, for each connected component we compute the number of black pixels above half of the index image. If this number is larger than a specific threshold, the component is considered as a letter or number. To improve the recognition, for each element we apply a *Gaussian blur filter*. Since the optimal kernel dimension changes for different index entries, we consider different kernel dimensions in a range between 1 and 19, considering only odd numbers. For each blurred image, we get the `Tesseract` result, taking into account the expected type of output (a letter for the first element and numbers for the following ones). At this point for each blurred image (ten in total) we consider the OCR output: a max-voting process will identify which one has the maximum occurrence that is most likely to be the correct one. There might be some problems:

- the "1s" in the index are not well recognized. We solve this problem computing the distance between vertical *upper* and *lower* of each element: if the distance is below a threshold it will be a 1 and the `Tesseract` process will not be performed. In case we are considering the first element, we change the 1 with an L;
- the distance between related *upper* and *lower* is too large. This means that the textline segmentation failed, not separating the elements in the correct way. In this case wee repeat the same process increasing the segmentation threshold until it reaches a maximum value: in this case we replace the result of the considered element with a blank space;

It may happen, in a few cases, that a text line has no index. In this case we just apply `Tesseract` for the whole line, without separating it in index and text part.

3   Corrections

In this section we will introduce some techniques that have been adopted to correct the OCR output and improve the results.

3.1   Dictionary

This technique is related to word correction regarding the `OCR` performed on the Main Text. To this purpose we consider an Italian dictionary[1] and a list of proper names. In addition, we created a python dictionary featured by bigrams as keys. For each bigram we define four lists that contain:

1. the words in which this bigram appears;
2. the occurrences of each word as detected by the OCR
3. the page referred in the index for the sentence containing the word
4. the line referred in the index for the sentence containing the word.

In order to populate the bigram dictionary we need to clean the `Tesseract` results that present some noise, like random punctuation or special characters. We first replace underscores and apostrophes with blank spaces and remove the other punctuations except for dots and commas, that might indicate an abbreviation. We therefore consider only dots and commas that have a character to their left and a white space to their right, but remove dots and commas that

---

[1] https://github.com/napolux/paroleitaliane/tree/master/paroleitaliane.

could be an abbreviation, but have to their left a word that is actually in the Italian dictionary.

After recognizing and indexing the whole text we can use the overall information to correct erroneous recognitions. For each phrase, we look only for non-dictionary words that are neither abbreviations or numbers (to avoid to modify correct words, numbers and abbreviations). For each selected word W, we select the words containing some bigrams of W, and compute the *Edit distance* between W and the words. The word with the lowest *Edit distance* is considered as a replacement for W. In case we have more than one word, we consider the one which has the maximum occurrences in the whole document. At this point, we replace the word to be corrected with the found one.

3.2   Punctuation

As already mentioned in the previous section, the OCR introduces some random punctuation while reading the images. What we tried to achieve is to remove this random factor with respect to the grammar rules: considering a punctuation, there will always be a character to its left and a space to its right. However, we tolerate two consecutive types of punctuation if one of them is an abbreviation dot (or an erroneous abbreviation comma when the OCR fails to recognize a dot properly). The random punctuation is then removed replacing it with a blank space. In addition, special characters are removed, except for the asterisks, which are needed for volumes comprehension. In Fig. 5, we can see the results of the two previous corrections. In particular, in blue we highlight the words corrections and in red the punctuation removal.

3.3   Index Correction

It is clear that for the correction of the index there is little information, if any, that can be provided by dictionaries, since any combination of numbers is in principle possible in an index. On the other hand, in the case of concordances it is not even possible to take into account the consistency of page numbers (that are usually increasing in table of contents).

The unique support to index correction is the main peculiarity of concordance where the context around the indexed word is printed as well. Taking into account this feature it is possible to adjust the page index looking for similar phrases in the rest of the book.

It is easy to notice that often the phrases contain abbreviations and therefore an exact match is not possible. We therefore consider trigram indexing to capture as best as possible similar textlines.

To this purpose, we first compute the trigrams in each textline. We then compute the hash address of the trigram in a space with 2^{16} slots and consider a vector representation of the textline where the vector contains values different from zero in positions corresponding to the trigrams in the textline.

Given this representation, we attempt to correct only the index entry for sentences with a wrong index structure. Let S be one of these sentences, with

d. ns. case si facciano . osterie	Dire... pa' ovvero **papàù(papà)**
ofttiene il princip. sopra gli altri	tenere in pace e quiete un popolo
ottenesse il principato: in voi	in pace factus est locus **eius(vis)**
vorr. ottenere g. che domandiamo:	in **paee(pare)** per quanto è possibile
non può ottenere ciò che vuole	ha fatto S. Antonio —da Padova...
I perseveranti e import. ottengono	Rev. Padre fra Battista da Crema
da Cremona, a. 8 di Ottobre 1538	in Xto Padre sempre osservandiss.
ovviare con ogni vostro potere	reverendo in Cristo Padre
fugge la leggerezza e l'ozio	ben è vero, caro Padre
la Scritt. non oziosamente narra	e così il **Padré(Padre)** Fra Bono
overe(opere) abbondanza .di oziosità	deh, caro Padre, non mi: abband.:
addormentata ovv. quasi 'oziosa	andiamo dal padre dell'anima ns.
si diffonde nei **parlarì(parlare)** oziosi	figlioli: del loro padre morto '
procede dalle parole oziose	Vi **pfega(prega)** il Padre Fra Bono
a. vedrete alcuni stare oziosi	mio da Padre onorando
	eariss. in Cristo .Padre e .Fratello
	carissimo. ad. Padre "in. Cristo

Fig. 5. Text and punctuation corrections in two pages. In blue words corrections, in red the punctuation removal. (Color figure online)

index I. We first compute the *Jaccard index* between the vectorial representation for S and all those of the other sentences in the document. The *Jaccard index* is used for computing the similarity of sets, that can be expressed using this formula, considering A and B as two hash vectors:

$$J(A, B) = \frac{|A \cap B|}{|A \cup B|} \qquad (1)$$

We take the first 50 sentences (with a syntactically correct index structure) having the highest *Jaccard index*. Afterwards, we compute the *edit distance* between S and the 50 sentences. The sentences S' with the minimum *edit distance* is selected, in case there are more than one sentence we choose the one with the highest *Jaccard index*. Finally, we can fix the wrong index I for sentence S on the basis of the information provided by the index I' for sentence S'. To this purpose we can distinguish three cases where we denote the three parts for index I as $I.L$ (for the letter), $I.1$ (for the first number), and $I.2$ (for the second number):

- If $I.L$ is missing then we copy this value from I' ($I.L = I'.L$);
- If $I.1$ is missing or is out of range then $I.1 = I'.1$;

Fig. 6. Word segmentation (left) and identification of bold words: on the center we show one bold word and the results of the erosion on the right.

– If $I.2$ (the line number) is out of range, it is replaced with $I'.2$, but only if $|I.2 - I'.2| > 2$. The latter condition applies to line numbers because similar phrases can have a close line number if some text wrap up.

It is interesting to notice that GPU has been used for index correction because the execution time for the *Jaccard index* computation would have been too long in CPU.

3.4   Identification of Bold Text

For each sentence in the concordances the index word is usually printed in bold. Extracting this feature is important for a good index reconstruction. The idea to find bold words is to first separate each word and then compute a morphological erosion of the word. The erosion is performed using an *elliptical kernel*. Therefore, considering NE as the number of pixels in the not eroded image and E as the number of pixels in the eroded one, the pixel ratio ($PR = \frac{NE}{E}$) will be smaller for bold words because the erosion will leave out some pixels for them with respect to non-bold words that will be master erased.

In Fig. 6 we show the bold word in both not eroded and eroded version. We can notice that in the eroded image of bold words we can still distinguish some black pixels, while for other words the result would have been almost empty. We use three different kernel size for making the algorithm more robust. Eventually, it may happen in very few cases that a phrase contains more than one bold word. In this case, after finding this latter, we check if there are any another pixel ratios, which are close to the one of the bold word. If so, also these words are marked as bold.

Document Transcription. The final step consists in the transcription of all document information to a final *docx* file. This process contains an intermediary step, which produces a *PDF* file as output. This is accomplished in the following way: for each page we transcript the text and indices in an HTML file, with a specific structure that divides the page in two main columns, one for the text and the other one for the indices. The index column is also divided in three columns. After merging the *PDF* files, using an online tool, we convert the *PDF* file to a final *docx* one, which can be modified if needed.

4   Experimental Results

In this section we describe the experimental evaluation that is performed on 20 random pages that have been manually annotated. In particular, we analyze the results from two different perspectives:

- recognition of indices and bold words without any correction;
- evaluation of text and punctuation correction.

The results concerning bold words and indices are very good, as shown in Table 1: the algorithms for identifying these two information were already robust and there were no needs for deeper corrections. As described in Sect. 3.3 we implemented one algorithm for indices, but the improvement was very marginal. For each information (bold words, indices, punctuation, text) we define E as the number of errors and N as the total number of that kind of information. The accuracy is then calculated as $Accuracy = 100 - \frac{E}{N} \cdot 100$.

Regarding the text correction we considered 3 different values of a threshold (α) which indicates the maximum allowed *edit distance* for word retrieval. Concerning the punctuation results, the correction leads to an improvement because the algorithm removes most of the random punctuation. Finally, increasing the text threshold, there are more words that can be chosen and also more chance to get an erroneous one. Accordingly, this behavior leads to a lower accuracy for $\alpha = 4$. Using $\alpha = 3$ or 2 instead, we get an improvement of 2%.

Table 1. Accuracy of the proposed method after different corrections.

	Accuracy	
Information	Before	After
Bold	–	98.50%
Indices	–	99.86%
Punctuation	86.06%	89.81%
Text ($\alpha = 2$)	93.44%	95.38%
Text ($\alpha = 3$)	93.44%	95.31%
Text ($\alpha = 4$)	93.44%	93.39%

Table 2. Execution times for different steps.

Phase	Time (s/page)
Pre-processing	11,9
Segmentation	5,85
OCR	154,2
Text correction	2,84
Indices correction	105,2
Bold extraction	6,6

In Table 2 we report the execution times of the various steps. As we can notice the most expensive phases are the OCR (performed by `Tesseract`) and the index corrections. The computer used in these experiments has a CPU Intel i7 7700HQ (Quadcore) and a GPU Nvidia GTX 1050 (4 GB) with 16 GB of RAM and a Samsung SSD 970 EVO Plus.

5   Conclusions

In this paper we presented a system for the recognition and indexing of a concordances book. Despite the good recognition of printed text by means of off-the shelf OCR tools the recognition of structured text containing short sentences with abbreviations and numbers is not perfect. We addressed the problem by considering specific correction techniques like punctuations and bold typefaces. For index correction we considered on the other hand the rendundancy of information of concordances.

For further studies, it would be good to focus also to non-italian words that appear in the document, like Latin ones, that may improve the text accuracy. Another idea is to correct the words depending also on the text context, because we noticed that several `Tesseract` errors concern the distinction between the letters o and a.

This approach can be extended also to deal with other indexes in books belonging to digital libraries, like table of contents that are the next target of this research.

References

1. Cagni, G.M.: Concordanze degli scritti di S. Antonio M. Zaccaria. Collana spiritualita barnabitica, 4 (1960)
2. Capobianco, S., Marinai, S.: Text line extraction in handwritten historical documents. In: Grana, C., Baraldi, L. (eds.) IRCDL 2017. CCIS, vol. 733, pp. 68–79. Springer, Cham (2017). https://doi.org/10.1007/978-3-319-68130-6_6
3. Cesarini, F., Gori, M., Marinai, S., Soda, G.: Structured document segmentation and representation by the modified X-Y tree. In: Fifth International Conference on Document Analysis and Recognition, ICDAR 1999, Bangalore, India, 20–22 September 1999, pp. 563–566 (1999)
4. Gatos, B.G.: Imaging Techniques in document analysis processes. In: Doermann, D., Tombre, K. (eds.) Handbook of Document Image Processing and Recognition, pp. 73–131. Springer, London (2014). https://doi.org/10.1007/978-0-85729-859-1_4
5. Likforman-Sulem, L., Zahour, A., Taconet, B.: Text line segmentation of historical documents: a survey. Int. J. Doc. Anal. Recognit. 9(2), 123–138 (2007)
6. Mandal, S., Chowdhury, S.P., Das, A.K., Chanda, B.: Automated detection and segmentation of table of contents page from document images. In: 2003 Proceedings of the Seventh International Conference on Document Analysis and Recognition, vol. 1, pp. 398–402 (2003)

7. Marinai, S., Marino, E., Soda, G.: Table of contents recognition for converting PDF documents in e-book formats. In: Proceedings of the 10th ACM Symposium on Document Engineering, DocEng 2010, pp. 73–76. ACM, New York (2010)
8. Otsu, N.: A threshold selection method from gray-level histograms. IEEE Trans. Syst. Man Cybern. **9**(1), 62–66 (1979)
9. Read, A.W.: Dictionary, Encyclopaedia Britannica (2016). https://www.britann ica.com/topic/dictionary. Accessed 30 Sept 2019
10. Smith, R.: An overview of the Tesseract OCR engine. In: Ninth International Conference on Document Analysis and Recognition (ICDAR 2007), vol. 2, pp. 629–633, September 2007
11. danvk: Finding blocks of text in an image using Python, OpenCV and numpy (2015)
12. Witten, I.H., Moffat, A., Bell, T.C.: Managing Gigabytes: Compressing and Indexing Documents and Images, 2nd edn. Morgan Kaufmann Publishers Inc., San Francisco (1999)

Open Science

RepOSGate: Open Science Gateways for Institutional Repositories

Michele Artini⬤, Leonardo Candela⬤, Paolo Manghi$^{(\boxtimes)}$⬤,
and Silvia Giannini⬤

Institute of Information Science and Technologies,
National Research Council, Pisa, Italy
{michele.artini,leonardo.candela,paolo.manghi,
silvia.giannini}@isti.cnr.it

Abstract. Most repository platforms used to operate Institutional Repositories fail at delivering a complete set of functionalities required by institutions and researchers to fully comply with Open Science publishing practices. This paper presents RepOSGate, a software that implements an overlay application capable of collecting metadata records from a repository and transparently deliver search, statistics, upload of Open Access versions functionalities over an enhanced version of the metadata collection, which include: links to datasets, Open Access versions of the artifacts, links to projects from several funders, subjects, citations, etc. The paper will also present two instantiations of RepOSGate, used to enhance the publication metadata collections of two CNR institutes: Institute of Information Science and Technologies (ISTI) and Institute of Marine Sciences (ISMAR).

Keywords: Institutional repository · Open Access · Open Science · Scholarly communication · OpenAIRE

1 Introduction

Open Science [3] publishing principles demand for a scholarly record that (i) is persistently stored into repositories and features all kinds of products, not only scientific literature, (ii) makes use of persistent identifiers for all scholarly entities (e.g. authors, organizations, scientific products, thematic services), (iii) keeps track of the semantic relationships between such objects in the metadata (e.g. citations, supplement material, versions), (iv) keeps an up-to-date record of science evolution, by continuously publishing such links within the metadata of the objects in the repositories, and (v) allows the deposition of multiple versions of a publication, each with its own access rights, to make it clear when a publication is also Open Access. Unfortunately, most institutional repository platforms (e.g. Eprints, DSpace, Invenio) are today unable to fulfill all such requirements at once [1, 2, 4, 6, 12]. Old releases, still broadly in use due, simply fail to provide support for PIDs and links, or in some cases make a difference between an Open Access and a Closed version of a publication; more recent releases, which may take these into account, fail instead to keep an up-to-date linking record as they do not

M. Ceci et al. (Eds.): IRCDL 2020, CCIS 1177, pp. 151–162, 2020.
https://doi.org/10.1007/978-3-030-39905-4_15

offer APIs to collect updates to the metadata records coming from trusted third-party sources.

This paper presents RepOSGate, a general-purpose software conceived to provide an Open Science view of a repository collection by transparently generating an intersection between the repository metadata collection and other public scholarly communication data sources. RepOSGate fetches the "pivot" metadata collection as exposed by a repository and performs an entity linking procedure based on publication DOIs to enrich such collection with properties and links from other sources: (*i*) the OpenAIRE Research Graph [7, 11] for collecting up-to-date information on publications metadata, and (*ii*) the OpenAIRE's Scholexplorer [5] for collecting up-to-date links between publications and dataset objects. As a result, repository users can access the RepOSGate portal, a gateway that transparently offers discovery and statistic functionalities to an enhanced version of the original repository metadata, including for example abstracts, links to Open Access versions, subjects, bibliographic references, links to datasets, links to software, links to projects, and, when missing, ORCID identifiers of the authors. The Gateway offers also OAI-PMH APIs [9], to expose the enriched metadata collection to third-party consumers.

We will also describe the deployment of RepOSGate to deliver the ISTI Open Portal[1], a gateway developed to promote the scientific publications of the Institute of Information Science and Technologies (ISTI)[2] - an institute of the Italian National Research Council (CNR) - by leveraging access to their open access versions. The ISTI Open Portal offers an Institutional Repository web-based user interface for discovery and statistics on top of an aggregation of multiple sources around the "pivot" collection of ISTI's publication metadata. Another installation of RepOSGate supports a gateway for another CNR's institutes, namely ISMAR, the Institute of Marine Sciences[3].

2   RepOSGate Architecture

RepOSGate has been conceived to make sure that scientists of an institution which already operates an institutional repository whose underlying platform cannot meet Open Science demands, can quickly, and at low cost, meet such demands. For example, the European Commission requires funded researchers to deposit in an Open Access repository, with links to project in the metadata, every article accepted for publication. Many repository platforms offered by institutions to researchers do not meet this basic requirement and researchers end up depositing in open shared platforms, such as Zenodo.org or Figshare. As a consequence, virtuous scientists deposit in two repositories, while others simply deposit once following their most urgent obligation. On a different aspect, but with similar drawbacks, such platforms do not leverage the good practice of providing links between datasets and articles, or of providing ORCID identifiers. For institutions this means they cannot support their researchers with the

---

[1] ISTI Open Portal https://openportal.isti.cnr.it/.

[2] *Istituto di Scienza e Tecnologie dell'Informazione*, https://www.isti.cnr.it/.

[3] *Istituto di Scienze Marine*, https://openportal.ismar.cnr.it/.

tools to comply with funders mandates and cannot provide their scientists with functionalities to keep their local collection of publications interlinked with the evolving
scholarly communication infrastructure.

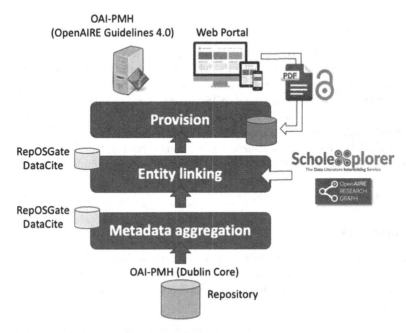

Fig. 1. High-level functional architecture.

RepOSGate was designed to deliver an overlay platform capable of enhancing
content in a repository with up-to-date metadata information regarding their interlinking with projects, datasets, ORCID IDs, Open Access versions, and more. Moreover, repository managers can upload Open Access versions of repository articles via
admin interfaces; to facilitate the adoption of RepOSGate, the Open Access files are
kept locally to RepOSGate, independently of the repository platform at hand. Ideally,
the resulting overlay repository makes the repository OpenAIRE compliant, hence
fitting with the OA mandate of the European Commission, and Plan-S compliant[4],
since all publications will be equipped with an Open Access version, if it exists.

RepOSGate's software builds on top of a D-NET Toolkit [10] instance. D-NET is a
framework where designers and developers can find the tools for constructing and
operating so-called aggregative infrastructures, namely systems for aggregating
(meta)data sources with heterogeneous data models and technologies. Designers and
developers can select from a variety of D-NET data management services, can con-
figure them to handle data according to given data models, and can construct auto-
nomic workflows to obtain personalized aggregative infrastructures. As shown in

---

[4] *Coalition S*, https://www.coalition-s.org/.

Fig. 1, RepOSGate adopts D-NET to deliver an aggregation system capable of: aggregation of metadata records from the repository collection, performing entity linking to build richer records, and index the records to expose them via a web portal or via OAI-PMH APIs that are compatible with the OpenAIRE Guidelines 4.0[5].

2.1 Aggregation

The repository must expose the publication metadata records as an OAI-PMH collection of Dublin Core metadata records, where `dc:identifier` should contain the DOI of the record. A D-NET aggregation workflow will be scheduled to harvest the records and transform them into the RepOSGate core metadata schema - the setting up of a D-NET workflow is described in detail in [10] and is not in the scope of this paper. The transformation includes standard harmonization rules to convert country codes, dates, DOI URLs/codes, author names, into a common representation; they can be fine-tuned to match peculiarities of the given repository, for example to include new `dc:subject` or `dc:resourcetype` terms into the vocabulary provided by RepOSGate.[6]

2.2 Entity Linking

The entity linking process is based on publications DOIs. The basic methodology is to send requests to external metadata source APIs so as to collect information required to enrich the records. Specifically, RepOSGate has been customized to collect information from three main sources:

- *OpenAIRE Research Graph*: entity linking collects abstracts, links to projects from 28 funders (including MIUR, the European Commission, NSF, Wellcome Trust, and others world-wide), links to other versions of the publication into other sources (possibly Open Access), ORCID identifiers, subjects according to standard vocabularies (e.g. MeSH, DEWEY, Arxiv, ACM, etc.), list of citations in the bibliography;
- *OpenAIRE Scholexplorer*: entity linking collects links from the publication to any dataset referring to it.

The degree of potential enrichment of the "pivot" collection is remarkable considering that:

- The OpenAIRE Research Graph aggregates today, November 2019, around 450Mi metadata records with links, which after deduplication and fine-grained classification narrow down to $\sim$100Mi publications [11], $\sim$8Mi datasets, $\sim$200K software research products, 8Mi other scientific products, with 480Mi semantic links between them. Such products are in turn linked to 7 research communities, organizations, and projects/grants from $\sim$30 funders worldwide. The Graph aggregates

---

[5] OpenAIRE Guidelines for Content Providers, http://guidelines.openaire.eu.

[6] Note that RepOSGate' vocabularies are the ones of OpenAIRE, which today has a complete coverage of transformation rules for more than 10,000 data sources world-wide.

sources such as CrossRef[7], DataCite[8], Microsoft Research Graph[9], Unpaywall, thematic repositories (e.g. ArXiv, RePEc, UK PMC, etc.), all known publishers, journals, data centers, research software repositories, research infrastructure archives/repositories, and all known registries (e.g. ORCID[10], GRID.ac, re3data. org, OpenDOAR[11], etc.). The graph is refreshed with new content every two weeks.

- The OpenAIRE Scholexplorer aggregates article-dataset and dataset-dataset links from publishers and data centers world wide, for a total of 480Mi links (a dump of Scholexplorer is available at [8]); its APIs are used by Scopus and tens of data centres and publishers to resolve DOIs to the relative linked objects. The Scholexplorer citation graphs is being kept refreshed every hour, with sync actions with DataCite and CrossRef EventData.

Each record in the repository with a DOI is enriched by the knowledge stored in the sources above, to build a richer record with up-to-date information.

2.3 Provision

The final step of data provision is that of indexing the enriched records and deliver an OAI-PMH API and Full-Text Index API with a web portal. This is performed by integrating in the D-NET workflow of aggregation and entity linking a final step of ingestion into the D-NET services designed for this specific purpose, namely the OAI-PMH Publisher (based on MongoDB[12]) and the Index Service (based on Apache Solr[13]). The RepOSGate portal is a general purpose UI, which can be configured to include custom branding and text in static pages, which offers search and browse functionalities and statistics on Open Access and Open Science, including integration with Altmetrics to show social media citations to the article DOIs. The user interface allows the upload of Open Access versions of the original PDFs.

The following section will showcase the portal as deployed for the CNR institutes ISTI and ISMAR, whose publication collection is available via People, the central institutional archive of CNR.

3 ISTI Open Portal

ISTI is the Institute of Information Science and Technologies of the National Research Council of Italy, counting around 250 members of staff. CNR researchers are mandatorily requested to yearly report their scientific publications, by depositing metadata and files into the central CNR archive called People. People stores and

---

[7] CrossRef, http://crossref.org.

[8] DataCite, http://datacite.org.

[9] Microsoft Academic, http://www.microsoft.com/en-us/research/project/academic/.

[10] ORCID Researcher Identifiers, http://orcid.org.

[11] OpenDOAR Repository Registry, http://opendoar.org.

[12] *mongoDB*, https://www.mongodb.com/.

[13] *Apache Solr,* https://lucene.apache.org/solr/.

exposes bibliographic metadata according to an internal qualified Dublin Core, where: (*i*) CNR author enroll numbers are kept with author CNR names, in turn kept separated from non-CNR author names (strings); (*ii*) grant names are kept in special fields as strings, with no reference codes; (*iii*) for each article the system can acquire multiple files, but no access rights are provided. People is only used for CNR and National research assessment programs, hence does not offer public search, browse, statistic portals nor public OAI-PMH APIs. This means that, unless the CNR will establish and embrace a roadmap to upgrade the current system, the institutes will not be capable of implementing Open Access and Open Science practices at the level required today by research organizations.

Luckily enough, CNR's People APIs are available on request. In order to offer a traditional institutional Open Access repository portal and OAI-PMH APIs, we have deployed an instance of RepOSGate to deliver the ISTI Open Portal[14]. A twin installation[15] has been made available for the ISMAR institute, the Institute of Marine Sciences. In the following we shall present the aggregation and entity linking workflow implemented by RepOSGate for ISTI but also show the numbers for ISMAR Open Portal, to demonstrate the gain in information enrichment.

3.1 Aggregation

RepOSGate collects from People OAI-PMH APIs only the metadata of publications provided by ISTI researchers, via a dedicated OAI-PMH Set. The transformation makes sure that:

- *CNR authors:* CNR Author information, which is properly structured, is included into the DataCite author metadata in such a way CNR enrollment number appears as author identifier;
- *non-CNR authors*: non-CNR Author information follows the same restructuring, but applying a case-driven function that attempts to transform the name into an "Surname, N." structure.
- *ISTI Laboratories*: Thanks to a custom author-laboratory map, CNR authors are also associated to their ISTI Laboratory, the information being kept into the affiliation field of the author structure.

Records from People are not clear in terms of Access Rights. This information is key to deliver an Open Access repository or view over the scientific production of ISTI and will be identified via the Entity Linking below.

3.2 Entity Linking

The entity linking process fetches from OpenAIRE Research Graph and Scholexplorer: links to projects, links to other versions of the publication into other sources (possibly Open Access), links from the publication to any dataset referring to it, bibliographic

---

[14] ISTI Open Portal http://openportal.isti.cnr.it.

[15] ISMAR Open Portal http://openportal.ismar.cnr.it.

references, and subjects according to standard vocabularies (enrichment with ORCID IDs is in the roadmap).

More specifically, by the 22nd of September 2019 the system collected 9329 publication records, out of which 2872 have DOIs (the majority of publications does not necessarily bear a DOI, for example technical reports, presentations, software, etc.). The administrator has uploaded 360 Open Access versions of non-OA articles. The entity linking phase enriched a total of 590 records by querying the OpenAIRE services, the numbers shown in Table 1. Of all information enrichments above, of great interest to the Open Access and Open Science mission of ISTI is in particular:

- The number of Open Access publications: such number could not be identified from the records in People and they are key to offer Open Access analysis and monitoring.
- Identification of Open Access rights: as long as an Open Access version of a non-Open Access publication in ISTI Open Portal will be collected by OpenAIRE, this version will also appear in the ISTI Open Portal as part of the publication metadata: researchers can freely deposit in EC compliant repositories like Zenodo.org to comply to the EC Open Access mandates and this version will be first collected by OpenAIRE and then fetched by ISTI Open Portal;
- Identification of links to funding: for the same reason, the projects funding the publication will be fetched from OpenAIRE by the ISTI Open Portal and will appear as part of the publication record.

Table 1. ISTI Open Portal: metadata enrichment statistics.

Properties and links	Original metadata	Enriched metadata	Difference
Articles with Open Access version	0	757 (360 added by administrator by depositing OA files)	757
Subjects	10752	12744	1992
Bibliographic references	0	6306	6306
Other versions	8146	9270	1124
Project links	610	770	160
Dataset links	0	54	54

Table 2 shows the numbers for ISMAR Open Portal. The 26th of September 2019 the system collected 5891 records, out of which 1898 have a DOI. Interestingly, the marine context features a richer set of datasets if compared to the Computer Science.

Table 2. ISMAR Open Portal: metadata enrichment statistics.

Properties and links	Original metadata	Enriched metadata	Difference
Articles with Open Access version	0	417 (no OA file deposited by administrator)	417
Subjects	7090	10454	3364
Bibliographic references	0	10038	10038
Other versions	4770	6068	1298
Project links	45	189	144
Dataset links	0	128	128

For both ISTI Open Portal and ISMAR Open Portal the aggregation and entity linking process is scheduled every night, thereby keeping the ISTI collection always up to date with the latest scholarly links and properties collected by OpenAIRE services.

3.3   Provision

RepOSGate's web portal offers a number of services including: (a) a per-publication page offering augmented information with respect to that natively stored in the institutional archive; (b) browsing options taking into account the ISTI authors and the research laboratories they belong; (c) a rich array of statistics including scholarly production indices, open access indices, and visits and downloads. It is worth highlighting that by aggregating content coming from several sources the portal is also conceived to provide its managers/curators with statistics and indicators on both information completeness and consistency to use to improve what's natively stored in the CNR archive as well as in the rest of providers. Static pages have been added to provide links to the Institute Open Access policy and curators of the site. The envisaged solution is suitable for any CNR institute as well as for any institution/community willing to build a repository by augmenting the content of its native repository(ies)/archive(s).

Figure 2 shows the home search page and the result list page with details on multiple versions of the article, access rights for each version, best access right for the article (following the ordering: Open > Restricted > Embargo > Closed), Altmetrics numbers, and links to projects in OpenAIRE.

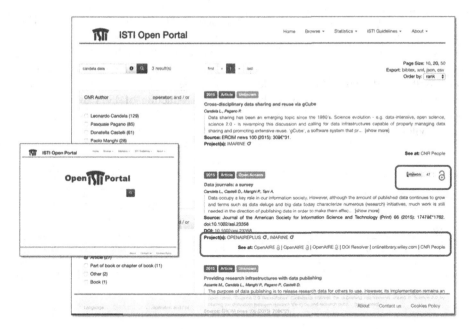

Fig. 2. ISTI Open Portal: home page and search result list.

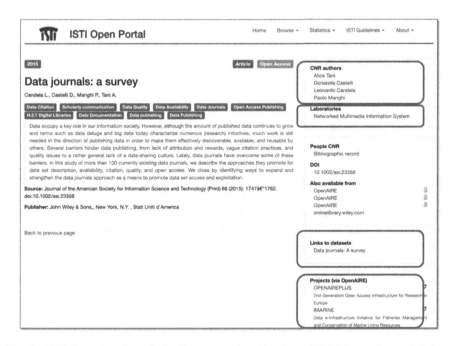

Fig. 3. ISTI Open Portal result details page: author identifiers, ISTI laboratories, and links to datasets.

Figure 3 shows the detail page of the publication "Data Journals: a survey". This record, which originally featured only the minimal metadata available from the People archive, includes today the link to the related ISTI laboratory, the link to ISTI authors, one DOI link to a dataset returned by OpenAIRE Scholexplorer, and the EC projects funding this work, with links to the detail project pages on the OpenAIRE web site. Figure 4 shows the statistics about the scientific production of ISTI over time, by access rights and by year, both in graph and tabular forms. Other statistics, by year/typology and by laboratory/typology, are shown in Fig. 5.

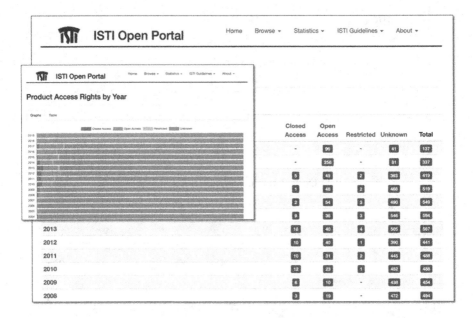

Fig. 4. ISTI Open Portal Open Access statistics by access rights/year: graph and table view.

The increase in open access versions in 2018 and 2019 is primarily due to the emission of the ISTI Open Access Policy since January 2018. From the date of entry into force of the Policy, each ISTI Author must deposit the metadata and a digital version for open access purposes in the CNR institutional archive. The import of the previous digital versions and their access rights is in progress. It should sharply limit the number of "Unknown rights."

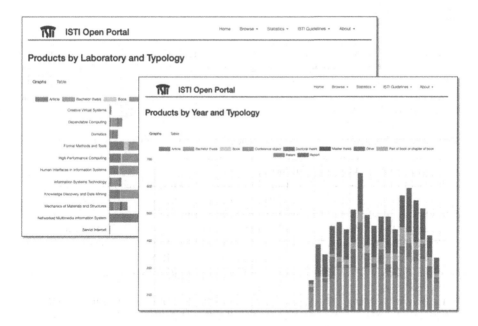

Fig. 5. ISTI Open Portal Open Access statistics by Laboratory/Year and Year/Typology of publications.

4   Conclusion and Prospects

RepOSGate has been developed to provide repository managers with a lightweight solutions easiying the development of their repository with respect to open science practices. This solution benefits from the large amount of knowledge that exists in the scholarly communication web to augment the information accompanying every repository artifact.

The adoption of this solution was instrumental for ISTI to develop and implement an Open Access policy. From 2018 on (the year the open access policy was signed) the Institute managed to make available more than 70% of its scholarly production.

The adoption of RepOSGate is currently being taken into consideration by other CNR institutes. Several enhancements are in the roadmap, such as exploiting entity linking to collect ORCID IDs and, most importantly, the possibility for authorized researchers to upload the Open Access version of an article rather than delegating one administrator of all the work.

Acknowledgments. This work was possible and co-funded by the EC H2020 project OpenAIRE-Advance (grant agreement 777541).

References

1. Arlitsch, K., Grant, C.: Why so many repositories? Examining the limitations and possibilities of the institutional repositories landscape. J. Libr. Adm. **58**(3), 264–281 (2018). https://doi.org/10.1080/01930826.2018.1436778
2. Assante, M., Candela, L., Castelli, D., Manghi, P., Pagano, P.: Science 2.0 repositories: time for a change in scholarly communication. D-Lib Mag. **21**(1/2) (2015) https://doi.org/10.1045/january2015-assante
3. Bartling, S., Friesike, S. (eds.): Opening Science - The Evolving Guide on How the Internet is Changing Research, Collaboration and Scholarly Publishing. Springer, Cham (2014) https://doi.org/10.1007/978-3-319-00026-8
4. Bashir, A., Mir, A.A., Sofi, Z.A.: Global landscape of open access repositories. Libr. Philos. Pract. (e-journal) **2445** (2019). https://digitalcommons.unl.edu/libphilprac/2445
5. Burton, A., et al.: The scholix framework for interoperability in data-literature information exchange. D-Lib Mag. **23**(1/2) (2017). https://doi.org/10.1045/january2017-burton
6. COAR Next Generation Repositories Working Group: Next Generation Repositories - Behaviours and Technical Recommendations of the COAR Next Generation Repositories Working Group (2017). https://www.coar-repositories.org/files/NGR-Final-Formatted-Report-cc.pdf
7. La Bruzzo, S., Manghi, P., Mannocci, A.: OpenAIRE's DOIBoost - boosting CrossRef for research. In: Manghi, P., Candela, L., Silvello, G. (eds.) IRCDL 2019. CCIS, vol. 988, pp. 133–143. Springer, Cham (2019). https://doi.org/10.1007/978-3-030-11226-4_11
8. La Bruzzo, S., Manghi, P.: OpenAIRE ScholeXplorer Service: Scholix JSON Dump [Dataset]. Zenodo (2019). http://doi.org/10.5281/zenodo.2674330
9. Lagoze, C., Van de Sompel, H.: The making of the open archives initiative protocol for metadata harvesting. Library Hi Tech **21**(2), 118–128 (2003). https://doi.org/10.1108/07378830310479776
10. Manghi, P., et al.: The D-NET software toolkit. Program: Electron. Libr. Inf. Syst. **48**(4), 322–354 (2014). https://doi.org/10.1108/PROG-08-2013-0045
11. OpenAIRE Research Graph. http://catalogue.openaire.eu/service/openaire.openaire_graph
12. Repository Platforms for Research Data Interest Group of the Research Data Alliance: Matrix of use cases and functional requirements for research data repository platforms (2016). https://doi.org/10.15497/rda00033

Training Data Stewards in Italy: Reflection on the FAIR RDM Summer School

Anna Maria Tammaro[(⊠)] and Stefano Caselli

University of Parma, Parma, Italy
{annamaria.tammaro,stefano.caselli}@unipr.it

Abstract. "Fair Research Data Management" Summer School in Parma focused on the skills gap in Italy for data stewards. A distinct feature of the Summer School was its aim to bring together participants from different backgrounds and from different countries. The paper is a reflection on the organization of the Summer School and the evaluation received by the participants.

Keywords: Research data management · Data stewards · Open Science

1 Introduction: Research Data Management Skills Gap

1.1 A Profile for Data Stewards

An understanding of the role defined by "data stewards", and the formal titles with which they typically operate (such as data librarians, data scientists, curators of research data, etc.), can vary considerably over time, between different institutional contexts and across international borders.

Research data must be managed and preserved for the long term. The support service for the management of research data, however, is not a simple "restyling" of preservation for new types of dynamic documents, but implies a role of the data steward that extends to all phases of the research cycle, starting with design and implementation of the research project. The most important feature of "data curation" is that it represents a socio-technological system: new partnerships of librarians and support staff with teachers and researchers are needed along with the technological infrastructure and institutional organization. The necessary approach is the systemic one defined by Borgman (2015) as a socio-technological system. We must not start from the granularity of the collection, but from the needs of users (scholars and re-users) and from the political and organizational context of the institution (Corrall 2012).

The vision of the academic libraries' service was clearly designed by ARL: *"In 2033, the research library will have shifted from its role as a knowledge service provider within the university to become a collaborative partner within a rich and diverse learning and research ecosystem"* ARL (2015).

A definition of data librarian proposed by the Project of the Library Theory and Research Section of IFLA is the following (Tammaro et al. 2019): *"Data librarians are supporters of data re-users, in the process of production, storage and access of data"*.

© Springer Nature Switzerland AG 2020
M. Ceci et al. (Eds.): IRCDL 2020, CCIS 1177, pp. 163–172, 2020.
https://doi.org/10.1007/978-3-030-39905-4_16

The activities characterizing the role and cited by the interviewees from the IFLA LTR Project, in order of decreasing importance, are in the first place activities in close contact with researchers such as training (70%), orientation (66%), communication (61%), followed by access (58%) preservation (58%), policy preparation (54%), data management plan (51%), information systems (44%), statistics (21%), copyright (18%), knowledge of the subject (26%). Most IFLA Project respondents work in universities (78%) and academic libraries (10%), a minority work in research centers (6%), public offices (5%), public libraries (1%) and other organizations. The majority of data librarian positions are for qualified roles and require a Master (35%) or even a PhD (6%).

Data stewardship is defined as *"the process and attitudes that make one deal responsibly with one's own and other people data throughout and after the initial scientific creation and discovery cycle"* (Mons 2018). Initially, the idea was that a domain expert had the responsibility of qualifying and documenting the data from their professional point of view. In fact, Data stewards share some responsibilities with data curator and data librarian.

1.2   Research Data Management in Italy: The Skills Gap

The mandate of the European Commission for Open Science states: "As open as possible, as closed as necessary". In practice, the European Commission asks the professors and researchers involved in projects for which public funding is requested and obtained to deposit research results, including scientific publications, in open access repositories and to produce a Data Management Plan for the data.

In Italy, after Law No. 112/2013 which launched a first political initiative for Open Access to scientific publications, a bill (called "Gallo" from the name of the speaker) is now being discussed in Parliament, which includes the research data among its topics of interest, as the first legal basis of a national policy for the research data infrastructure, starting from the existing network of institutional repositories.

Even in Italy, some research data management pioneering experiences are born, many linked to the IOSSG group. The characteristic that distinguishes the service of these Italian universities has been defined as: "single point of entry". This model of open data support services, developed by the IOSSG Group, highlights the social role of the data librarian, who must work with the other University offices involved in the research cycle. However, adequate skills are lacking in Italy, and moreover new roles are needed for support services. Only two training experiences have been carried out at the Universities of Bologna and Padua, where the Library Systems have trained staff involved in support services.

Most of the professional literature believes that the librarian's background includes fundamental skills for the data librarian, but often does not describe them. During the Stelline Conferences in 2018 and 2019 two Seminars were held on the Data Librarian profile to understand the needs of Italian universities that pioneered the research data management service. The organizers of the two Seminars were DILL (International Master in Digital Library Learning) together with IOSSG, OpenAire and RDA. The good practices of some of the major Italian universities were illustrated during the seminar by Elena Giglia (University of Torino), Paola Galimberti (University of Milan), Elena Bianchi (University of Padua), Marialaura Vignocchi (University of Bologna).

The questions on which the organizers wanted to start the discussion were: What are the activities necessary for research data management? and what skills are consequently necessary for the training and updating of the data librarian? Before the first Seminar in 2018, a questionnaire was distributed on the skills of the data librarian. A conversation before and after the Seminar took place online, and helped to clarify the different opinions of librarians.

The questionnaire that preceded the Stelline Seminar allowed to highlight the opinions of 165 librarians who responded to the survey (Tammaro 2018). The competencies listed in the questionnaire had to be classified by the respondents as: fundamental (core identity of the librarian), specialized (emerging competencies of the data librarian), important (common to librarians in different roles) and not important. The objectives that had been set were:

- Understand the skills that require specialized training for the data librarian;
- Highlight the core skills that each librarian curriculum should propose.

The results of the questionnaire for the first macro-area of the support activities highlight as core skills in order of importance: cataloging (59%) including classifications and ontologies (28%), evaluation and selection of resources (28%) and preservation (28%). It is interesting to note that the management of research data (35%) is considered both a core competence and an emergent competence: librarians believe that the management of research data is part of the professional profile.

Technological skills are also considered important for all librarians. In particular, in order of importance we highlight: institutional repositories (35%), user experience (33%), interoperability (41%), semantic web (46%), information architecture (40%).

All management skills are considered important: research methods for user studies and service evaluation (50%), support for institutional services policies (49%), resource management (47%), legal aspects and ethical (42%), costs and business plans (39%). It is interesting to note that many librarians consider the business plan a specialist competence of the data librarian (44%). Even the organizational culture is a competence of common importance and considered fundamental: as an aptitude to work in a group (72%) and ability to network (68%), orientation to problem solving (68%), multiculturalism (55%).

Other skills that have been added by respondents concern aspects that had been neglected in the questionnaire such as: statistics, humanistic skills to understand the social value of research results, knowledge of international good practices, information literacy, empathy, ability to delegate and to ask questions if something is not known.

2 FAIR Research Data Management Summer School

The planning of the "Fair Research Data Management" Summer School in Parma began during a management meeting of the ROMOR Project in Brighton (16–18 January 2019) with an initial discussion of the learning objectives from the partner institutions. Since the Summer School would take place in the last year of the ROMOR project (http://romor.iugaza.edu.ps), the partners agreed on the dual objective of consolidating the knowledge of Open Access Institutional Repositories (OAIR) topics and developing the data stewards skills on more advanced topics. From the Stel-line

Seminars survey on learning needs and from documentary research, it was highlighted that currently no training offer is available in Italy on the management of research data. In agreement with the ROMOR Project coordinator, it was decided to open the Summer School also to external participants.

The purpose of this paper is to evaluate what has been done for the Italian participants and discuss how to improve the curriculum of the Summer School in the next experience.

2.1 Learning Objectives

In developing the Summer School program, there were some actions that had a prominent role, both as a process of self-learning of the Parma team and as an outcome of the ROMOR project (Awadallah et al. 2019), where the Parma team had the opportunity to collaborate with the most experienced European and Palestinian partners in the management of research outputs.

One of the first activities was an applied documentary research (benchmarking) on the teaching of "data management" and "FAIR principles", together with conversation with experts involved in teaching in ROMOR (Peter Burnhill, Janet and David Anderson, Susanna Mornati, Joseph Torn, Ilaria Fava, Marialaura Vignocchi, Marisol Occioni, Emma Lazzeri) and together with Paola Gargiulo, Elena Giglia: all of them allowed us to identify different education and training proposals on the management of research data, which was a key point for analysis of the needs and the planning phase of the program.

The broad context of the Summer School at the University of Parma covered the FAIR principles relating to interoperability and re-use of research data.

FAIR data are data which meet standards of findability, accessibility, interoperability, and reusability. The expected learning outcomes were:

– Planning a management campaign of research results
– Re-use of research data for the entire research life cycle.

2.2 Learning Material

The materials and the bibliography of the Summer School were selected from various sources: the reference materials of the previous training courses of the ROMOR Project and the presentations used for the lessons that were regularly taught. A variety of educational material has been used for the study schools, such as videos, links, documents to adhere to the learning objectives and the expected outcomes.

Copyright was taken into consideration, providing all the material that the students of the Summer School could be used in open access with a CC-By license. All teaching material was available from the FAIR RDM Study School website (http://fair-rdm. unipr.it).

2.3 Course Content

A combination of frontal and laboratory lessons has been planned. The first day was an introduction to the FAIR principles for the quality of research data together with a focus on the user of the data and the needs for re-use and interoperability. The second day was dedicated to the new generation of institutional repositories and OpenAire with practical exercises for evaluating different types of needs. The third day focused on the legal issues of copyright and privacy together with policy impact on the organization of support services. A "Data Carpentry" laboratory was planned and managed in collaboration with Data Carpentry team in the last two days (http://datacarpentry.org).

Other mobility activities included visits to the libraries of Italian Universities of Bologna and Venice (the latter visited virtually) to learn about the management of research data.

The final assignment (group activity) was based on the planning of an information website for accessing from a single point the support service for the management of research data.

The course structure is reported in the Appendix.

2.4   Selection of Participants

Data stewards are support staff and subject-specific experts and often have different skills and knowledge that they bring to the research data management team. However, this also means that data stewards may have varying degrees of understanding of general needs and expectations in the field of research and Open Science data management. However, the Summer School focused on an intensive training program on topics of common interest for different backgrounds.

The Summer School was planned for a total of 40 Palestinian participants and a maximum of 20 external participants. Meeting rooms and facilities have been planned based on the expected size of the class. Three tutors (Computer Engineering students with personal interest in the School topics) were also recruited to support laboratory activities, as recommended by the Data Carpentry laboratory methodology.

The criteria for the selection of the participants in the School of Study were the following. Staff and researchers from the Palestinian institutions affiliated with ROMOR were selected by the ROMOR partners based on their previous involvement in the project, the role within the university and their knowledge of OAIR issues.

The criteria for Italian candidates were based on their background and role (librarians, researchers, IT staff, etc.) declared in their online application, together with their motivation to participate. The applications were accepted according to the order of the applications received. The window for the application of participants remained open for 10 days.

A total of 63 qualified applications were received (40 Palestinian participants and 23 Italian participants). All candidates were admitted with an official invitation, as the total number was close to the maximum expected and all candidatures showed adequate motivation and background.

2.5   Attendance

The duration of the Summer School was 5 days, from 1 to 5 July 2019. Participation in the lessons was very constant, despite the hot temperature of the Italian summer and the very dense Summer school program. Participants enthusiastically participated in all the lessons, engaged in discussions, mixed in working groups, were stimulated to active and proactive interactions between them and with the teachers.

2.6   Institutional and Media Coverage

The Summer School was opened with a welcome speech by the Vice-Chancellor for Research of the University of Parma. In the coming days, it included brief statements by the Vice-Chancellor for International Relations and the Director of the Center for International Cooperation at the University of Parma.

The Summer School was advertised on the University of Parma website and in specialized mailing lists. The Summer School has also been marked with interviews, photos and articles from local newspapers and TV.

3   Summer School Final Evaluation

At the end of the Summer School, two types of assessment were carried out with the 63 participants with differentiated questionnaires for Palestinian participants and Italian participants.

All participants were asked to evaluate the general programme structure and organization of the contents on the various aspects of the Summer School to gather their opinions, as well as their advice for future editions of the School.

3.1   Evaluation of Summer School Programme

Many Italian participants declared that they were very satisfied with the open format of the School. As for the relevance of the contents, a great degree of satisfaction has been reported, which allows us to affirm that the topics have been well selected (Figs. 1 and 2).

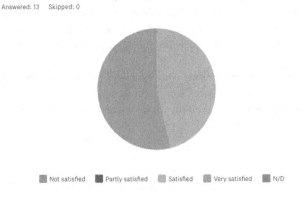

How do you rate the overall Summer School programme?

Answered: 13   Skipped: 0

Not satisfied   Partly satisfied   Satisfied   Very satisfied   N/D

Fig. 1. Satisfaction for the Summer School programme.

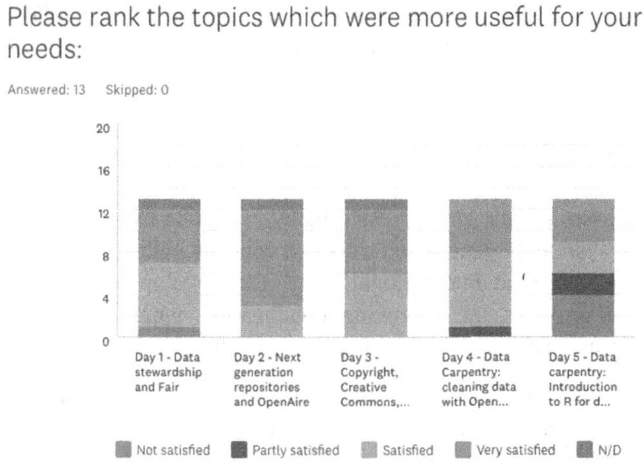

Please rank the topics which were more useful for your needs:

Answered: 13   Skipped: 0

Fig. 2. Satisfaction for the different topics of the Summer School.

The contents (Fig. 2) that received the highest satisfaction (69% very satisfied) were in the second day in the Next Generation repositories and OpenAire, together with the fourth day (60% satisfied) in Data Carpentry using Open Refine. Both of these sessions were based on practical exercises following a theoretical introduction.

The contents proposed in all other days of the Summer School satisfied on the average about 50% of the participants, including the Introduction to FAIR and Copyright and privacy.

Some problems can be noticed on the last day, devoted to the application of R, in which satisfaction fell to 24% and very satisfied to 31%, with 31% partially satisfied. This session was somehow more technical and perhaps not fully suitable for all attendees, in the short time available.

The Summer School organization received the highest percentage (70%) of satisfaction, together with classroom and accommodation (61%).

About the mastering of the subject by the speakers, 60% of the participants stated that they were very satisfied. The pedagogical approach of all the teachers and tutors was highly appreciated. Also the learning material obtained the following evaluation: very satisfied by 46% and satisfied by 36% of respondents, partly satisfied by 15% of respondents.

In general, it can be concluded that the School had many positive elements and that it can be repeated making some adjustments, mainly in the distinction between theory and practice.

Open comments and suggestions from participants include:

- *A more practical focus on the long term preservation of digital objects, with example of software and formats to be used.*
- *Other platforms and tools (open and free if possible) for data repository.*
- *More practical applications of RDM on a technical point of view, for instance through case studies, working groups and labs.*
- *Keep technical sessions separated from the rest of the training for those really interested in hands-on training.*

– *Software and tools for data management as lecture on a handful programmes focusing on the concept and tasks or assignment that those tools can accomplish.*

4 Conclusions

Courses with classes of this size generate many expectations in the participants, who can interact and share experiences and establish contacts with colleagues from different institutions at national and international level. The development of the FAIR RDM Summer School provides the following conclusions, which should be taken into account in other education and training projects of this style:

– The role of the data steward is truly *international*, with FAIR principles and homogeneous organizational criteria that can be applied to various contexts. The multicultural aspects of the Summer school were very gratifying, for both Palestinian and Italian participants.
– Another important aspect is the need to include *flexibility* in the programme. In a course open to participants with different backgrounds and from different institutions, the times, beyond their programming, should allow and give attendees the opportunity to develop assignments and do exercises at different times, although such an organization involves a greater demand for teachers and tutors.
– In a study school developed with different teachers and tutors there must be a permanent *communication and coordination* effort in order to guarantee homogeneity in delivering content and provide full support to participants.

Appendix

Data Stewardship and FAIR principles - Monday 1st July

9.30-11.00	*Welcome, Introduction to the Study School, Data stewardship core* Stefano Caselli, Anna Maria Tammaro, Janet and David Anderson
11.30–13.00	*Data Stewardship (1): Introduction and Overview of FAIR* Peter Burnhill
14.00–15.30	*Data Stewardship (2): Focus on the Data User. Provision for Access. Relationship to Articles, Books and Web resources* Peter Burnhill
15:30-16:30	*Group work* Group task and to be presented in class by end of the School

Next Generation repositories - Tuesday 2 July

9.30– 11.00	*Behaviours and Technical Recommendations of the COAR Next Generation Repositories Working Group - Part 1 - Behaviours* *Behaviours and Technical Recommendations of the COAR Next Generation Repositories Working Group - Part 2 - Technologies and Implementations* Susanna Mornati
11.30– 13.00	*OpenAIRE and RDA: community driven tools and support for research data access and reuse* Emma Lazzeri
14:00- 16:30	*Library system organisation for RDM: Visit to the University of Bologna* Marialaura Vignocchi

Copyright, CC and Privacy - Wednesday 3 July

9.30– 11.00	*Copyright, creative commons, privacy issues for research output management* Janet Anderson and David Anderson
11.30- 13.00	*Data stewardship (3). Use, preservation and citation of 'web resources': a look into the future* Peter Burnhill
14.00– 15:00	*Single point of entry: RDM management at University of Venice* Marisol Occioni (Videoconference)
15:00- 16.30	Group work

Data carpentry - Thursday-Friday 4–5 July

Data carpentry Laboratory and Group work
Marianne Corvellec, Nilani Ganeshwaran
Day 1:
9:30 am-1 pm : *Introduction to data, and best practices in using spreadsheets*
2 pm-4:30 pm : *Cleaning data with Openrefine*
Day 2:
9:30 am - 1 pm : *Introduction to R for data analysis*
2 pm - 4:30 pm : *Using R for data visualization and generating reports*

References

ARL: Strategic Thinking + Design Initiative report (2015). https://www.arl.org/wp-content/uploads/2015/02/strategic-thinking-design-full-report-aug2014.pdf

Awadallah, R., et al.: Setting Up Open Access Repositories: Challenges and Lessons from Palestine, iPRES, Amsterdam (2019)

Borgman, C.: Big Data, Little Data, No Data: Scholarship in the Networked World. MIT Press, Cambridge (2015)

Corrall, S.: Roles and responsibilities: libraries, librarians and data. In: Pryor, G. (ed.) Managing Research Data, pp. 105–133. Facet, London (2012)

Mons, B.: Data Stewardship for Open Science: Implementing FAIR Principles. CRC Press Taylor and Francis Group, London, New York (2018)

Tammaro, A.M.: Una proposta non sovversiva. Biblioteche oggi **36**, 65–71 (2018)

Tammaro, A.M., Matusiak, K., Sposito, A., Casarosa, V.: Data curator's roles and responsibilities: an international perspective. Libri **69**(2), 89–104 (2019)

Creating Digital Cultural Heritage with Open Data: From *FAIR* to *FAIR^5* Principles

Nicola Barbuti$^{(\boxtimes)}$

Department of Humanities (DISUM), University of Bari Aldo Moro, Bari, Italy
nicola.barbuti@uniba.it

Abstract. The Art. 2 of the *EU Council Conclusions of 21 May 2014 on cultural heritage as a strategic resource for a sustainable Europe* (2014/C 183/08) states the existence of the new Digital Cultural Heritage (born digital and digitized). Starting from this assumption, we must rethink digitization, digitalization and digital transformation as recording and representing the processes of contemporary life cycles, no longer as simple tools to improve access to reality. So, we must define clear and homogeneous criteria to validate and certify what among contemporary digital magma we can identify as Digital Cultural Heritage (DCH). This paper outlines a proposal in such way starting from the extension of the *R: Reusable* requirement of *FAIR Principles* to *R^5* adding the requirements: *Readable, Relevant, Reliable and Resilient*. These requirements should lead the design and creation of descriptive metadata in open format for indexing and managing digital cultural resources. The *Terra delle Gravine between sharing economy and experiential tourism* project was a case study for testing this proposal. Three digital libraries of the municipal libraries of Massafra, Mottola and Grottaglie were designed and implemented by creating an open data schema for indexing and describing the digital resources.

Keywords: Digital Cultural Heritage · Born digital · Digitization · R^5 · Reusable · Readable · Relevant · Reliable · Resilient · Metadati descrittivi

1 Introduction

The art. 2 of EU *Council Conclusions of 21 may 2014 on Cultural Heritage as a Strategic Resource for a Sustainable Europe (2014/C 183/08)* states:

> *"cultural heritage consists of the resources inherited from the past in all forms and aspects - tangible, intangible and digital (born digital and digitized), including monuments, sites, landscapes, skills, practices, knowledge and expressions of human creativity, as well as collections conserved and managed by public and private bodies such as museums, libraries and archive"*.[1]

Starting by this assumption, we must necessarily change our approach to digital and digitalization starting to consider them representations that identify the digital transformation that characterizes the contemporary age. So, we need to identify and classify

---

[1] https://eur-lex.europa.eu/legal-content/EN/TXT/?uri=CELEX%3A52014XG0614%2808%29.

© Springer Nature Switzerland AG 2020
M. Ceci et al. (Eds.): IRCDL 2020, CCIS 1177, pp. 173–181, 2020.
https://doi.org/10.1007/978-3-030-39905-4_17

among the massive digital resources we produce, either they are single computational artefact or complex digital libraries or 3D systems, those that we can recognize as the new Digital Cultural Heritage (DCH).

However, the current approach to digital creation does not concern the evolution of digitization, which today has become a complex process driven by defined and shared rules. The quality of the digital data is also completely undervalued in relegating their function to mere mediation tools for fostering the fruition of analogical artefact by their virtual representation. This instrumental use still negatively direct the creation of digital data and, above all, the structuring of metadata schemes for indexing digital artefacts and of their composition and descriptions of elements, that are formulated as merely codes for searching and retrieving data on the web. On the contrary, we should identify the digital data as records by recognizing the transformation of their function linked to their reuse over time, giving them some essential requirements for their sustainability.

Therefore, the metadata and descriptions associated with them needs to be focused with special care, since they are the only source that can record and represent in an intelligible way the digitization, digitalization and digital transformation processes that characterize the data life cycle, and to preserve the information necessary to know them and qualify them as digital resources with cultural functions for future generations.

The essential function of metadata for the management and use of digital data is the focus of the *FAIR Guiding Principles for Scientific Data Management and Steward-ship*[2], the guidelines for the management of scientific data published in 2016. This is one of the major topics interest in the wider debate on the possibility to apply *data science* methodologies to the creation and management of *data humanities*[3].

A workshop on the effectiveness of the *FAIR Principles* with regard both to the scenarios that digitization today poses, and that are already imminent was held at the CIDOC Conference 2018[4]. This paper summarizes some reflections matured by that fruitful comparison, related to the need to provide for an extension of the requirement *R: Reusable* of the *FAIR* to the requirements R^5: *Reusable, Readable, Relevant, Reliable and Resilient*. This extension aims to facilitate the applicability of the *Principles* to data humanities and, consequently, to foster the identification and certification as Digital Cultural Heritage of the data meeting these requirements in the formless digital magma in which today we float.

2   From *FAIR* to *FAIR*^{5}

The starting assumption of this reflection is that digital data are *records*, that is: *Digital data are dynamic and diachronic resources that record and preserve in their composition and descriptions the processes of their creation and the information about their life cycle.*

---

[2] https://www.go-fair.org/fair-principles/.

[3] https://www.rd-alliance.org/open-consultation-fair-data-humanities-until-15th-july-2019; https://www.go-fair.org/implementation-networks/overview/co-operas/; https://operas.hypotheses.org/.

[4] http://www.cidoc2018.com/sites/default/files/CIDOC2018-BookOfAbstracts-Final-v-1-2.pdf.

Therefore, descriptive metadata become fundamental and inseparable for full identification and intelligibility of digital artefacts, since the accuracy and quality of their descriptions qualify them as *records* and make them digital resources designed and created for diachronic use and reuse by both contemporary and future users, and all of them should understand what the data represents.

We think that an approach to *data humanities* adopting the *FAIR Principles* in their state of the art has some issue. First of all, we are not entirely convinced that *Findability*, *Accessibility* (this one absolutely cannot be identified with *Open*) and *Interoperability* are suitable requirements to qualify metadata and data as *records* and digital resources.

A findable, accessible and interoperable data does not provide any guarantee of quality, completeness and reliability of the information that it contains. Moreover, the *findability* and, consequently, the *accessibility* and *interoperability* that originate by the one, mean when a data interests the users. The interest in a data is today strictly linked not to its function as access key to a simple or complex digital artefact, but to its role of cognitive and informational resource due to the correct quantity and quality of descriptive contents of metadata that it provides to users.

We think that the *FAIR* requirement that give meaning to first three, and by which those depend, is *Reusability*. The non-stop use and reuse of data are the requirements that guarantee their sustainability over time and, therefore, their survival, as *Reusability* is characterized by dynamism and diachrony which imply transformations of the functions of digital artefacts: to get an idea using an analogical paradigm, we have to think to Coliseum and to its life cycle.

The descriptive metadata become essential to guarantee quality and persistence of digital resources, when their contents are based on balanced quantitative/qualitative relation and respond to further requirements which, in our opinion, are just as essential as *Reusability*. In fact, this one does not constitute in itself a guarantee of the quality of data and of their value as information and cognitive resource. Indeed, the variability of data due to their reuse could become a cause for distortion and discrepancy of the contents, whose informative and cognitive value can therefore no longer be certified as *reliable*.

So, we propose to extend the *R* of *Reusable* into R^5 by adding the following requirements:

- *Readability*: this has not the semantic meaning of *legibility*, but the conceptual one of *intelligibility* of digital data for all the possible user targets who are interested in using them; this requirement is based on the well-balanced quantitative/qualitative relation among the descriptive metadata elements and formal, stylistic and linguistic accuracy of their content, and it is essential for giving metadata the informative and cognitive functions needed to qualify them as *records* and *cultural resource*;

– *Relevance*: this requirement is linked to users interest for the informational and cognitive contents recorded in the metadata; it is closely linked to reuse and to the functional transformations of data recorded in the descriptions over time; therefore, this requirement is indispensable so that we can recognize and identify the form and descriptive structure of data usually created with no cultural purposes even when their functions vary over time, evolving them into a source of knowledge about the processes recorded in descriptions and, therefore, in Digital Cultural resources;
– *Reliablility*: this requirement is related to the quality certification and validation of digital resources detected by their recorded descriptions throughout their life cycle, as related to all the functional transformations they can have; therefore, it is closely connected to recording and preserving in metadata descriptions the contents which can guarantee their informative and cognitive quality, also in the variation and evolution of their functions and forms over time;
– *Resilience*: this is a fundamental requisite for giving digital resources the new cultural dimension; stating the definition commonly used in information technology[5], it is *"the ability of a digital resource to adapt to use and reuse, to resist wear, to be flexible in case of transformation or evolution of its functions, in order to guarantee its cognitive and informative potential over time"*; therefore, it is indispensable to guarantee the sustainability and reuse of digital resources in the long term, providing to preserve both the information useful to know the processes of their creation, and those on their original function, and, finally, the recordings of functional transformation and evolution that characterized their life cycle.

The *Terra delle Gravine* project for creation of digital libraries in open data, below illustrated, has been the case study to test application of R^5 requirements in drafting descriptive metadata.

3 The *Terra delle Gravine* Project

Terra delle Gravine tra sharing economy e turismo esperienziale[6] is a project for creation of digital libraries of different kind of cultural heritage carried out in 2018 by a consortium of twelve municipalities in land of Taranto, Puglia, thanks to a grant from the Regione Puglia.

As project activities, D.A.BI.MUS. Ltd. and the Department of Humanities – DISUM of University of Bari Aldo Moro carried out the design and implementation of three digital libraries in open data for enhancement of book collection preserved in the libraries of the Municipalities of Massafra, Mottola and Grottaglie.

The metadata schema and datasets were designed referring to national standard of ICCU and ICCD and according to the schema defined for the national project *dati.gov*.

---

[5] https://it.wikipedia.org/wiki/Resilienza.

[6] https://terradellegravineprogettazioneperlacultura.wordpress.com/il-progetto/.

it^7 and by the Regione Puglia for its *Puglia Digital Library*[8]. The project engaged the students of some high schools of the three Municipalities in creation of contents related to the original resources treated to fill descriptive metadata elements.

Previously, students were trained on:

– methods and techniques for cataloguing and for digital description of books;
– open data ontologies and metadata standards used by ICCD[9] and ICCU[10] for their digitization projects;
– methods and techniques for structuring metadata schema using open data.

Then, the students were engaged in the creation of metadata schema for description of both original books and of the digital objects produced by their scanning.

The activities included the following phases:

1. transferring to students know-how for creation of metadata schema in open data;
2. supporting the students for design and creation of their metadata schema in open data following rules and standards used at national and regional level;
3. creating cataloguing contents and inserting descriptions within metadata elements;
4. editing digital libraries on CKAN platform.

The monitoring of project progress and interaction with student teams was achieved by activating specific groups through *Telegram* messaging app, that is fast, secure, simple and free.

The digital libraries with their open data and descriptions are currently published on the regional platform *Terra delle Gravine*[11] and on the national platform *dati.gov*[12].

4   Designing Digital Libraries in Open Data for Creation of DCH

The open data schema used for indexing the digital resources was developed integrating and rationalizing elements extracted by ICCU and ICCD metadata standards. The descriptive contents were elaborated according to R^5 requirements with the aim to create digital resources that can be identified as DCH.

To this goal, we preferred to distinguish the descriptive metadata relating to the digital objects from cataloguing descriptions of the books reproduced in the images carried out by the scanning.

We used elements of Dublin Core[13] standard for descriptive section both of the books reproduced and of the digital objects, integrated with elements taken from other

---

[7] https://www.dati.gov.it/.

[8] http://www.dataset.puglia.it/.

[9] http://dati.beniculturali.it/altre-ontologie-utilizzate/.

[10] http://dati.culturaitalia.it/.

[11] http://www.terradellegravine.eu:3389/dataset.

[12] https://www.dati.gov.it/dataset/digital-library-biblioteca-comunale-comune-massafra; https://www.dati.gov.it/dataset/digital-library-biblioteca-comune-mottola; https://www.dati.gov.it/dataset/digital-library-biblioteca-comunale-comune-grottaglie.

[13] https://www.dublincore.org/resources/glossary/application_profile/.

standards, in particular as reported in the rules defined by the ICCU for *Cultura Italia* project. Some other elements were taken from the ontologies of the ICCD Linked Open Data project, in order to create a schema that represents both the full process of creation and the life cycle of each digital resource integrating the R^5 requirements necessary to validate them as digital cultural entities.

The sequence of elements was organized focusing on the goal to provide information as intelligible as possible to both user operators in charge of entering descriptions in each element, and to any future users who, accessing to the metadata, will look for information on the creation process and on the life cycle of the digital resource they managed.

As an example of the solution used for the three digital libraries, the DL layout of the Municipality of Massafra is reported as Table 1.

The correct format in XLS or CSV can be viewed online at the *URL* indicated in the above note to the text.

The project is currently undergoing and open data sustainability is constantly monitoring to define, by this way, if digital resources can effectively maintain the requirements that allow their identification as Digital Cultural Heritage in their diachronic evolution.

Table 1. Digital Library Biblioteca Comunale di Massafra – Open Data schema

Titolo della risorsa digitale	Identificativo risorsa digitale	Genere risorsa digitale	Livello di descrizione	Soggetto responsabile della digitalizzazione	Stato della digitalizzazione	Progetto di digitalizzazione	Descrizione risorsa digitale	Genere_1	Argomento_1	Argomento_2	Argomento_3
P. Catucci, Massafra sue epigrafi, Tecnografica 1986	TA0012_M_00001	Text	Monografia	Biblioteca Comunale di Massafra	In corso	Terra delle Gravine		DigitalObject	Storia e monumenti		
F. Ladiana, La pietra della fame, Stampa Sud 1984	TA0012_M_00002	Text	Monografia	Biblioteca Comunale di Massafra	In corso	Terra delle Gravine		DigitalObject	Massafra - stroria 1901-1922		
C. D. Fonseca, comprensorio civiltà rupestre, Stampa Sud (1985?!)	TA0012_M_00003	Text	Monografia	Biblioteca Comunale di Massafra	In corso	Terra delle Gravine		DigitalObject	Massafra - cultura e storia		
P. Ladiana, Uomini, fatti e cose della vecchia Massafra,Tipolitografia B.M. s.n.c. - Massafra 1995	TA0012_M_00004	Text	Monografia	Biblioteca Comunale di Massafra	In corso	Terra delle Gravine		DigitalObject	Massafra - cultura e storia		

Categoria_1	Categoria_2	Titolo della risorsa analogica rappresentata	Autore	Contributore_1	Contributore_2	Contributore_3
Libro a stampa	Libro moderno	Massafra e le sue epigrafi – fra cronaca e storia -	Paolo Catucci			
Libro a stampa	Libro moderno	La pietra della fame - Massafra/ borghesia e popolo tra ottocento e novecento	Fernando Ladiana			
Libro a stampa	Libro moderno	Il comprensorio della civiltà rupestre	Cosimo Damiano Fonseca			
Libro a stampa	Libro moderno	Uomini, fatti e cose della vecchia Massafra	Paolo Ladiana	Vito Serio		

(continued)

Table 1. *(continued)*

Data	Editore e Luogo di edizione	Descrizione fisica	Soggetto_1	Soggetto_2	Soggetto_3	Note	Genere risorsa analogica	Materiale	Localizzazione logica della risorsa analogica
1986	Tecnografica, Massafra	247 pag ; 25 cm	Storia-Monumenti-Massafra	Storia-Personaggi Illustri-Massafra		In calce al front.: Amministrazione Comunale di Massafra, Assessorato alla Cultura	PhysicalObject	Carta	Biblioteca Massafra CRSEC TA/50 I B 16
1984	STAMPASUD Posa, Mottola	219 pag. ill ; 26 cm	Massafra	Storia		In calce al front.: Regione Puglia Assessorato alla Cultura C.S.P.C.R. Massafra	PhysicalObject	Carta	Biblioteca Massafra CRSEC TA/50 I B 09
1985 (?!)	STAMPASUD Posa, Mottola	91 pag. ill ; 29 cm	Massafra	Insediamenti rupresti - Massafra		In calce al front.: Regione Puglia Assessorato alla Cultura C. S. P. C. R. Massafra	PhysicalObject	Carta	Biblioteca Massafra XV 4 21
1995	Tipolitografia B.M. s.n.c., Massafra	241 pag. ill ; 24 cm	Massafra	Monumenti e personaggi			PhysicalObject	Carta	Biblioteca Massafra XVII B 6

Thesaurus PICO 4.3_1	Thesaurus PICO 4.3_2	Descrizione del contenuto	Lingua	Ambito cronologico	Soggetto conservatore
http://www.culturaitalia.it/pico/thesaurus/4.3/thesaurus_4.3.0.s kos.xml#http://culturaitalia.it/pico/thesaurus/4.2#libri		Testimonianze degli avvenimenti che le epigrafi ricordano: un richiamo alla conservazione della memoria storica, di cui gli studiosi locali, come l'autore, sono con la loro opera diligente e appassionata, i vigili custodi.	Ita	decennio 1980 - 1986	Biblioteca comunale-Paolo Catucci-Massafra
http://www.culturaitalia.it/pico/thesaurus/4.3/thesaurus_4.3.0.s kos.xml#http://culturaitalia.it/pico/thesaurus/4.2#libri		Il volume racconta la drammatica realtà vissuta della popolazione massafrese negli anni a cavallo tra i due secoli (dalla fine dell' Ottocento all'avvento del Fascismo) , quando la fame, la miseria è l'incertezza occupazionale erano dominanti. Addirittura c'era chi, durante un breve intervallo di lavoro nei campi non aveva non un tozzo di pane per colazione e si appartava per la vergogna, nascondendo nel suo fazzoletto una pietra per camuffare il desco : La pietra della fame	Ita	decennio 1980 - 1984	Biblioteca comunale - Paolo Catucci - Massafra
http://www.culturaitalia.it/pico/thesaurus/4.3/thesaurus_4.3.0.s kos.xml#http://culturaitalia.it/pico/thesaurus/4.2#libri		Tra gli aspetti specifici e per tanti versi appariscenti che definiscono l'identità categoriale della "Pugliesità" e senza alcun dubbio quella della " Vita in Grotte", ormai entrata in pieno titolo nella letteratura storica, dopo gli studi del prof. Cosimo Damiano Fonseca, con il suggestivo nome di "Civiltà Rupestre". Infatti l'elemento di continuità che lega dalla preistoria all'età moderna la vita delle popolazioni pugliesi è la pietra: dal Gargano allo Ionico, dalla Linea Ofantina sino al Salento, pur con differenti tipologie, l'escavazione degli invasi grottali si ripete con una impressionante seriazione.	Ita		Biblioteca comunale - Paolo Catucci - Massafra
http://www.culturaitalia.it/pico/thesaurus/4.3/thesaurus_4.3.0.s kos.xml#http://culturaitalia.it/pico/thesaurus/4.2#libri		Raccolta del materiale dove vede protagonisti monumenti e personaggi della vecchia Massafra, distretto diocesano con i suoi vescovi e con il suo clero e le chiese.	Ita	1500-1950	Biblioteca comunale - Paolo Catucci - Massafra

Regione	Provincia	Comune	Indirizzo	Latitudine	Longitudine	Formato della risorsa digitale pubblicata	Data e ora di creazione della risorsa digitale	Dimensioni della risorsa digitale	Profilo ICC	Profondità di colore	Livello qualitativo	MIME Type
Puglia	Taranto	Massafra	Via Lopizzo n.38	40.58711	17.11152							
Puglia	Taranto	Massafra	Via Lopizzo n.38	40.58711	17.11152							
Puglia	Taranto	Massafra	Via Lopizzo n.38	40.58711	17.11152							
Puglia	Taranto	Massafra	Via Lopizzo n.38	40.58711	17.11152							

Accessibilità	Direzione di lettura	Numero di immagini	Sequenza delle pagine	Versione SW di produzione	Detentore dei diritti della risorsa digitale	Licenza per la risorsa digitale	Collezione digitale	Identificativo collezione digitale	Scheda Puglia Digital Library
Uso pubblico	Sinistra - Destra	1	Da 1 a 247						
Uso pubblico	Sinistra - Destra	76	Da 1 a 219						
Uso pubblico	Sinistra - Destra		Da 1 a 91						
Uso pubblico	Sinistra - Destra	30	Da 6 a 249						

5   Conclusions

The adoption of the *FAIR Principles* requirements with the extended R in R^5 is an indispensable prerequisite for the creation of digital resources and their metadata, to characterize them as the new DCH by making them sustainable, permanent, reliable, resilient sources of knowledge about process and transformations that characterize their evolution over time.

Not the data itself, in fact, but the interest of present and future users in the data as informative and cognitive resources must become the assumption on which we have to base the entire process of design, creation, publication and preservation of digital cultural entities. Therefore, we must focus on the application of the R^5 requirements already from the analysis and design phase of both digitization and of creation of metadata schema for indexing and managing digital objects.

By this way, the identification of DCH among the massive data that today overlaps in the web can start in the medium term and, at the same time, homogeneous and shared guidelines for the creation of digital resources can be defined having clear from the beginning how we can give them the value of cultural entities.

We think this is the way to create and recognize over few years the DCH as defined by the 2014 EU *Conclusions*. Otherwise, we will continue to consider digitization, digitalization and digital transformation only as different and captivating instruments for enjoy the tangible and intangible heritage, losing sight that all of them are already today the humus that, at different levels, identifies the contemporary Digital Age.

References

1. https://www.go-fair.org/fair-principles/
2. https://www.go-fair.org/implementation-networks/overview/co-operas/
3. https://operas.hypotheses.org/
4. http://www.unesco.org/new/fileadmin/MULTIMEDIA/HQ/CI/CI/pdf/mow/unesco_ubc_vancouver_declaration_en.pdf
5. https://eur-lex.europa.eu/legal-content/EN/TXT/?uri=CELEX%3A52014XG0614%2808%29
6. http://www.interpares.org/
7. Agenzia per l'Italia Digitale (AgID), Presidenza del Consiglio dei Ministri, Linee guida sulla conservazione dei documenti informatici, Versione 1.0, p. 45, dicembre 2015. http://www.agid.gov.it/sites/default/files/linee_guida/la_conservazione_dei_documenti_informatici_rev_def.pdf
8. Bailey, L.: Digital Orphans: The Massive Cultural Black Hole on Our Horizon, Techdirt, 13th October 2015. https://www.techdirt.com/articles/20151009/17031332490/digitalorphans-massive-cultural-blackhole-our-horizon.shtml
9. Barbuti, N.: Le nuove entità culturali digitali tra Intangible Cultural Heritage e Patrimonio Culturale Immateriale, in the Creative Network – Conferenza GARR, Firenze, 30 novembre–02 dicembre 2016 (2016). https://www.eventi.garr.it/it/conf16/home/materiali-conferenza-2016/paper/19-conf2016-paper-barbuti/file
10. Barbuti, N.: Dalla Digital Culture al Digital Cultural Heritage: l'evoluzione impossibile? In AIUCD 2017 Conference – Book of Abstract. Il telescopio inverso: big data e distant reading nelle discipline umanistiche, pp. 14–17. AIUCD (2017). http://aiucd2017.aiucd.it/wp-content/uploads/2017/01/book-of-abstract-AIUCD-2017.pdf

11. Barbuti, N.: Niente memoria, niente storia. Conservare le Digital Libraries oggi per co-creare il Digital Cultural Heritage di domani, IRCDL (2017)
12. Barbuti, N., Marinucci, L.: Dal Digital Cultural Heritage alla Digital Culture. Evoluzioni nelle Digital Humanities, DH 2018 (2018). https://dh2018.adho.org/dal-digital-cultural-heritage-alla-digital-culture-evoluzioni-nelle-digital-humanities/S. Cosimi, Vint Cerf: ci aspetta un deserto digitale, Wired.it, 16 febbraio 2015. http://www.wired.it/attualita/2015/02/16/vint-cerf-futuro-medievale-bit-putrefatti/
13. Daga, E., Isaksen, L.: Proceedings of the 1st Workshop on Humanities in the Semantic Web, co-located with 13th ESWC Conference 2016 (ESWC 2016), Anissaras, Greece, 29th May 2016 (2016). http://ceur-ws.org/Vol-1608/paper-05.pdf
14. Duranti, L., Shaffer, E. (ed.): The memory of the world in the digital age: digitization and preservation. In: An International Conference on Permanent Access to Digital Documentary Heritage, UNESCO Conference Proceedings, Vancouver, 26–28 September 2012 (2012). http://ciscra.org/docs/UNESCO_MOW2012_Proceedings_FINAL_ENG_Compressed.pdf
15. Gambetta, V.: La conservazione della memoria digitale, [Rubano], Siav (2009)
16. Guercio, M.: Gli archivi come depositi di memorie digitali, "Digitalia", Anno III, n. 2, ICCU Roma, pp. 37–53 (2008)
17. Guercio, M.: Conservare il digitale. Principi, metodi e procedure per la conservazione a lungo termine di documenti digitali. Roma-Bari, Laterza (2013)
18. Joint Steering Committee for Development of RDA. Resource Description and Access (RDA) (2015). http://www.iccu.sbn.it/opencms/export/sites/iccu/documenti/2015/RDA_Traduzione_ICCU_5_Novembre_REV.pdf
19. Kool, W., Lavoie, B., van der Werf, T.: Preservation Health Check: Monitoring Threats to Digital Repository Content. OCLC Research, Dublin (Ohio) (2014). http://www.oclc.org/content/dam/research/publications/library/2014/oclcresearch-preservation-health-check-2014.pdf
20. Lavoie, B., Gartner, R.: Preservation Metadata, 2nd edn. DPC Technology Watch Report, DPC Technology Watch Series, 03 May 2013. http://www.dpconline.org/docman/technology-watch-reports/894-dpctw13-03/file
21. Library of Congress, PREMIS – Preservation Metadata: Implementation Strategies, v. 3.0. http://www.loc.gov/standards/premis/v3/premis-3-0-final.pdf
22. Marzano, G.: Conservare il digitale. Metodi, norme, tecnologie. Editrice Bibliografica, Milano (2011)
23. OCLC. PREMIS (PREservation Metadata: Implementation Strategies) Working Group (2005). http://www.oclc.org/research/projects/pmwg/
24. Sustainable Economics for a Digital Planet: Ensuring Long-Term Access to Digital Information, Final Report of the Blue Ribbon Task Force on Sustainable Digital Preservation and Access (F. Berman and B. Lavoie, co-chairs), La Jolla, February 2010. http://brtf.sdsc.edu/biblio/BRTF_Final_Report.pdf

Nanocitation: Complete and Interoperable Citations of Nanopublications

Erika Fabris[1][(✉)] [ID], Tobias Kuhn[2] [ID], and Gianmaria Silvello[1] [ID]

[1] Department of Information Engineering, University of Padua, Padua, Italy
{erika.fabris,gianmaria.silvello}@unipd.it
[2] Department of Computer Science, VU University Amsterdam,
Amsterdam, The Netherlands
t.kuhn@vu.nl

Abstract. Nanopublication is a data publishing model which has a great potential for the representation of scientific results allowing interoperability, data integration and exchange of scientific findings. But this model suffer of the lack of an appropriate standard methodology to produce complete and interoperable citations providing both data identification and access. In this paper we introduce *nanocitation*, a framework to automatically get human-readable text-snippet snippet and machine-readable citations of nanopublications.

Keywords: Nanopublication · Data citation · DisGeNET

1 Introduction

We have recently witnessed a transition to the data-intensive scientific research paradigm – i.e. the fourth paradigm [8] of science – which led to a change in the nature of scientific discovery and publication. This paradigm shift has made it necessary to adapt the infrastructure for managing the growing amount of scientific data, led to the definition and adoption of open access policies for the access to scholarly data, to new concepts of data scholarship [3] and sanctioned the transition to data-intensive research where data are as essential as scientific publications [8].

One of the grand challenges of data-intensive science is to ease knowledge discovery, evaluation, propagation and reuse. To this end, international initiatives together with academia, industry and publishers designed the so-called

The full paper was presented at TPDL 2019 [5].

The work was partially funded by the "Computational Data Citation" (CDC) STARS-StG project of the University of Padua. The work was also partially funded by the EXAMODE (contract n. 825292) part of the H2020-ICT-2018-2 call of the European Commission.

M. Ceci et al. (Eds.): IRCDL 2020, CCIS 1177, pp. 182–187, 2020.
https://doi.org/10.1007/978-3-030-39905-4_18

FAIR (Findability, Accessibility, Interoperability and Reusability) principles to be followed when producing and storing data.

In this scenario, the nanopublication model has been proposed as a means to represent and publish individual scientific claims or statements together with their provenance specification and publication information. This model allows individual scientific results to be uniquely identifiable, accessible, attributable, citable and reusable [7,11].

Alongside the improvement of scientific data management and infrastructure, another problem has gained importance: data citation [15]. Citations are one of the main "driving force" for scientific progress and, since data has gained the same scholarly status of traditional publications, even data citation has become a "driving force" for scientific progress as well. Data citation is central to enable: (i) credit attribution to database creators and curators not only to papers authors; (ii) connection between scientific papers and used data; (iii) identifiability, reachability and accessibility of data; (iv) knowledge sharing and propagation; (v) evaluation of the impact of the data; (vi) reproducibility of the experiments. To date, two are the facets of data citation which have been studied: the definition of data citation principles and the development of solutions for computational problems related to the automatic or semi-automatic generation of citations. Two main international initiatives (CODATA [1] and FORCE 11 [6]) have defined core principles and criteria for data citation which are: (i) through the citation data should be identifiable on variable granularity; (ii) both citation metadata and cited data should be persistent and accessible; (iii) every citation should come with a citation reference (text-snippet) which describes the cited data and should be complete enough to attribute credit and to interpret the data content; (iv) citations should be flexible and both machine- and human-readable. Moreover, data citation and the design of systems for the automatic creation of data references are considered a computational problem [4]. Some solutions to automatically generate data citations have been proposed in the literature, mostly to create citations of subsets of relational and graph databases [14,16].

Nevertheless, up to now there is no automatic solution to create complete, consistent, interoperable textual citations to single nanopublications. Thus, we introduce a framework to automatically create a citation text-snippet and a machine-readable citation given a single nanopublication and a landing page where all the information within the nanopublication is shown to the user.

The rest of the paper is organized as follows: Sect. 2 introduces the concept of nanopublication, Sect. 3 presents the *nanocitation* framework to obtain citation of a single nanopublication and Sect. 4 draws some conclusions and presents an outlook to future work.

2 Background

A nanopublication is a granular-level publication containing an individual scientific claim (an atomic statement in the form of subject-predicate-object, e.g. *malaria is transmitted by mosquitoes* together with its provenance (its origin and generation process) and publication information.

The nanopublication model makes use of Linked Data W3Cs Resource Description Framework(RDF) specification representing its contents (scientific statement, provenance and publication information) within three graphs in the form of RDF triples (two entities/resources with a certain relation) where each element or ontology term is represented through an Internationalized Resource Identifier (IRI). The potential of the nanopublication model is that each scientific claim can be individually represented, linked to its evidence and can be independently addressed allowing fine-grained citation metrics on the level of individual claims and enable article-data connections [7].

Today, over 10M nanopublications are freely accessible and hosted on a nanopublication network[1] [9] and other 200M are available as independent private datasets. Published nanopublications represent data and scientific claims extracted from datasets from several domains, mostly from Life Science domain dataset including DisGeNET [13], neXtProt [10] and WikiPathways [12], but also smaller nanopublication datasets from digital humanities domain (philosophy, archaeology and music) have published.

Nowadays all the solutions to cite nanopublications (through their identifiers or citing the data papers or the whole dataset where they are stored) guarantee only up to two data citation requirements, i.e. the accessibility of data and persistence of data. But these solutions do not guarantee completeness and interoperability requirements, they do not provide necessary information or provide partial information to attribute the credit to all contributors nor provide content information as well as they raise up issues about the loss of specificity. We tackle these problems by proposing a citation framework which meets all the citation criteria.

3   The Nanocitation Framework

We design *nanocitation*, a framework to automatically obtain citations of nanopublications as illustrated in Fig. 1. This framework concerns the creation of citations for single nanopublications (see violet and blue components in Fig. 1).

The nanocitation framework is composed of four main components, as input it receives the identifier of the nanopublication to be cited (i.e. the URI) and a set of citation policies and produces three outputs:

1. a text-snippet citation to be included in reference lists;
2. the nanopublication citation metadata in machine-readable formats (i.e. XML and JSON);
3. a landing page where the user can explore the content of the nanopublication in a human-readable form.

Dereferencing and Enrichment – The first module of the framework aims at dereferencing all the identifiers of the resources and entities within the nanopublication RDF triples of the nanopublication and aims at searching for all the

---
[1] http://npmonitor.inn.ac/ accessed on 09/25/2019.

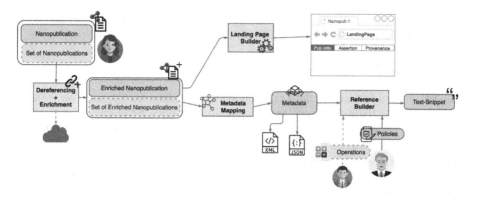

Fig. 1. Framework schema for nanopublication citation. Violet and blue nodes represents the components involved in citation creation, whereas green and blue nodes concern citation creation for a set of nanopublications. (Color figure online)

relevant information related to them from external sources. At the end of the process, the module produces a human-readable and enriched version of the nanopublication, i.e. the *enriched nanopublication*.

Metadata Mapping – Human-readable information within the enriched nanopublication are structured as metadata. For data citation, several metadata formats are proposed by the literature. The most recent and widely recognized metadata format for citing data, DataCite [2] needs to be extended in order to represent the nanopublication citation metadata since several data within the enriched nanopublication do not find any correspondent metadata fields and some metadata fields would need to be overloaded. Thus, we define the semantics and constraint of the metadata by defining an *ad-hoc* metadata schema as a Dublin Core Application Profile. Once the metadata has been created, this can be used as a machine-readable serialization of the content of the nanopublication.

Reference Builder – The reference builder module performs the creation of the citation text-snippet according to some citation policies, which has to be defined by the database administrator in the form of selection, ordering of the fields of the metadata and fields operations (e.g. concatenation).

Landing Page Builder – Moreover, the enriched nanopublication is the input of the landing page builder component which is employed to create the landing page. The landing page is provided to the user to better and fully explore the content of the nanopublication. Through the landing page the user can browse all the content information and, throughout provided links, get to the original sources used to build the nanopublication. The landing page provides a user-friendly interface and human-readable visualization of the complete and specific information about the nanopublication together with the possibility to get the machine-readable form of the landing page content and citation serialization.

We implemented the *nanocitation* framework as a web application freely accessible at nanocitation.dei.unipd.it and we provide also a RESTful API which enables programmatic requests of text-snippet citations, landing pages and citation metadata serializations in JSON and XML format.

4   Discussion

The requirements which a data citation system has to meet: (i) identification of the cited data; (ii) persistence and accessibility of both cited data and citation metadata; (iii) complete and understandable citation text-snippet; (iv) interoperability of the citation in both human- and machine-readable format. Unlike existing solutions to cite nanopublications, our framework satisfies all the above requirements. The identification of the nanopublication is guaranteed by its unique identifier which is reported in the landing page, in the citation metadata and text-snippet. The data is persistent due to the nature of the nanopublication and by the nanopublication network and specification [9], besides, the citation is persistent due to the one-to-one correlation between a given nanopublication and its citation metadata and landing page (a nanopublication is always associated to the same metadata). Moreover, the citation completeness is guaranteed by the presence of all the information relative to the nanopublication in the citation metadata as well as in the landing page, which provides all the information needed to attribute the credit to whom was committed to the creation of the nanopublication and its scientific claim. Furthermore, the human- and machine-readable citations provided as outputs of the framework ensure the interoperability requirements.

To date, our implementation of the framework allows a user to cite single nanopublications, but we are committed to extending the framework to handle the creation of citations of sets/aggregations of nanopublications. Thus, we have to face several problems which are the following: (a) ensure the presence of information of the overall content of the set of nanopublications in the citation even on a situation of heterogeneous content of the single nanopublications; (b) guarantee the completeness of the citation and the creation of a text-snippet concise enough to be integrated in a reference list, which is threatened by the volume of information contained in the set; (c) ensure the presence of the identifiers of all the nanopublications of the set in the citation. To solve all these problems we plan to extend the framework by considering some improvements as shown in Fig. 1 (green and blue nodes). Each nanopublication in the given set undergoes a dereferencing and enriching process and then is mapped into a separate metadata schema. Afterwards, the set of separate metadata are aggregated to form single metadata containing citation information common to all the nanopublications in the set. This cannot be done by performing a mere concatenation of the metadata, but by performing some operations at field-level in the set of metadata. As for the citation policies, the operations to be executed are defined by the system administrator. Then, by applying citation policies to the metadata of the overall set the text-snippet is created. Additionally, the landing page provides complete and understandable information about the content of the nanopublications in the set, alongside the link to the access to landing pages and citations of the single nanopublications.

References

1. Out of Cite, Out of Mind: The Current State of Practice, Policy, and Technology for the Citation of Data, vol. 12. CODATA-ICSTI Task Group on Data Citation Standards and Practices, September 2013
2. DataCite Metadata Schema Documentation for the Publication and Citation of Research Data, Version 4.0. Technical report, DataCite Metadata Working Group (2016)
3. Borgman, C.L.: Big Data, Little Data, No Data. MIT Press, Cambridge (2015)
4. Buneman, P., Davidson, S.B., Frew, J.: Why data citation is a computational problem. Commun. ACM (CACM) **59**(9), 50–57 (2016)
5. Fabris, E., Kuhn, T., Silvello, G.: A framework for citing nanopublications. In: Doucet, A., Isaac, A., Golub, K., Aalberg, T., Jatowt, A. (eds.) TPDL 2019. LNCS, vol. 11799, pp. 70–83. Springer, Cham (2019). https://doi.org/10.1007/978-3-030-30760-8_6
6. FORCE-11: Data Citation Synthesis Group: Joint Declaration of Data Citation Principles. FORCE11, San Diego, CA, USA (2014)
7. Groth, P., Gibson, A., Velterop, J.: The anatomy of a nanopublication. Inf. Serv. Use **30**(1–2), 51–56 (2010)
8. Hey, T., Tansley, S., Tolle, K. (eds.): The Fourth Paradigm: Data-Intensive Scientific Discovery. Microsoft Research, Redmond (2009)
9. Kuhn, T., et al.: Decentralized provenance-aware publishing with nanopublications. PeerJ Comput. Sci. **2**, e78 (2016)
10. Lane, L., et al.: Nextprot: a knowledge platform for human proteins. Nucleic Acids Res. **40**(Database-Issue), 76–83 (2012)
11. Mons, B., et al.: The value of data. Nat. Genet. **43**(4), 281–283 (2011)
12. Pico, A.R., et al.: WikiPathways: pathway editing for the people. PLoS Biol. **22**, e184 (2008)
13. Piñero, J., et al.: DisGeNET: a comprehensive platform integrating information on human disease-associated genes and variants. Nucleic Acids Res. **45**(D1), D833–D839 (2017)
14. Silvello, G.: Learning to cite framework: how to automatically construct citations for hierarchical data. J. Am. Soc. Inf. Sci. Technol. (JASIST) **68**(6), 1505–1524 (2017)
15. Silvello, G.: Theory and practice of data citation. J. Am. Soc. Inf. Sci. Technol. (JASIST) **69**(1), 6–20 (2018)
16. Wu, Y., Alawini, A., Davidson, S.B., Silvello, G.: Data citation: giving credit where credit is due. In: Proceedings of the 2018 International Conference on Management of Data, SIGMOD Conference 2018, pp. 99–114. ACM Press, New York (2018)

Correction to: Identifying, Classifying and Searching Graphic Symbols in the NOTAE System

Maria Boccuzzi, Tiziana Catarci, Luca Deodati, Andrea Fantoli,
Antonella Ghignoli, Francesco Leotta, Massimo Mecella,
Anna Monte, and Nina Sietis

Correction to:
**Chapter "Identifying, Classifying and Searching Graphic
Symbols in the NOTAE System" in: M. Ceci et al. (Eds.):**
Digital Libraries: The Era of Big Data and Data Science,
CCIS 1177, https://doi.org/10.1007/978-3-030-39905-4_12

The original version of the chapter 12 was previously published non-open access. It has now been changed to open access under a CC BY 4.0 license and the copyright holder has been updated to 'The Author(s).' The book has also been updated with the change.

The updated version of this chapter can be found at
https://doi.org/10.1007/978-3-030-39905-4_12

© Springer Nature Switzerland AG 2020
M. Ceci et al. (Eds.): IRCDL 2020, CCIS 1177, p. C1, 2020.
https://doi.org/10.1007/978-3-030-39905-4_19

Author Index

Printed in the United States
By Bookmasters